# EURYDICE AND THE BIRTH OF MACEDONIAN POWER

Recent Titles in

# WOMEN IN ANTIQUITY

*Series Editors: Ronnie Ancona and Sarah Pomeroy*

# EURYDICE AND THE BIRTH OF MACEDONIAN POWER

*Elizabeth Donnelly Carney*

OXFORD
UNIVERSITY PRESS

# OXFORD
## UNIVERSITY PRESS

Oxford University Press is a department of the University of Oxford. It furthers the University's objective of excellence in research, scholarship, and education by publishing worldwide. Oxford is a registered trade mark of Oxford University Press in the UK and certain other countries.

Published in the United States of America by Oxford University Press
198 Madison Avenue, New York, NY 10016, United States of America.

© Oxford University Press 2019

First issued as an Oxford University Press paperback, 2022

CIP data is on file at the Library of Congress
ISBN 978-0-19-028053-6 (hardback)
ISBN 978-0-19-767229-7 (paperback)

*For my brother, James T. Carney*

# Contents

# *Acknowledgments*

This book is a project I've been contemplating and yet avoiding (although I have carved off bits of it to discuss at one occasion or another) for a very long time because its subject, Eurydice of Macedon (who was born in the late fifth century and died in the 340s BCE; all dates hereafter are BCE unless otherwise stated) is elusive and yet compelling. I owe Ronnie Ancona and Sarah Pomeroy, the editors of the Women in Antiquity series, and Stefan Vranka, Oxford University Press's editor for Ancient History, Archaeology and Classical Studies, my thanks for their continued support and assistance, not to mention patience, in bringing this to completion.

The discoveries of Manolis Andronikos (the royal tombs under the Great Tumulus at Vergina in 1977 and 1978, the sanctuary of Eucleia in 1982, and the "Tomb of Eurydice" in 1987) changed the nature of doing ancient Macedonian history generally and made this particular project possible, not simply because they introduced new evidence about Eurydice but also because the discoveries provided greater context for long-familiar literary evidence relevant to Eurydice. Critical to this project was the work of Chrysoula Saatsoglou-Paliadeli on the Eucleia sanctuary, the site of at least two dedications of Eurydice. Recently, I have been fascinated by Athanasia Kyriakos' and Alexandros Tourtas' discussion of what amounts to the ancient memory history of the Eucleia site. I am grateful to Drs. Saatsoglou-Paliadeli and Kyriakos for allowing me to use some images from the Eucleia site and for their asistance in acquiring them. Andronikos' and Angeliki Kottaridi's description of the intriguing tomb they attribute to Eurydice has illuminated this fascinating space. The scholarship and conversation of a number of scholars have helped me to think about Eurydice and her time. Bill Greenwalt and I have talked about Eurydice and disagreed about her, part of the time, for many years. Kate Mortensen stimulated my thoughts early on. Olga Palagia has helped me in innumerable ways, as have conversations with Sheila Ager and Sabine Müller and Daniel Ogden and Jeanne Reames and Peter Schultz. The analysis of two very different historians of ancient Macedonia, Eugene Borza and Militiades Hatzopoulos, has informed my own, though I have rarely agreed with either. As always, my husband and daughter have listened patiently to my latest scholarly worries and interests, even in the course of a Manhattan emergency room visit. I learned my first Latin when my brother began to study it and later listened to him practice his declamation of Cicero's First Catlinarian. It might seem a long way from Cicero's orations to the narrative of Justin (the subject of much discussion and condemnation in this study), but the distance from another of Cicero's speeches, the *Pro Caelio*, to some of the more lurid points in Justin's account of Eurydice is actually short.

I have spent my professional career in a history department and though I often wished that I were a member of a classics department, the fact that my academic anchor was, in fact, in the history department turned out to be stimulating. My colleagues, mostly historians of the last few centuries, were often bemused by my field and by the comparative paucity of evidence that is the normal situation for those who study antiquity. Nonetheless I learned a great deal from the questions they asked and the ways, blessed with more abundant evidence, they interrogated their sources. But, now that I no longer teach regularly, I am also newly aware of how much I learned from having to describe and explain the ancient world to students. Coincidentally, I taught a course on Alexander and ancient Macedonia for the first time in January 1978, a month or so after the first news of the finds at Vergina/Aegae appeared. For me, teaching about ancient Macedonia has always involved integrating the material and political history of the kingdom. The present work attempts to do the same.

# Abbreviations

| | |
|---|---|
| AA | Αρχαιολογικά ἀνάλεκτα ἐξ Ἀθηνῶν (Athens Annuals of Archaeology) |
| ACD | *Acta Classica* |
| AE | *Archaiologika Ephemeris* |
| AEMTH | Το Αρχαιολογικό Έργο στη Μακεδονία *και τη* Θράκη |
| AHB | *Ancient History Bulletin* |
| AJP | *American Journal of Philology* |
| AM | *Ancient Macedonia (Archaia Makedonia)* |
| AncSoc | *Ancient Society* |
| AncW | *Ancient World* |
| AnnPisa | *Annali della Scuola Normale Superiore di Pisa* |
| BCH | *Bulletin de correspondance hellénique* |
| BSA | *Annual of the British School at Athens* |
| CA | *Classical Antiquity* |
| CB | *The Classical Bulletin* |
| CJ | *Classical Journal* |
| CP | *Classical Philology* |
| CQ | *Classical Quarterly* |
| C&M | *Classica et Mediaevalia* |
| FGrH | *Die Fragmente der griechischen Historiker* |
| FlorIlib | *Florentia Iliberritana* |
| GRBS | *Greek, Roman and Byzantine Studies* |
| JHS | *Journal of Hellenic Studies* |
| LCM | *Liverpool Classical Monthly* |
| REG | *Revue des études grecques* |
| RhM | *Rheinisches Museum für Philologie* |
| RSA | *Rivista storica dell'Antichità* |
| SEG | *Supplementum Epigraphicum Graecum* |
| SIG | W. Dittenberger, *Sylloge Inscritioneum Graecarum*, 3rd edition, Leipzig, 1915–24 |
| ZPE | *Zeitschrift für Papyrologie und Epigraphik* |

# Chronology

| | |
|---|---|
| 410–404 | Eurydice born |
| 394/3 | Amyntas III takes the throne |
| 393/2–390 | Eurydice marries Amyntas III |
| 388? | Alexander II born |
| 384–343? | Perdiccas III born |
| 383 or 382 | Philip II born |
| 370/69 | Amyntas III dies and Alexander II (370/69–368/7) takes throne* |
| 368/7 | Despite attempt of Pelopidas to bring peace, Ptolemy kills Alexander II Perdiccas III may be king, or Ptolemy, or it may be disputed between them |
| July–autumn: | Pausanias threatens to take the throne; Eurydice appeals to Iphicrates |
| November?: | Pelopidas returns, forces Ptolemy to be regent; Alexander II clearly king |
| 365 | Perdiccas III kills Ptolemy |
| 360/59 | Perdiccas III dies in battle against the Illyrians and Philip II takes over |
| 350s | Eucleia complex and Eurydice dedications |
| 343 | Aeschines, recounting a 346 speech to Philip, refers to the Iphicrates incident and says that he told Philip he could ask others present about it, but does not tell him to ask his mother |
| 338 | August: Philip's victory at Chaeronea; decision to build Philippeum, including Eurydice statue |
| 336 | Philip II is killed and Alexander III takes the throne |

*If Eurydice married Ptolemy, it may have happened after Amyntas III's death or more likely after Alexander II's death or after Pelopidas forced Ptolemy to be regent.

# King List

Alexander I c. 498–54
Perdiccas II c. 454–414/13
Archelaus 414/13–399
Orestes? 399
Aeropus 399–396/5
Pausanias 396/5
Amyntas II 395/4
Pausanias 394/3
Amyntas III 394/3–370/69
Alexander II 370/69–368/67
Perdiccas III 368/7–360/59
Philip II 360/59–336
Alexander III (the Great) 336–323
Philip III (Arrhidaeus) 323–317
Alexander IV 323–c. 309

# The Agread Dynasty in the era of Eurydice

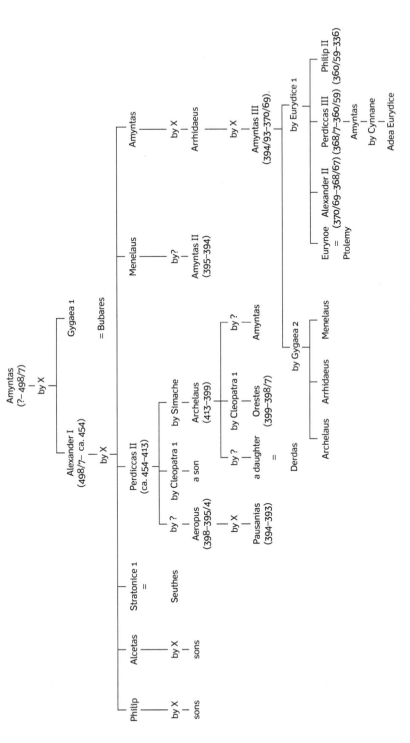

*Map*

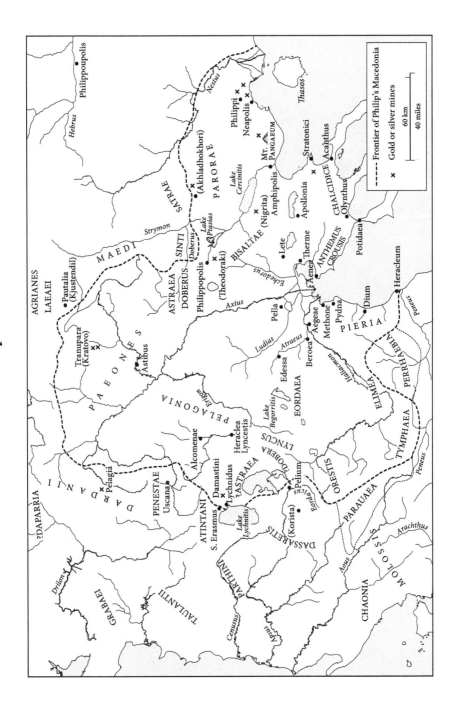

# EURYDICE AND THE BIRTH
# OF MACEDONIAN POWER

# 1

# *Introduction*

Eurydice, the daughter of Sirras (c. 410–c. 340s BCE), the wife of Amyntas III, king of Macedonia, and the mother of Philip II and grandmother of Alexander the Great, played a notable role in the public life of ancient Macedonia. She is the first royal Macedonian woman known to have done so, although she would hardly be the last. Her career marked a turning point in the role of royal women in Macedonian monarchy, one that coincided with the emergence of Macedonia as a great power in the Hellenic world. These two phenomena coincided but were not the result of coincidence: the same circumstance that led to Eurydice's prominence also led to the growth of Macedonian power: dynastic crisis. This study examines the nature of Eurydice's public role, the factors that contributed to the expansion of her role (and that of subsequent royal women), and how that expansion related to the growth of Macedonian power.

An element of the arbitrary always prevails in the survival of evidence from antiquity. The arbitrary element, however, is particularly strong in terms of material about the lives of individual women, given the degree of male dominance present in ancient societies, a dominance particularly powerful in relation to written records. Nonetheless, chance has occasionally preserved a considerable body of material about individual women. One thinks, for instance, of Enheduanna (2285–2250 BCE), daughter of Sargon King of Akkad. She was the high priestess of the goddess Nanna in Ur. Enheduanna is one of the first poets whose name we know and, remarkably, a considerable body of her work has survived despite her apparent involvement in political controversy. There are also two seals with her name and a disk depicting her.[1] Somewhat similarly, many traces of Plancia Magna, a woman who lived in the late first and early second centuries CE in Perga in western Asia Minor, still exist: at least five portrait statues survive and many inscriptions.[2] Both of these women were members of a ruling elite and both performed religious functions of great importance to their communities. Something similar can't be said of Eurydice. In this sense, so much material about her and these other women did not survive entirely by chance; only women from elite groups with distinctive roles could possibly have produced or had created for them so many material and literary remembrances.

In fact, a surprising amount of evidence relevant to Eurydice's life and actions has been preserved or discovered, some of it dating from her lifetime or very soon after her death. Aeschines (389–314 BCE), an Athenian politician and orator, in a speech delivered to the Athenian assembly in 343, provides a vivid, if highly rhetorical account of her resourceful actions in support of her young sons at a critical moment in Macedonian affairs (Aeschin. 2.26–29). Aeschines delivered the speech a generation after the incident it describes (see Chapter 4). Three dedicatory inscriptions by Eurydice survive (two preserved on statue bases, the third included in an essay attributed to Plutarch). In addition, excavators have found the base of a portrait statue of Eurydice, as well as (at a slightly different location) another statue that some also consider a portrait of Eurydice (see Chapter 5). Philip II constructed an unusual building at Olympia that once housed gleaming images of some members of his immediate family (Philip himself, Alexander, Amyntas III, Olympias, and Eurydice). Pausanias' description of this construct survives, as do the lower sections of the structure itself, including most of the statue bases. Finally, a splendid and eerie Macedonian-type tomb at Vergina (widely considered the site of the ancient Macedonian capital of Aegae) may have belonged to Eurydice (see Chapter 6).

Narrative sources of a much later date also recount her supposed actions and crimes and those of her close kin (see Chapters 3 and 4). We should approach these narratives with caution and skepticism. Upon what, for instance, do these later, largely Roman-era, writers depend? Even if we (optimistically) conclude that their ultimate sources were fourth century and that the extant authors do not create events out of whole cloth but rather select material for their own purposes (often the teaching of moral lessons), we must recall that the original fourth-century narratives themselves (e.g., Theopompus or Ephorus) had marked political perspectives, often Athenocentric or focused on Theban concerns, not Macedonian.[3]

Presumably, all of these depended, in turn, either on Macedonian court sources (thus people themselves likely involved in court factions; see Chapter 4) or on foreign visitors to the court, often members of embassies visiting Macedonia. These foreigners might have misunderstood customs and actions reported to them and also failed to recognize partisan opinion when they heard it. A court source, by definition, involves participants in the politics of Macedonia, but, so far as we know, none of the extant written sources depend on eyewitness accounts. For instance, neither Theopompus nor Marsyas (who was an elite Macedonian, but of a later generation), though each was familiar with the court, was personally present for the major events of Eurydice's life.[4] Antipater wrote a history of Perdiccas III's Illyrian campaigns, but we have none of it.[5]

Moreover, since the narrative sources were written mainly by non-Macedonian authors either never or rarely present in Macedonia, and since Macedonia was not, during most of the period covered by this work, a great power, we should not assume that these sources knew exactly when certain events happened or exactly how long they took to happen. If a man died and his son succeeded him without any known dispute, then we can probably take our sources at their word about who was king, but if a king died unexpectedly or without an obvious adult heir, or if a rival claimant appeared, it may have taken awhile before widespread agreement developed about who was indeed king, and somewhat longer before such recognition spread abroad.

Macedonian monarchy and history were anything but stable, particularly in the era under consideration: conspiracies, assassinations, multiple claimants to the throne, and assorted foreign threats were commonplace. The court was faction ridden, but we cannot always identify to which group an individual belonged or assume that this was an unchanging allegiance or presume, at any given time, that we really understand the basis for that allegiance. Did, for instance, supporters of the mysterious Ptolemy (see, particularly, Chapter 4) always support him, or did they simply join him in reaction against the policy of Alexander II (Philip II's older brother)? Having once supported Ptolemy, did they remain faithful and, if they did not, did Perdiccas III (the next of Eurydice's sons to rule) and his brother Philip accept them back into the group of their *philoi* (friends)? Some may have belonged to the same "faction" for different reasons: personal loyalty or ambition, family loyalty, or connection to families or governments outside of Macedonia proper.

Chronological problems relating to Macedonian events in the first half of the fourth century compound our source problems. It is not simply that the absolute date of many incidents is uncertain because of contradictory testimony, but that the relative chronology of events is unclear. We cannot always tell if someone—for instance Eurydice—is reacting to something or whether that event has yet to happen. The relative chronological context of the incident involving Eurydice narrated by Aeschines and the actions of Pelopidas in Macedonia as described by Plutarch is unclear (see Chapters 3 and 4). Understanding what happened and why, in this case, is further complicated by uncertainty about whether Eurydice married the enigmatic Ptolemy and, if so, when (see Chapter 4).

Finally, gender stereotyping plays an important role in virtually all material relevant to Eurydice. Some sources accuse her of sexual infidelity (and thus either directly or indirectly question the legitimacy of her sons), treachery, and murder (of two of her own sons), whereas Aeschines and her own dedicatory inscriptions (see Chapter 5) picture her as a loyal and heroic mother. Roman writers, fond of employing stories about royal women to teach moral lessons, may have preserved and stressed the tales about Eurydice's bad behavior, although Plutarch, for instance, preserves one dedicatory inscription by Eurydice (see Chapter 5) because he wants to teach a lesson about good parenting. Until the 1990s (and to some degree to this day) scholarship uncritically accepted the negative stories about Eurydice, reflecting persistent discomfort with politically active women. Discussions of Eurydice's possible marriage to Ptolemy often implicitly assume that this marriage would have functioned like a modern marriage in the sense that it would have been collaborative and that the marriage was something Eurydice chose. Perhaps both assumptions are valid, but perhaps not. Certainly they require discussion before their validity is accepted.

Thus, despite the comparative abundance of material related to Eurydice, some of it contemporary with her lifetime, the more one reflects, the less certain one becomes about not only her actions but her public persona. What seems at first straightforward becomes anything but. Interpretation of virtually all this material about Eurydice is contested. Much like her namesake in the Orpheus tale, as we turn back to look at her, her image blurs and threatens to fade away, partly because of controversies about her that originated in her own day, but partly because of current issues including the construction of modern

Greek national identity. The abiding dispute about the identity of the individuals who were once interred in tombs at Vergina widely considered to be royal contributes to the problem as well. Moreover, our uncertainty about the nature and order of many Macedonian events during her lifetime, as well as the identity of many important individuals, makes it difficult to understand aspects of her social and historical context. But we can try.

Let me turn to a critical aspect of her historical context, Macedonian monarchy. Tradition puts the origin of Macedonian monarchy in about the seventh century BCE. According to much later and non-Macedonian literary accounts, the monarchy was founded by descendants of Heracles (Heraclids) from Argos. This founding dynasty, the Argeads—or, as they are sometimes called, the Temenids—ruled, at least in name, from the seventh century until the last of the male line, Alexander IV (the son of Alexander III, better known as Alexander the Great), died c. 309 BCE.[6] Little, however, is known about individual kings or events until the reign of Alexander I, who ruled at the beginning of the fifth century (c. 498–454). At the time of the Persian Wars, Macedonia was to some degree a vassal state of the Persian Empire; Alexander I and Macedonian troops actually fought on the Persian side, though the king managed, nonetheless, to maintain friendly relations with the Athenians. Once the Persians were defeated, Alexander I took advantage of their departure to expand his territory considerably. He competed at the Olympics, issued a considerable coinage, and made himself and his court more connected, especially politically, to the wider Hellenic world, not simply the northern Aegean.[7]

Alexander I seems to model a kind of royal Macedonian type: the wily, much-contriving king who tried, often successfully, to turn his country's weakness into strength by playing one major foreign power against another. Often these kings had a knack for successful image building. Pindar (frag.120) termed Alexander I "θρασύμηδες" (bold thinking or planning) and Hammond rightly spoke of his skill at playing a "double game."[8] The game is "double," of course, seen from the point of view of the major powers; from a Macedonian point of view, it is simply practical policy for a kingdom not yet a great power. If the tale of Alexander I's tricky elimination of the Persian ambassadors sent to demand Macedonian submission (Herod. 5.17–21) is, indeed, a fictional construct of Alexander I himself, then Alexander may have promoted his own image as a royal schemer.[9] Many of his descendants fit his

Odyssean prototype.[10] These qualities enabled survival for some, like Perdiccas II,[11] while others, most notably Philip II, were employed these same traits with much greater success. Was there a female version of this prototype? This question is unanswerable about any royal woman before Eurydice, but, as we shall see, she could indeed be understood as somewhat Penelopean, perhaps particularly in her treatment of Ptolemy of Alorus (see Chapters 4 and 6).

When Alexander I died after a long reign, his son Perdiccas II succeeded him but was considerably more embattled both internally and externally, though he too reigned a long time (c. 454–c. 414/13). Only gradually did Perdiccas II establish central control over his kingdom, initially having to share rule with several of his brothers. Meanwhile, the Peloponnesian War had commenced and, in order to survive, Perdiccas ricocheted between alliances with the competing great powers, the Athenians and the Spartans.[12]

Whereas Perdiccas II's internal dynastic problems were dealt with gradually and comparatively nonviolently, his son Archelaus (414/13–399) reached or at least retained the throne only through violence. Archelaus, however, benefited from the decline in Athenian power during his reign and thus from reduced foreign interference in Macedonian affairs. Archelaus centralized the kingdom and improved its infrastructure and military. He probably added a second capital, close to the coast, at Pella, though some would date this alteration to the reign of Amyntas III.[13] Archelaus patronized major Greek intellectual and artistic figures: his palace held splendid paintings and Euripides became a member of his court. Archelaus' very success, as well as a combination of individual grievances against him, led to his assassination c. 399.[14] Immediately after Archelaus' death, his young son Orestes succeeded him, but he was soon eliminated in favor of a series of short-lived Argeads.[15] Greater dynastic stability was achieved only gradually, after Amyntas III, husband of Eurydice, took the throne (394/3), followed, in turn, by all three of his sons by her. None of these men, however, ruled without Argead challengers, and all endured external threats including multiple invasions, and each had to make humiliating (at least initially) concessions to leading Greek powers. All three of Eurydice's sons died by violence (see Chapters 2, 3, and 4).

Before we consider this period from 399 (the death of Archelaus) to 336 (the death of Philip II) and the role of Eurydice in the events of this period, we need first to examine the nature of the kingdom of

Macedonia, the character of its monarchy, the pattern of succession to the throne, and the role of royal women in Macedonian monarchy. The kingdom expanded and contracted in response to the ever-changing power of the Argead rulers and their neighbors, but the foundation of the kingdom apparently lay in the Pierian foothills, where the original capital, Aegae (modern Vergina), was located. Despite the presence of Greek colonies on the coast, Argead rulers often controlled much of lower Macedonia (the coastal plain). Upper Macedonia (predominantly a mountainous area) was divided into principalities (including Lyncestis, Elimeia, Orestis, and Tymphaea), each with its own dynasty. Only in the reign of Philip II (360/359–336) did Upper Macedonia entirely pass into the control of the Argead kings. Until then, the Upper Macedonian princes often weakened Argead rule and certainly made Argead rulers more vulnerable.[16]

To the southeast of Macedonia lay Thessaly, a region economically and culturally similar to Macedonia; both areas had pastoral economies and were dominated by horse-riding elites.[17] To the north and east were a collection of peoples generally called Thracian. Thracian influence on Macedonia, particularly in matters related to religion, was considerable, though relations with various Thracian leaders were sometimes friendly and sometimes not.[18] To the north and northwest were a people Greeks and Macedonians called Illyrians though they were, in fact, not one people but many. Despite some Argead intermarriage with members of the Illyrian elite, Illyrian peoples frequently raided and sometimes invaded Macedonia. West of Macedonia, on the other side of the Pindus range, was the Molossian kingdom; it resembled Macedonia in a number of respects, but it was more remote, had a smaller population, a weaker monarchy, and fewer resources.[19] Historically, Macedonia functioned as a buffer between peoples to the north and those south of them; it was frequently invaded, whereas until late antiquity the peninsula to the south was relatively rarely invaded by peoples from outside the peninsula.[20]

The kingdom of Macedonia had tremendous potential for wealth and thus power. Whereas the southern Greek peninsula was heavily deforested, Macedonia was rich in timber. Today that would certainly be advantageous, but in antiquity it was far more so because timber (and its related product, pitch) built ships and the oars that propelled them in battle. The ability to trade in these vital products was an advantage but also attracted the interest and intervention of more powerful peoples, most consistently of the Athenians, the great naval power of the Greek world in the fifth and fourth centuries. Macedonia contained considerable fertile land, and so horses and horse warfare were important to a degree they could not be for most of the rest of the peninsula, except for Thessaly with its similar excellent pasture land. For good and for bad, Macedonia lay on the major land route north and east (thus the invading Persian army passed through it and then retreated through it) and along the sea route to the Black Sea and its many grain-producing Greek colonies. Depending on which areas an Argead ruler controlled at a given period, there was considerable access to mineral wealth, a resource that Philip II would use to great advantage. Potentially the larger land area and population offered up the possibility of a much larger military force, though this potential was certainly not consistently realized until the reign of Philip II.[21]

Macedonian monarchy was personal: the king led the army into battle and was apparently also the chief judicial official and a kind of religious figure as well. *Hetairoi* (companions; our extant sources often refer to them as *philoi*) accompanied the king in peace and in war.[22] How many of them there were and how many were, at a given moment, in personal attendance at court is not clear and would doubtless have varied. In battle, they served on horseback. Probably old Companion families had hereditary lands, but the king could also create new Companions (not necessarily men born in Macedonia) and assign them lands. Kings and their children sometimes married members of the elite, though it is impossible to establish how extensive this intermarriage was. Older scholarship used to assume there was some sort of national army assembly, but now most would agree that the king made decisions on his own, though often with or against the advice of a varying number of advisors, who were sometimes but not always hereditary members of the Companion group. Kings seem to have been acclaimed by some part of the populace, but the populace did not initiate the choice of the king. Opinions vary as to whether there was a formal council in this period—my own view is that there was not—but there were certainly advisors, and in order to reach the throne or keep it, the support of some group or faction was necessary. Kings' sons grew up within the context of the elite. Conspiracies and assassinations often involved members of the elite, though they usually acted in support of some member of the Argead clan.

As far as we can tell, only male Argeads ruled Macedonia until there were no more, but it is sometimes hard to determine. A ruler or would-be ruler typically appears in Greek historical texts with a personal name and often but not always with a patronymic; sometimes an ancient author provides enough information so that we can be certain exactly which "Amyntas" (a name lamentably common in the Argead dynasty and in Macedonia generally) is intended, but often this does not happen. Thus, while we may assume a given ruler or claimant is an Argead, which branch of the family he came from may be unknown and thus subject to endless scholarly surmise.

We can make rough generalizations about the pattern of succession in Macedonia, but they are only that. Eurydice, as well as subsequent royal women, sometimes played a role in succession. Legitimacy in terms of the Macedonian throne was not an absolute concept but rather something situationally determined and sometimes re-determined.[23] I will not, therefore, term someone a "legitimate" or "rightful" heir nor refer to anyone as a "usurper," though I will describe men not currently recognized as kings who are attempting to become kings as "claimants." The latter term is not a negative judgment on their right to rule but simply recognition that this person had not yet acquired widespread recognition as monarch but was trying to acquire it.

Often a man was succeeded by his oldest son, not because of any abstract principle, let alone law, like primogeniture, but because of demographic realities. Given ancient life expectancy (not to mention the perilous careers of Argead rulers, few of whom died in their sleep), a man would be lucky if he had even one adult son by the time he died. Macedonia was rarely stable and so the luxury of a child king, particularly a very young child king, was not affordable. Some sources report the elimination of child kings by guardians who supplanted them as kings, though it is possible that the youthful "kings" were never kings at all.[24] In any event, these young kings' sons were often murdered by their guardians, whatever the guardians' status. Members of more distant branches of the royal family, for instance men whose great-grandfather, perhaps, had been a king, might try to become king, and they sometimes succeeded, even against adult candidates. Amyntas III, Eurydice's spouse, was not the son of a king and perhaps not even the grandson of a king (his line of descent is disputed; see Chapter 2). Sometimes the path to the throne (or to its retention) lay in violence; frequently, foreign powers sponsored Argead claimants, supporting them with military forces. Scholars have tended to term such men "puppets," but I will resist that terminology because, in practice, it is applied only to failed contenders for the throne with foreign support. Amyntas III, for instance, received help from, at different times, the Spartans and the Athenians, but no one ever calls him a "puppet," because he gained and retained (or regained) recognition as king. A king with military or political problems—Argead kings often had both—was vulnerable to such attempts. We tend to assume that it was immediately clear who was king, but the events of Eurydice's life suggest that this was not always the case; different populations could acclaim someone king, but only events would determine whether this acclamation endured.

But what if a king had more than one son of an age to rule? We know that Philip II and Alexander the Great were polygamous and it is very likely that earlier Argeads, at least as far back as Alexander I, were as well (see Chapter 2).[25] It is possible that Alexander I was the first king to practice polygamy.[26] Polygamy tends to produce more male heirs than monogamy (a significant advantage considering the many threats against the life of the ruler) and enabled a king, by his multiple marriages, to establish or confirm multiple alliances; but the practice, over generations, also contributed to numerous struggles for the succession. As Daniel Ogden has noted, succession struggles typically pitted a king's sons by one mother against the ruler's sons by another woman (Ogden termed these struggles between sons by different mothers "amphimetric"), whereas full siblings (not just full brothers, but their sisters as well) tended to work in relative concert.[27] We do not know how a successor was chosen—probably a combination of the last king's views and the support of important groups within the elite was critical—but if circumstances warranted, whatever initial decision had been reached, it might subsequently be overturned.[28]

It was the polygamy of Argead kings that, more than anything else, contributed to the growing role of royal women in Argead monarchy. A king might have sons by several women and could favor one or several sons over others, but a royal mother was more closely tied to her sons and tended to have greater power through influence in the reign(s) of her son(s) than in that of her husband. (This factor makes any scenario which imagines a royal woman prioritizing a new or potential husband over a son implausible if not absolutely impossible, as we will see in the case of Eurydice.) Royal mothers (and sometimes sisters) functioned as succession advocates; they were more closely connected to their sons than their husbands could ever be, for the very practical reasons I have outlined.[29] Indeed, as we shall see in the case of Eurydice, sometimes the public images of the royal son and his mother were linked (not only before the son became king but subsequently as well), both by the efforts of the king and his mother and also by those of his enemies. In Argead Macedonia, the issue was not merely managing to make it to the throne, but also retaining the throne against the claims (military and political) of rival Argeads. Royal mothers contributed to both efforts.

Ogden has pointed to a phenomenon he connects to royal polygamy and the perpetual dynastic strife it engendered: royal contenders and their families would denigrate the birth and status of their rivals. Such denigration might involve charges of bastardy or slurs about the low status or ethnicity or bad acts of mothers of candidates. Ogden sometimes terms this phenomenon "bastardizing," though the charge may not literally be that these men are not the sons of their alleged fathers.[30] Ogden argues that subsequent ancient authors preserved these contemporary political attacks without, necessarily, realizing that they were not literally true or that they were made as part of a political campaign of sorts. In addition, we cannot be certain that the terms used in our extant sources were those used in Macedonia or that even the original source of these insults meant them in an absolute sense, though they have subsequently been taken literally, especially by later authors. For instance, Plutarch (*Alex.* 9.4–5) says that Attalus, the guardian of Philip II's last married bride (Cleopatra), asked the Macedonians to pray to the gods for a "legitimate" successor (γνήσιον . . . διάδοχον), a request that so enraged Alexander that he demanded to know whether Attalus was calling him a bastard (νόθος). Did Plutarch's Attalus mean that Alexander was literally not Philip's son? Alternatively, was he simply indicating that, in his view, Alexander was a less legitimate candidate for the throne than any child by Attalus' ward, Cleopatra, whether because Alexander's mother Olympias was foreign or because he felt that a child by Attalus' ward would be a *more* legitimate candidate than Alexander because, from Attalus' self-interested point of view, his ward would be a more appropriate king's mother?

"Bastardizing" is thus perhaps too narrow a term to describe the phenomenon in question. Rarely do these attacks assert that a man is not the son or descendant of an Argead king. Instead, more often they simply denigrate the status of the mother of the man in question. This denigration may take the form of asserting that she was a slave or that her son was one and thus she must have been (e.g., Aelian *V. H.* 12.43) or that she was a prostitute or of low birth or, perhaps, that she was foreign (see Chapter 2). As we shall see, the negative tradition about Eurydice focuses primarily on her murderous and treacherous acts; one ancient author, Justin, does picture her as an adulteress, but her adultery in Justin happens only after her daughter is married, so Justin's narrative does not directly question the literal legitimacy of her sons; rather, it vividly pictures how evil Eurydice was. The *Suda* s.v. "Karanos" is aware of sources that do question the legitimacy of Eurydice's children, but none of these are extant. Rather than terming such attacks attempts to "bastardize" candidates, I prefer to speak of them as attempts to defame the candidates and their mothers. The existence of this phenomenon demonstrates not only the importance (negative as well as positive) of mothers as succession advocates but also that, in practice, a royal candidate's worthiness was not understood simply in patrilineal terms; the status and descent of the mother was important as well and, given the wide availability of male Argeads, more variable from one candidate to another. A combination of royal decisions and chance made the identity of royal mothers and women more important from the reign of Amyntas III on than previously, but it was an issue at least as early as the reign of Archelaus.

Various other factors may have contributed to the influence and thus power of a royal woman: family status; production of offspring, particularly if the offspring were male; national and international politics; ethnic identity; and perhaps the affection of the monarch for a wife. There is no evidence for a title for royal women in the Argead period; indeed, Argead kings did not themselves use a title until the reign of Alexander. Thus there was no official or institutionalized chief wife.[31]

Instead, the situation of a royal woman was fluid and varied over time. If a royal woman's husband died before a son was able to rule on his own, the situation could empower the mother, as to some degree it did Eurydice, but it might also render her more vulnerable, something probably also true of Eurydice. Virtually all royal marriages came into being in some sort of political context, most often toward the completion of peace or an alliance, but it is less clear to what degree these "marriage alliances" (the term ordinarily used about them in English) remained important over the long term.[32] Did, for instance, Eurydice's marriage continue to be a factor in Macedonian/Illyrian/Lyncestian relations for a generation after its inauguration (see Chapters 2, 3, and 4)? Did a royal wife function as an advocate or at least a means of access to the king for her kin and friends? Was her role in the alliance simply symbolic, or in some ways meaningful and of practical use? Did a royal wife have a group of supporters and kin with her at court? Little information survives to help provide answers to these questions and, of course, the answer might have been different at various times and in differing situations. More information survives about Hellenistic royal women (though not about those in Macedonia), but we should be very cautious in using later information to fill out a picture of Argead women,[33] particularly since we know that the role of royal women in the Hellenistic period varied from one dynasty to another, and from one generation to another. Eurydice is the first Argead royal woman for whom we have more information than the simple fact of her marriage; this may be significant—she may have shaped a new role that affected subsequent royal women—or it may simply be a matter of the chance survival or disappearance of evidence.[34]

The lives of royal women—or at least some aspects of their lives—played out, or may have played out, in public. Elite women in the Hellenic world often played prominent roles as priestesses, patrons of shrines and festivals, and dedicators of votives. No direct evidence survives that any Argead woman served as a priestess, though some scholars have concluded that certain female burials at Aegae imply this (see Chapters 5 and 6), but both epigraphic and literary evidence survives for them for the other categories of religious activity. Female patronage in its various forms advertised both the woman and her kin and helped to shape her public image as well as that of the royal family.[35] We know that the funerals and burials of Argead women were public and often rich (see Chapter 6), and their weddings and other events in their life cycles (the birth of children, the marriage of their children) may have been as well. Royal women had some funds at their disposal, as their patronage might suggest, and had relationships with other members of the court; we do not know how much they appeared in public at court or if they heard petitions in a public way, but it seems likely they did both, at least at times.[36]

# 2

# *The Marriage of Eurydice and Her Husband's Rule*

Although Macedonian history in the Argead period was always some-what disordered, the assassination of Archelaus in 399 precipitated the kingdom's descent into dynastic chaos that, at its worst, lasted about seven years. The ruler we know as Amyntas III (394/3–370/69), hus-band of Eurydice and father of Philip II, emerged from this chaos and managed to rule for a lengthy period. Macedonian kings tended to "die with their boots on,"[1] so the fact that Amyntas died a natural death, in old age, was an accomplishment, one with consequences. Though not without contention, his descendants ruled the kingdom until there were no males left in his line of descent.

Amyntas' own reign, however, was characterized by foreign invasion and intervention and he suffered a host of other, if lesser, indignities, though the later stages of his reign were more stable than the earlier. He demonstrated resilience in the face of these assorted crises, often managing to persuade a greater power to come to his aid at a critical moment. Amyntas stayed in the game until the very end of his reign and probably acted to smooth the path to the throne for his successor, the eldest of his sons by Eurydice, Alexander II. Historians used to treat Amyntas III with some contempt, primarily because ancient sources do, but Zahrnt has rehabilitated his reputation, arguing that comparison to Philip and Alexander III had exaggerated Amyntas III's weaknesses.[2] Macedonia had chronic problems with outside pressure and with the princes of Upper Macedonia, particularly at times of transition in rule and especially when the unsettled dynastic situation at the time Amyntas took the throne all but invited foreign powers to try to take advantage.

During his reign, Amyntas demonstrated considerable coping skills, though these were stronger in terms of diplomacy than in terms of the military.

## Source Problems for the Reign of Amyntas III

The wider Greek world apparently found events in Macedonia in this period particularly incomprehensible. One wonders how much, even at the time, people outside Macedonia knew about current Macedonian affairs, particularly if events in Macedonia did not immediately involve the great powers of the Greek world.[3] Struggles within the royal clan and at court must have seemed especially obscure to those not present at court. Partly because of this original obscurity, but also because so many contemporary narratives and documents have been lost, surviving ancient sources have proved as confusing as the events they attempt to record. Not only do narrative histories contradict each other and other literary sources in important ways but they also often differ from ancient chronographic writing, not only about the dates and lengths of reigns but even about whether someone was king. Eugene Borza rightly termed the period a "historiographical nightmare."[4] Given the number of times several men vied for the throne, exactly when one contender counted as king and another did not may not have been clear or even generally agreed upon.[5]

Our sources for events in Macedonia (see general remarks in Chapter 1) are poor for Amyntas' reign and poorer yet for those of his two eldest sons. The most important extant narrative source is the first century BCE "universal" historian Diodorus Siculus, who probably depended heavily, but not exclusively, on Ephorus (c. 400–330), an earlier universal historian. Justin (a Roman writer of disputed date who wrote an epitome of the work of the Augustan-era Pompeius Trogus) also offers a narrative, though one much more abbreviated and highly colored than that of Diodorus (see further Chapter 4). Xenophon's pro-Spartan *Hellenica* contains material on Macedonian events, and there is also a smattering of references in other fourth century writers like Isocrates. Only a few relevant inscriptions from the period survive and these do not necessarily end the confusion.[6] The coin evidence, however, suggests relative stability during Amyntas' reign.[7]

It is not simply that the sources provide little consensus about the absolute dates of reigns and events,[8] but also that even the order of events and indeed whether they happened at all is subject to disagreement, given the apparent contradictions preserved in surviving written sources. For instance, as we shall see, we cannot be certain whether the Illyrians invaded Macedonia and forced Amyntas to flee once or twice during his reign or when either of these possible invasions might have happened. Since two such humiliating events, especially if they happened many years apart, would imply a much more fundamentally troubled reign than one such upset, this is a vital issue. The identity of several rulers or claimants to the throne during this period remains uncertain. More importantly, the line of descent of Amyntas III himself is not agreed upon and while we know the name of Eurydice's father, her wider genealogy and her ethnicity are subject to great controversy (see following section). A reader who consults other works on this period will therefore encounter differing king lists, regnal dates, and family trees and thus widely different analyses of the motivation of major figures and powers.[9]

Given the severe nature of our source problems, it is easy for any discussion of the reigns of Amyntas III and those of his first two sons to turn into a series of technical puzzles. While I will sometimes prefer some explanations to others, and some chronologies and genealogies to others, my goal here is to give the reader a sense for the big picture and for the major forces driving events in the reigns of Amyntas and his two elder sons and thus to create a context for Eurydice's actions and supposed actions.

In attempting, despite the weaknesses of our sources, to understand this big historical picture and thus Eurydice's historical context, it helps to take note of some political patterns. One or two of the various men who tried to reach the throne during this period may not have been Argeads, but it is more likely that all, in some sense (for instance, in the maternal line), were. The dynasty had acquired and retained a collective legitimacy whereas few individual Argeads possessed such broad support and acceptance.[10] If, as appears to have happened in the case of Amyntas III, a man not closely related to recent rulers attempted to claim and then hold the throne, he was likely to experience greater difficulty than if he had simply been the son of the most recent king. This difficulty, however, was a practical one; it did not mean that such a succession was impossible or that someone like this was somehow not a "rightful" king. Eurydice played a part, active and passive, in her husband's and sons' ability to take and hold the throne, despite their persistent difficulties.

## The Reign of Amyntas III (394/3–370/69)

Amyntas III was hardly Archelaus' immediate successor; enduring dynastic disarray followed the death of Archelaus. Diodorus (14.37.6) recounts that, after Archelaus' death, Orestes, a boy, succeeded him.[11] Young Orestes was killed by his guardian, Aeropus, who then ruled for six years. No patronymic survives for Aeropus, but he would probably not have been chosen as guardian if he were not close kin to Orestes and an Argead.[12] Orestes is nowhere called the son of Archelaus, but it seems very likely he was because of his ability to succeed as a child. It is possible that Diodorus has conflated the role of guardian and that of regent, that Orestes was never king, and that Aeropus became king immediately after the death of Archelaus; in this reading, he would have killed Orestes not to insure his own succession but rather to make more likely that this own son would follow him to the throne.[13] Other than some abortive attempts, apparently in alliance with the Thessalians, to oppose the Spartans (Polyaen. 2.1.17, 4.4.3; Xen. *Hell.* 4.3.10), nothing further is known of Aeropus. Diodorus asserts (14.84.6) that Aeropus died of illness and was in turn succeeded by his son Pausanias, though Pausanias ruled for only a year before he was assassinated by a man named Amyntas (Diod. 14.89.1–2). Diodorus' subsequent narrative makes it clear that he believed that this particular Amyntas was the father of Philip II and the man historians call Amyntas III. Amyntas III, Diodorus says, ruled for twenty-four years.[14] Further complicating the matter, the chronological lists include another ruler—worse yet, another Amyntas (hereafter Amyntas II)—between Aeropus and Pausanias.[15] Thus Amyntas III took the throne after more than five years of dynastic confusion and mayhem.

Important for this study is that Amyntas III's parentage, let alone his ancestry, remains quite unclear. Diodorus (15.60.3; see also Syncellus p. 500 as emended by Dindorf) terms him the son of Arrhidaeus, but Justin (7.4.3) calls him the son of Menelaus, brother of Alexander I. Aelian (*V. H.*12.43) not only calls Amyntas the grandson of Menelaus (whom Aelian considers a bastard), but he also asserts that Amyntas was the servant and slave of Aeropus. Inscriptions (*SIG* 135, 157), however, confirm that Amyntas was the son of Arrhidaeus.[16] If he was the son of Arrhidaeus, Amyntas III was not the son and not necessarily the grandson of a king, indeed possibly only a great-grandson or perhaps even more remotely related to an Argead king.[17] For what it's worth, the sources seem to agree or at least imply that he was part of the royal clan, and the material in Aelian, as Ogden has noted, indicates an attempt—in this case literally so—to bastardize Amyntas' lineage and generally denigrate it, an attempt that was doubtless originally the work of a rival claimant to the throne.[18]

Often, in the Greek world, the eldest son was named after his paternal grandfather and the next eldest after the maternal grandfather. Such a practice, in Amyntas III's case, might confirm his patronymic, but, in his case, it is not helpful. Amyntas III had two sets of sons by two wives, but the birth order of the two sets, relative to each other, is not entirely clear, as we shall shortly see. Justin (Just. 7.4.5), however, at least lists them in what appears to be birth order within the amphimetric sets: Eurydice's sons were Alexander, Perdiccas, and Philip, and Gygaea's sons were Archelaus, Arrhidaeus, and Menelaus. Since neither of the eldest sons in the series was named Menelaus or Arrhidaeus, his sons' names do not help. Amyntas obviously did not follow traditional naming practice for either set of sons; instead, the name choices for his sons imply an inclusive understanding of the dynasty and perhaps suggest that Alexander I was indeed his ancestor and make it even less likely that his father was named Menelaus.

It should be evident that there are too many Amyntases, too much uncertainty, to create any even passably secure reconstruction of the descent of the contenders to the throne during this period. The death of a king whose son was apparently too young to rule on his own triggered a descent into dynastic chaos, but the child king/heir was probably not the only factor in the chaotic succession pattern of the 390s. Archelaus' assassination was, as we have seen, politically motivated at least in part; it may be that those who supported the assassins preferred to have someone on the throne who was not of the line of Archelaus or someone who did not embrace the policies of Archelaus. Since at least two and possibly three lines of descent from the sons of Alexander I apparently battled for domination in the years after Archelaus' murder, Upper Macedonian rulers of Elimeia or Lyncestis may have involved themselves in these Argead conflicts, although this was primarily a struggle within the royal house. (These regions of Upper Macedonia, it will be recalled, were not yet under Argead control and had their own princely houses.)

Diodorus (14.89.2) somewhat cryptically comments that Amyntas did away with his predecessor Pausanias, son of Aeropus, by some sort of trick or treachery. Even if we accept the validity of Diodorus' testimony, we must also note that the actions he ascribes to Amyntas were fairly typical of Argead succession struggles, as subsequent events will demonstrate. Presumably, Amyntas III knew there was dissatisfaction with Pausanias (perhaps as much because of dissatisfaction with Aeropus than with Pausanias himself, since Pausanias ruled so briefly), and was aware of some support for himself, and so acted to claim the throne.

The reign of Amyntas III ultimately generated greater dynastic stability in Macedonia, but not at once and not without a struggle. Given the recent disarray of the dynasty, Amyntas and his line established authority only gradually. Amyntas constituted another example of the wily ruler type so common in the dynasty. He suffered defeats but somehow always managed to recover, typically by calling in the help of an outside power. Much like Perdiccas II, the foreign powers he convinced to assist him were often rivals, like Sparta and Athens. Thus he avoided being entirely dependent on one great power by being dependent on more than one. Amyntas also had variable dealings with regional powers, Thessaly and the Chalcidian League (dominated by Olynthus).

Soon after Amyntas III had, in a manner now more or less traditional for an Argead, likely murdered his way to the throne, the Illyrians invaded Macedonia and Amyntas was forced to flee the country.[19] Diodorus (14.92.3–4) specifies that Amyntas, having given up as hopeless his kingdom, made a gift of territory that bordered Macedonia to the Olynthians. Within a short time, Diodorus says, he recovered his realm with the help of the Thessalians and ruled for twenty-four years. Diodorus notes, however, that some sources say (not, he implies, his main sources) that after Amyntas was forced out, a certain Argaeus ruled for two years, and only after that interlude did Amyntas regain his kingdom. Argaeus is mentioned in historical narratives only in Diodorus, yet chronographic sources also give Argaeus a two-year reign.[20]

The start of Amyntas' reign would have been the most vulnerable period for him in terms of internal as well as external threats, so a claimant, possibly sponsored by the Illyrians, who had some brief period of authority is not implausible. Argaeus' name is Argead, but speculations about which branch of the royal family he might be connected to seem futile,[21] particularly since many doubt his historicity, though I am not among them. To my mind, the existence of a claimant of the same name early in the reign of Philip II (see Chapter 3) lends credence to the historicity of this Argaeus, whether he was the same man or a son or grandson.[22]

Diodorus' narrative also contains a second account of an Illyrian invasion that forced Amyntas to flee; scholars have differed as to whether to conclude that Amyntas really was twice forced into exile by an Illyrian invasion or whether Diodorus accidentally created a doublet and so transformed one event into two.[23] Diodorus' second account of an Illyrian invasion (15.19.2–3) seems, given its location in Diodorus' narrative, to happen c. 383/2, about ten years after the first. As in the first narrative, the Illyrians invade and Amyntas gives the Olynthians territory on their shared border.[24] At this point, this second account begins to differ from the earlier one: when Amyntas unexpectedly recovers his kingdom, the Olynthians, having come to enjoy the territory from their new lands, will not return it. Amyntas forms his own army, allies with the Spartans against the Olynthians, persuades the Spartans to send a general and a military force against the Olynthians, and together the Macedonian and Spartan force (with allies) make war against Olynthus (Diod 15.20.3, 21.1–3).

Xenophon's *Hellenika* (5.2.11–13, 37) supports some aspects of Diodorus' second invasion narrative (Spartan aid) but instead of invading Illyrians, it tells of invading Olynthians who had taken a number of Macedonian sites including Pella itself (in other words, in this version they did more than simply attempt to retain territory they already controlled). In Xenophon, it is not Amyntas who takes the initiative in seeking Spartan assistance but rather Acanthus and Apollonia, unfriendly neighbors of Olynthus who were also threatened by Olynthian power.[25] An Acanthian ambassador supposedly tells the Spartans that Amyntas has withdrawn from many of his cities and is all but driven out of Macedonia.[26] The Spartans come north under Teleutias, who has instructed Amyntas to hire mercenaries and to persuade neighboring kings to join the effort by funding them and he has encouraged Derdas, the king of Elimeia, to join the effort. Xenophon reports that it was the Elimiote cavalry rather than Amyntas' that contributed to Olynthus' defeat and the disbandment of the Chalcidean League (*Hell.* 5.2.37–3.2, 3.8–9, 18).[27]

Isocrates (6.46) further complicates matters by asserting that a defeated Amyntas initially planned to abandon Macedonia but, inspired by a dubious aphorism, instead seized a small fortress, used it as a base to send for reinforcements, got back all of Macedonia in three months, and then spent the rest of his life on the throne, dying an old man. The Isocrates passage cannot easily be reconciled to the Diodorus passage or to Xenophon.[28]

While there can be no certainty, I am inclined to think that the second Diodorus passage is a partial doublet: Amyntas was indeed driven from his kingdom twice, but only the first time by the Illyrians, though there may well have been other Illyrian raids.[29] Diodorus (16.2.2) says that after his defeat by the Illyrians (which defeat is not clear), Amyntas paid them off, presumably to keep them at bay (see following). There are certainly doublets in Diodorus, quite apart from this possible one.[30] The Illyrians had often pressed against Macedonian territory, and Macedonian kings had repeatedly catered to the needs of one great power or another, but never before had a king been compelled to abandon all his territory, as Amyntas was apparently twice forced to do, if not twice by Illyrians.[31] The second time it was the Olynthians. As Zahrnt argues, in the 380s when Amyntas was in a more stable situation, he asked for the land back that he had ceded to them at the time of the first invasion, and the Olynthians refused: as Xenophon says, the Olynthians were initially successful, took a number of cities, and drove Amyntas out of Macedonia, but he regained his kingdom with the help of the Spartans and Elimeia, and the Chalcidean League which Olynthus dominated was disbanded in 379.[32]

For the rest of his reign Amyntas' Macedonia remained, at best, a regional power, though dramatic misfortune was behind Amyntas. Argead dealings with the Thessalians, usually but not always in alliance with the Aleuad clan of Thessaly, had been and would remain close. At one point, apparently switching from one Thessalian faction to another, Amyntas allied himself with Jason of Pherae, getting Perrhaebia (the border region between Macedonia and Thessaly) in return for abandoning his former allies, the Aleuads (Diod. 15.57.2, 60.2; Xen. *Hell.* 6.1.11). Like Perdiccas II before him, Amyntas courted the Athenians as well as the Spartans (thus leading to his "adoption" of one Athenian admiral, Iphicrates; see Chapter 4 for discussion), concluded a treaty with

Athens involving supplying timber to them,[33] acted as an arbitrator in a regional border dispute between Elimeia and Doliche,[34] and later joined the congress of the Hellenes (he sent a representative to vote for him) that led to the Common Peace of 371 (Aeschin. 2.32–33).[35] A late source reports, perhaps correctly, that the people of Pydna built a sanctuary to Amyntas.[36]

In sum, Amyntas' reign was less than glorious and yet, however inglorious his means, Amyntas III got what he wanted in a minimal sort of way.[37] Nothing suggests that he did anything to improve infrastructure, and the poor performance of even his cavalry during the Spartan campaign (unless that is simply a slur of Xenophon's) demonstrates that during his reign Macedonia was a comparatively negligible power, able to remain independent only through the endless intrigues of its ruler. While Xenophon's account of Amyntas is anything but flattering, as we have seen, Diodorus' Amyntas is reasonably competent and certainly not passive. Justin (7.4.4–6) provides an astonishingly positive verdict on Amyntas: he was aggressive and a good general (see further Chapter 4). As we examine the reigns of Amyntas III's sons and the career of his widow Eurydice, we can reflect on how the indignities of Amyntas' reign as well as his demonstrable survival skills may have shaped the goals and policies of his sons and the strategies of Eurydice. It is probably true that Amyntas' reputation suffers by comparison to that of his famous son Philip.[38] Philip would never have been king had his father not demonstrated those remarkable survival skills.

### The Marriages of Amyntas III

Let us now turn to the marriages of Amyntas III. Justin (7.4.5) says that he had two wives: Gygaea (by whom he had three sons: Archelaus, Arrhidaeus, and Menelaus) and Eurydice (by whom he had three sons and a daughter: Alexander, Perdiccas, Philip, and Eurynoe). Given that Amyntas may have been middle-aged when he became king and considering the apparent ages of his two sets of sons (and thus the likely marriage dates for their mothers), Amyntas may well have had an earlier wife and possibly children by her as well.[39]

We do not know for certain which woman of the two Justin names he married first. True, it is often assumed that Gygaea was his first wife,[40] but since her sons did not, so far as we know, challenge any of

Eurydice's sons until early in the reign of Philip II (Just. 8.3.10–11), the third of Eurydice's sons to rule, it seems more likely that Gygaea's were younger, not older, than Eurydice's sons.[41] Amyntas may have married both women within a short period of time (see further in following sections), just as Philip II seems to have married four or possibly five of his wives within two or three years.[42] If Amyntas had produced three sons by Gygaea before becoming king, he would not likely have married Eurydice soon after taking power and would not have rejected Gygaea and her sons before Eurydice had any.[43]

Some other factors also imply that Eurydice's marriage preceded Gygaea's. Justin mentions Eurydice's sons first. Two sources call Alexander II the eldest of Amyntas III's sons (Diod. 16.2.4; Just. 7.4.8), and another (Aeschin. 2.26) speaks of Alexander II as Philip's oldest brother. Perhaps all three sources are thinking only of full brothers, but perhaps not. If Justin listed the two sets of children in birth order, then, as we have already observed, Amyntas did not follow common naming practice, so his naming habits do not help to resolve this issue. There is no direct evidence that Amyntas was polygamous, but it seems quite likely.[44]

Virtually nothing is known of Gygaea other than her name, and only Justin tells us that.[45] Nonetheless, because the only other Gygaea known was an Argead, the sister of Alexander I (Herod. 5.17–18), it has been assumed that Amyntas' wife was also a member of the royal family.[46] Given that none of Gygaea's sons ruled and all of Eurydice's did, this is an especially problematic assumption to make: one must assume that something about Eurydice and her connections was so important that it merited privileging Eurydice's sons over those of another Argead. If, however, as I have argued, Gygaea's sons were significantly younger than Eurydice's, the dominance of Eurydice's sons is easily explained, even if Gygaea was indeed an Argead by birth. Let us bear this issue in mind as we consider Amyntas' marriage to Eurydice. Since Justin attributes no ethnicity to Gygaea, whether or not she was Argead, she was probably Macedonian.

### The Identity of Eurydice and Her Marriage to Amyntas III

Whereas the problem with Gygaea is that we know too little about her, the problem with Eurydice is that, in a sense, we know too much, but much of what we "know" is profoundly contradictory. Let us begin with the thorny issue of Eurydice's identity, primarily her ethnic identity, and whether it mattered in ancient times. Strabo (7.7.8) explicitly states that Philip's mother, Eurydice, was the granddaughter of Arrhabaeus, having just explained that Arrhabaeus' family, the Lyncestian princely line, was the part of the Bacchiad dynasty from Corinth. In short, in genealogical terms, they—like the Argeads and Aeacids (the Molossian royal family to which Olympias, mother of Alexander belonged)—counted as Greek and claimed a heroic founder; indeed, both the Argeads and Bacchiads were supposed descendants of Heracles. During the Peloponnesian War, in the reign of Perdiccas II, Arrhabaeus, in alliance with Illyrians (Thuc. 4.125), opposed the Spartans and Macedonians; the ultimate result was an unhappy one for Perdiccas II. Like the other princely families of Upper Macedonia, Arrhabaeus and his line resisted Argead control. Thus, on her mother's side, Eurydice came from an upper Macedonian dynasty that claimed heroic Greek descent.

It is her father's family and ethnic descent that is at issue. Strabo also states that Eurydice's father was Sirras, a patronym confirmed by three inscriptions from Vergina (see Chapter 5).[47] Unfortunately, we do not know who Sirras was or where he came from. He has been variously identified as Elimiote, Orestian, Lyncestian, or Illyrian.[48] The *Suda* s.v. "Karanos" not only says that Eurydice was Illyrian, but also that some sources claim her children were suppositious (see also Lib. *Hypoth.* c. 18 and discussion in Chapters 3 and 4).[49] A third passage attributed to Plutarch (Plut. *Mor.* 14c) describes her as Illyrian and "three times a barbarian."[50] Aristotle (*Pol.* 1311b) refers to a war Archelaus fought against Arrhabaeus and Sirras but offers no explanation of the identity of the Sirras he refers to.[51] The name "Sirras" otherwise appears in only one inscription.[52] "Sirras" may or may not be a Greek name, but since some personal names were used by both non-Greek and Greek peoples of northern Greece, this particular issue may not be very relevant to understanding Eurydice's identity. Terming Eurydice Illyrian could refer to her general or majority line of descent rather than specifically to her father. Athenaeus (13.560f)—in a passage that cites Duris of Samos—describes Cynnane as Illyrian, though she was one of the daughters of Philip II by an Illyrian wife and so only half Illyrian. Given the known alliance between Arrhabaeus and the Illyrians and the tendency of elites to seal alliances with marriages, it seems likely enough that the granddaughter of a Lyncestian ruler was also partly Illyrian.[53]

The only really compelling argument against attributing at least a partly Illyrian identity to Eurydice has to do with a notorious dispute that happened many years later, near the end of the reign of Philip II (in 338 or 337), a dispute already discussed (in Chapter 1).[54] According to Plutarch (*Alex*. 9.4), at a symposium celebrating Philip's marriage to his last bride, Cleopatra, her guardian Attalus wished for the Macedonians to beg the gods for a legitimate successor to be produced from the marriage of Philip and Cleopatra. Plutarch next describes an incensed Alexander who asks if he is then a bastard. Athenaeus (13.557e), in a slightly different version of this incident, has Attalus state that now (presumably after Philip's marriage to Cleopatra) legitimate, not bastard, kings will be born (the same Greek terms are employed about legitimacy and bastardy as found in Plutarch). Generally, Attalus' insult has been understood not to charge Olympias with adultery, but rather with not being Macedonian, that is to say that it was an ethnic rather than a personal insult. Philip, in both of these accounts, either tolerates Attalus' remarks or actively supports him.

The argument has been that Attalus would not have dared to utter these remarks and Philip would not have supported him if Philip himself had had a foreign mother, let alone one from a people Greeks considered barbarian. If Eurydice was partly Illyrian, then Philip II, not Alexander III, would have been the first Macedonian king who had a foreign mother. But it is not clear that Attalus' insult to Alexander was about ethnicity any more than it was about Olympias' adultery. Attalus' remark may have been based on his presumption that he and his family were superior—and thus more legitimate—than the family of Olympias.[55] When one recalls that Philip II married seven women, only two of whom could count as Macedonian, one begins to wonder. It seems unlikely that Philip would have married so many women whose children could not have been considered legitimate if ethnicity was the sole determinative in legitimacy.[56]

As we've already noted, "Illyrian" is a term Greek writers employed about the peoples to the north and northwest of Macedonia, though in actuality there was no unified Illyrian state in Argead times and no reason to think that those in this region understood themselves as one people rather than many.[57] The Illyrians are, in other words, literally a constructed "Other." Groups (but not necessarily the same groups) of these Illyrian peoples drove Amyntas III out of his kingdom and later defeated and killed his son Perdiccas III in battle. Given that Argeads certainly married into/with other peoples who had been (internal and domestic) enemies and would do so again, the problematizing of Eurydice's family background can't be related to their past military opposition. Moreover, Arrhabaeus, Eurydice's maternal grandfather, had certainly fought the Argeads, and in alliance with the Illyrians.[58]

Describing Eurydice as "Illyrian" when she can at most have been only partly Illyrian could be the consequence of a kind of racialized thinking, similar to that in many slave societies, where even a drop of African blood led to a categorization of someone as "black." On the other hand, as may be the case with the description of Cynnane, it may reference a cultural identity rather than specific lines of descent. Cynnane, the daughter of Philip by his Illyrian wife Audata, apparently learned from her mother to be a warrior and she in turn passed this skill on to her daughter Adea Eurydice. While we know of nothing that associates Philip II's mother Eurydice with warfare, she was certainly an assertive woman, at least some of the time, and the careers of Audata, Cynnane, and Adea Eurydice do imply that Illyrian elite women played a less circumscribed role in society than Greek and Macedonian women did.[59] Moreover, the pseudo-Plutarch passage exaggerates Eurydice's supposed non-Greek ethnicity to make its point: even the very Illyrian, very barbarian Eurydice modeled good behavior for her sons. Remnants of the rivalry between the two sets of Amyntas III's sons, and thus surviving "bastardizing" kinds of stories (see Chapters 3 and 4)—probably intensified by subsequent resistance to and resentment of Philip's success—have been preserved in these later authors,[60] but none of this rhetorical or political exaggeration prevents the possibility that Eurydice actually was part Illyrian.

The problem of Eurydice's alleged Illyrian identity merges into a larger discussion about whether or not ancient Macedonians were Greek. The second problem complicates the first. Alexander I, by his participation in the Olympics, seems to have gotten some formal recognition of the Argeads as Greeks, in keeping with their mythic Heraclid origin. Greek authors sometimes recognized the Macedonians as a Greek people and sometimes did not. Many of our written sources derive from the period in which Philip was gradually coming to dominate the Greek peninsula and reflect the political hostility against him, particularly in Athens.

Most modern analysis of ethnic identity treats the category not as an absolute but rather as a fluid, frequently changing construct, having little to do with modern notions of ethnicity, tied as they are to the evolution of the nation-state.[61] Little survives of the ancient Macedonian language, but it does seem likely that it was a Greek dialect.[62] Macedonian religious expression had mixed aspects, ones that varied over time. The Olympian deities were honored in Macedonia, but so were some Thracian religious experiences.[63] By the middle of the sixth century, their burial practices, despite some shared aspects, were distinct from those of their Thracian and Thessalian neighbors.[64] How Macedonians themselves, apart from the royal family, felt about their Greekness is comparatively unknown because our extant sources are not Macedonian. Obviously, considerable differences existed within the groups usually considered Greek: Spartans and Athenians and Boeotians had very different ways of life. The issue is, in a sense, at what point regional difference becomes something more fundamental. Though Macedonia had important urban centers before the fourth century, it was less urban than many other regions of Greece, retained a monarchy when most other areas had given that institution up, and preserved (or more likely consciously embraced) more archaic customs than was common in central and southern Greece. Views of Macedonia from other regions of Greece seem to vary depending more on their hostility or friendliness toward Macedonian political power than on any fixed belief about Macedonian ethnicity.[65] Thus Eurydice's complex genealogy may have proved more of a political problem for her sons—particularly Philip—in terms of the wider Greek world, as Macedonian power grew, than it was for her. The solution he (or they) found, as we shall see (Chapters 5 and 6), was to stress her public role; in effect, they took the offensive.

The marriage of Amyntas III and Eurydice happened in the context of the aftermath of the Illyrian invasion of c. 393/2. Eurydice likely had married Amyntas III by 390, might well have married him a year or two earlier than that,[66] and had to have married him by the very early 380s, given that her oldest son ruled on his own c. 370 and must have been at the least in his late teens at the time of his ascension to the throne. As I have suggested, Amyntas married twice, both times relatively early in his reign. One marriage was directed at the external problem of the Illyrians (and Lyncestians) and the other, especially if Gygaea was not only Macedonian but Argead, aimed to address internal problems: the consolidation of the dynasty. This internal marriage alliance may also have happened in the post-invasion context.

What did the marriage of Amyntas III and Eurydice mean, particularly in political terms? Its initiation apparently relates to Macedonian recovery from the Illyrian invasion (indeed, some deduce that the invasion was actually a joint Lyncestian-Illyrian enterprise),[67] whether Eurydice was simply Lyncestian or a combination of Lyncestian and Illyrian.[68] The marriage probably happened as part of an attempt to bind Amyntas more closely to one of the problematic regions of Macedonia and to those bordering it. We do not hear of trouble with the Lyncestians again until the reign of Alexander II, though whether Eurydice's marriage had anything to do with these improved relations one can only speculate.

If the supposed second Illyrian invasion of Amyntas' reign was indeed a doublet, then the Illyrians did not again trouble Macedonia during the reign of Amyntas even though they did invade Molossia and were repulsed only with considerable effort. During the reign of Eurydice's son Alexander II there was some trouble with the Illyrians and in the reign of Perdiccas III, there was another very serious Illyrian invasion, as we shall shortly see (see Chapters 3 and 4). No proof exists, of course, that the "Illyrians" who drove Amyntas out are the same "Illyrians" who gave the Molossians or later Alexander II and particularly Perdiccas III such trouble. Moreover, if Eurydice's marriage was part of some general accord between Amyntas and the Lyncestians and perhaps Illyrians, the subsequent peace could have been the result of that accord, not simply the marriage. On the other hand, the marriage seemed to be an integral part of the arrangement.[69] In effect, trying to distinguish the two may be impossible; this is the kind of chicken-and-egg problem that makes assessing the importance of marriage alliances so difficult.[70]

For practical purposes, we know nothing further of Eurydice's life during the reign of Amyntas III, apart from the spurious charges of adultery against her (see Chapters 3 and 4)—charges that may postdate the reign of Amyntas III, given the smooth accession of Eurydice's son Alexander II immediately following the death of Amyntas III. Considering that the story that Philip II, at very young age, served as a hostage to the Illyrians is usually regarded as false (see Chapters 3 and 4), it is likely that all of Eurydice's children remained in Macedonia during her marriage. Eurydice probably remained at court, doubtless promoting the future of her sons and, perhaps, the marriage of her daughter. Her inscription commemorating her own education after her sons had matured, preserved in the corpus of Plutarch (*Mor.* 14c), could date from this period, but it more likely, given its diction, dates to the period after Amyntas III's death (see further Chapter 5). As discussed in the first chapter, royal wives likely brought with them something of an entourage and may have been expected to speak for or represent or at least liaise with their birth families. Since, soon after the death of her husband, we hear that Eurydice has *philoi* (see Chapters 3 and 4), she almost certainly had a base at court, though, like all factions, this one was probably ever-shifting in membership.

While we do not have specifics about how the next king was chosen, it would appear that kings did sometimes indicate whom they desired as successor and ordinarily a king's oldest son—if an adult—might expect to follow his father, but such decisions did not always endure, and even if they did, they did not endure without challenge. The presumption is that a candidate for the throne had to have support from some groups within the elite and then retain that support. Since the eldest of Eurydice's sons took the throne immediately after his father's death and references in our sources (see Chapter 3) imply that, initially, he had support within the elite that he subsequently lost, it seems reasonable to assume that Alexander II was the choice of his father (as inscriptional evidence may indicate) and that some elite groups did support him, initially.[71] Alexander II soon experienced difficulty and lost much of that support, but this loss was, as we shall see, a consequence of events after the death of Amyntas III.

Why were the sons of Eurydice prioritized? [72] As I have argued, one possible factor in the preference for Eurydice's sons over Gygaea's would have been their ages, but this factor alone does not explain the continued predominance of Eurydice's sons through two more reigns. The actions of her two younger sons, as we shall see, sometimes contributed to their continued predominance, whereas when Alexander II became king, neither he nor his brothers were, so far as we know, proven candidates.

Why then, at that early stage, prefer the sons of a Lyncestian and perhaps partly Illyrian woman over those of a woman almost certainly Macedonian and possibly Argead, given that none of Amyntas' sons by either mother had, as yet, a track record? Eurydice and her connections must have mattered more than Gygaea's, probably because Eurydice's Lyncestian connection was just as important as her possible Illyrian one. Eurydice herself may have been a better succession advocate than Gygaea, but the only evidence for her advocacy originates in the period after Amyntas' death.

When, after the assassination of her son Alexander II, Eurydice appears in the sources, she participates in a faction focused on her and her sons and battles to preserve the throne for them. She seems familiar with international diplomacy and her husband's past dealings and is certainly familiar with court politics (see Chapter 4). That knowledge and familiarity cannot have been acquired overnight; she must have become knowledgeable about court affairs and international dealings while her husband was alive.[73] Was she at the "center of a faction" that supported normalized relations with the Illyrians?[74] Perhaps. My own view is that she had *philoi* who supported the candidacy of her son Alexander II. No one became king without some elite group behind him, and Alexander II became king, originally, without a serious contender for the succession, so he must have had a faction behind him.

Whether this faction had an Illyrian policy or not we do not know. Especially if Gygaea was not an Argead, Eurydice could have been perceived as simply having the more prestigious descent. As this might suggest, I believe that the status of the mother was a factor in the ability of a king's son to succeed to the throne, though not the only one (obviously, for a king with multiple sons, the king's judgment of the character and skills of his possible heirs must also have been an issue).[75] Müller rightly speaks of the "symbolic capital" royal wives accumulated and wielded.[76] The attempts to denigrate Eurydice (see following and Chapter 4) speak to that, as do events involving Alexander III and his mother Olympias at the end of Philip's reign.[77]

By the closing days of Amyntas' reign, Eurydice and her sons had clearly won the first round of the succession battle with Gygaea and her sons. The extraordinarily hostile tradition about Eurydice preserved in Justin and some other sources is testimony to the original succession battle between Gygaea and Eurydice, whenever it began, and its perpetuation into the reign of Philip, possibly supplemented by the dynastic challenges of Ptolemy Alorites, Pausanias, and Argaeus (see Chapters 3 and 4).[78] Justin (7.4.7–8) pictures an adulterous Eurydice plotting to kill her husband (her son-in-law has become her lover), thus betraying her daughter and her sons, and he claims that she even planned to murder her sons.[79] This is a classic example of an amphimetric dispute where dynastic rivals "bastardize" their half-siblings by smearing the half-siblings' mother. (While it is likely enough that Gygaea and her supporters promoted her sons and denigrated those of Eurydice, the amphimetric struggle, at least the fragmentary remains we have of it, seems primarily to date from the period after the death of Amyntas and therefore it is discussed in Chapter 4.)

Amyntas died old, of natural causes, having kept his kingdom together and even prospered in a modest way in the later years of his reign, and appearing to leave a clear succession behind him. Eurydice, at the time of his death, was probably toward the end of her thirties.[80] Given that her marriage likely post-dated the Illyrian invasion at the beginning of Amyntas' reign, her situation during her married life had been comparatively secure (apart from the apparently brief Olynthian invasion or incursion), especially if Amyntas had made it clear that her eldest son was his preferred successor. For Eurydice and for the rest of Macedonia, this security would rapidly end.

# 3

# *The Rule of the Eurydice's Sons*

## *Alexander II, Perdiccas III, and Philip II*

On the face of it, Amyntas III would not seem like a hard act to follow. True, he did manage to save his kingdom from long-term foreign rule and the later stages of his reign were free of dynastic strife. Although he proved comparatively adept at coping with disaster and the threat of it, his chronic military weakness meant that he was rarely if ever proactive, presumably because he was not able to be. In practice, he always had to react to trouble by working in concert with and in de facto subordination to other powers. On the other hand, he had a long reign for a Macedonian king (even allowing time off for flight/s from the kingdom) and, unlike so many Argeads, he died old and not by violence. In practice, he did prove hard to equal, at least hard to equal for his first two sons by Eurydice.

Judging by their actions, Amyntas III's three sons by Eurydice tried to avoid their father's often parlous situation by pursuing more aggressive policies, but they did so with comparatively little success until Philip II stabilized the kingdom c. 357. Before that point, dynastic instability once more enabled (or invited) interference and invasion by assorted foreign powers and assorted ambitious Argeads. Alexander II ruled little more than a year before he was murdered by a Macedonian faction. Perdiccas III perished in a massive defeat, having ruled longer than his brother but nowhere nearly as long as his father. Consequently, there was little or no internal or external stability in Macedonia between 370 and 357. Amyntas' first two successors, the elder sons of Eurydice, were, arguably, even less successful than he had been. It was not immediately apparent that his third son, Philip II, would fare any better; certainly the odds seemed against him at the time he took the throne. It was in this prolonged period of internal and external instability after the death of Amyntas III that Eurydice would play an important role.

### Alexander II (370/69–368/7)

Diodorus (15.60.3) remarks on the coincidence that Amyntas III died in the same year that Jason of Pherae, the ambitious ruler of Thessaly, was murdered. The battle of Leuctra, spelling astonishing defeat to Sparta and new-found great power status to Thebes, had happened the year before these two deaths. The combination of these three events shaped Alexander II's brief reign, not only because he had to deal with the consequences of all three, but also because he had to cope with a new and in some ways unprecedented situation that arose at the time he became king, a situation that altered the balance of power in the Greek peninsula, particularly in the north.[1]

Despite his youth,[2] Alexander II succeeded his father without any internal resistance that we know about. Soon after he took the throne, however, presumably hoping to take advantage of his inexperience, some Illyrian peoples may have invaded or threatened to do so until he somehow placated them. He supposedly had to pay them off, possibly though, not probably, offering his youngest full brother, the future Philip II, as a hostage (Just. 7.5.1; see also Diod. 16.2.2).[3] In contrast to this vulnerability and his avoidance of conflict in terms of the Illyrians, when the Aleuads of Larissa in Thessaly asked Alexander II for help against their new and tyrannical Thessalian overlord, Alexander of Pherae, Alexander II obliged and took the offensive. While Alexander of Pherae was preparing to invade Macedonia, Alexander II, with his Thessalian allies, took Larissa (partly by betrayal, partly by siege) and Crannon too. Doubtless Alexander II hoped to win military glory at the very start of his reign. Apart from the general acclaim that this campaign might give the new king, Alexander II may also have been thinking of reversing the relatively subordinate relationship with Thessaly that had existed under Amyntas III.[4] Initially, as we have noted, Alexander II retained his family's "traditional" alliance with the Aleuads. After this success at Larissa and Crannon, however, the young king then refused to relinquish to his Aleuad allies the towns he had taken, though he had promised to do so (Diod. 15.61.3–5).[5] Retention of areas conquered may have been his plan, or at least his hope, from the start.[6] Just as his father Amyntas III had abandoned the Aleuads for the sake of territorial gain (see Chapter 2), so now did Alexander II.

The Aleuads, betrayed by their ally, next sought aid from the newly powerful Thebes (Plut. *Pel.* 26.1; Diod. 15.67.3). Alexander II had not, apparently, considered the possibility of Theban intervention. According to Diodorus (15.67.3–4), the Thebans instructed Pelopidas (a general who, in association with Epaminondas, had transformed Thebes into the dominant military power in the Greek peninsula) to settle things in Thessaly to the best interests of Thebes. By the time Pelopidas arrived, Alexander II had apparently already departed.[7] Pelopidas found Alexander II's garrison at Larissa, expelled it, and marched on to Macedonia.[8] Diodorus asserts that Pelopidas then made an alliance with Alexander II. It can hardly have been one between equals. Not only had Alexander II been humiliated militarily, but he now had to turn over his brother Philip to Pelopidas as a hostage. Pelopidas, having settled matters in Thessaly and Macedonia to his liking, then returned to Thebes.[9]

Whereas Diodorus implies that Pelopidas' intervention in Macedonian affairs came as a consequence of and probably as a punishment for Alexander II's activities in Thessaly, Plutarch's description of Pelopidas' activities in Thessaly (*Pel.* 26.3–5) makes no mention of Alexander II or his intervention in Thessalian affairs and instead states that Alexander II and a rival invited Pelopidas to Macedonia. Plutarch also provides much more detail than Diodorus about Pelopidas' actions in Macedonia. Plutarch specifies that after Pelopidas had settled things in Thessaly, he went to Macedonia because Ptolemy (Plutarch gives the man in question no patronymic) was at war with Alexander II[10] and both men had asked Pelopidas to come as arbiter, judge, and give aid to whichever side he determined to have been wronged. According to Plutarch, Pelopidas supposedly settled their differences, returned Macedonian exiles (which ones and by whom exiled are not specified by Plutarch, but probably people expelled by Amyntas III), and took not only Philip, as Diodorus had reported, but also thirty sons of the most distinguished Macedonians as hostages.

Thus Diodorus' narrative, even though only Philip is mentioned as a hostage, implies that Pelopidas took a hostage as punishment for Alexander II's behavior, but in Plutarch, the more extensive hostage taking he mentions appears to happen to guarantee the success of Pelopidas' settlement of the dispute between Alexander II and Ptolemy.

This being so, it would be interesting to know if the thirty hostages belonged to both sides in the dispute (i.e., that of Alexander II and that of Ptolemy). Given that Plutarch does not name a hostage from Ptolemy's side and does say that Alexander II's brother Philip was taken, Alexander II (not surprisingly, given Pelopidas' role as Thessalian protector) seems the one more severely punished, and Ptolemy the one favored. On the other hand, simply because it was a settlement between two sides, hostages from both were probably required, though Ptolemy's side may have gotten off more lightly. One may also wonder whether it is true, as Plutarch (*Pel.* 26.4) asserts, that both Ptolemy and Alexander II summoned Pelopidas or whether Alexander II simply put the best face he could on Pelopidas's appearance in Macedonia, quite possibly invited by Ptolemy alone. The Theban general clearly acted in his own and Theban self-interest, furthering Theban ambitions in Macedonia and certainly weakening Alexander II's position even more, presumably to advantage Thebes at the expense of Macedonia.[11] Despite Plutarch's somewhat hagiographical approach to Pelopidas, his account does much more than that of Diodorus to put this series of events in the context of wider Macedonian politics.

Pelopidas's first settlement of Thessalian and Macedonian affairs was quickly overturned. Diodorus (15.71.1, 16.2.4) reports that Ptolemy (here termed "Alorites," meaning from Alorus) treacherously killed Alexander II (whom Diodorus describes as Ptolemy's brother) and says that Ptolemy was himself king for three years (see following and Chapter 4). Marsyas (*FGrH* 135/6 F 11 = Ath. 14. 629d), presumably Marsyas of Pella,[12] states that Alexander II, while watching a performance of a Macedonian dance, was killed by those "around Ptolemy," that is to say Ptolemy's faction.[13] Plutarch (*Pel.* 27.1–3) recounts that matters in Macedonia had once more become disordered—Ptolemy had killed the king and come into control of the kingdom—and that the king's (i.e., Alexander II's) friends were calling upon Pelopidas for help, whereas Demosthenes (19.195–196) refers to a certain Apollophanes of Pydna as one of those who had killed Alexander II; he does not mention Ptolemy but his wording indicates that Apollophanes was part of a group of assassins. Justin (7.5.4–5), as part of a larger narrative that blames Eurydice for other crimes, claims that Eurydice treacherously killed her son Alexander. The scholiast for Aeschines 2.29 says that Ptolemy and Eurydice worked together to bring about the death of Alexander II (the scholiast is also the sole source for the idea that Ptolemy married Eurydice).

Why did Alexander II's reign unravel with such striking speed? We will deal with Eurydice's role in these events in the next chapter and also discuss at greater length the identity of the mysterious Ptolemy (who may or may not have been an Argead). Given the very different natures of our extant accounts, it is impossible to tell whether Ptolemy actually objected to Alexander II's failed imperialistic policy in Thessaly and had previously accepted or even supported Alexander II or whether Ptolemy simply took advantage of the trouble Alexander's failure and its aftermath generated to pursue long-existing goals. I incline to the latter view. Ptolemy would not have been able to start what may, even before the assassination, have been a civil war (if Plut. *Pel.* 26.3 is taken literally) unless he already had fairly broad support.

In fact, the remarks of Marsyas and Demosthenes indicate that a faction, not simply Ptolemy himself, was responsible for the assassination of Alexander II, as does the number of hostages Pelopidas required on both the first and second (see following) occasions he tried to settle Macedonian matters. Thus, the likelihood is that Alexander II was purposefully assassinated by a court faction led by Ptolemy and possibly involving his mother Eurydice (on her role, see further Chapter 4).[14] Whether or not Ptolemy himself was simply self-serving, the support he seems to have had behind him demonstrates that Alexander II's Thessalian escapade (whether because it had involved the betrayal of the Aleuads or more likely because it had led to humiliation at the hand of the Thessalians and Thebans) lost the young king much of the support with which he had begun his reign. One can easily surmise that many Macedonians saw him as a rash, impulsive, and inexperienced young king and that Ptolemy gained followers by portraying himself as more mature and less inclined to overreach. Alexander II must have been quite young when he took the throne but, though Alexander III and Philip II were both about the same age when they did so, they exercised much better judgment and were able, however gradually, to establish and maintain a broad base of support, whereas Alexander II's rapidly eroded.

A possible policy of Alexander II's might also have contributed to the loss of support. A well-known fragment of Anaximenes (*FGrH* 72 F 4) attributes the creation of the *petzhetairoi* (Foot Companions) to a king named Alexander. Difficulties exist with connecting this innovation— the initiation of the first serious infantry in Macedonia, with a name implying a similar relation between the king and this infantry as that between the king and the *hetairoi* (Companions; see Chapter 1)—to any of the Macedonian kings named Alexander. Alexander II could be the king referred to, and thus the motivation (or at least support) for Alexander II's assassination could have developed because the innovation threatened the existing order, particularly the thoroughgoing domination of the Macedonian elite because of its virtual monopoly on military might.[15] None of our narratives mentions such a connection, but then none demonstrates much understanding of Macedonian internal affairs. Hatzopoulos suggests that Ptolemy's conspiracy was inspired by the coastal cities and their ruling elites, as part of a regional dispute.[16]

### *Perdiccas III (368/7–360/359) and Ptolemy*

What happened immediately after the murder of Alexander II is questionable in virtually every respect.[17] We do not even know who was king or whether any one person was immediately and generally recognized as king. Our sources contradict each other about whether Ptolemy ever ruled in his own right or whether immediately after the assassination of Alexander II he simply became regent for Perdiccas III, the second son of Amyntas III and Eurydice. The order of events in the period of the aftermath of Alexander II's assassination is disputed. Perhaps most confusing of all is that the scholiast for Aeschines 2.29 asserts that Ptolemy and Eurydice murdered Alexander II and that Eurydice married Ptolemy. If, however, Eurydice did marry Ptolemy, willingly or not, the other sources seem unaware of it (see further discussion in Chapter 4.)

I argue for the following order of events: soon after Alexander II's murder, a certain Pausanias tried to claim the throne, but the Athenian general Iphicrates prevented him and safeguarded the throne for Eurydice's remaining children; Ptolemy attempted to rule on his own until, for a second time, Pelopidas intervened and compelled Ptolemy to accept the regency alone.[18] All of these events likely happened within a short period time, a matter of months. If Eurydice did indeed marry Ptolemy, I believe that the marriage happened after the death of Alexander II, most likely after Pelopidas's second settlement of Macedonia, but it could, though this is less likely, have transpired soon after Alexander II's murder (see further discussion in Chapter 4).

I further suggest that Ptolemy probably tried to achieve recognition as king but failed. In my view, soon after the assassination, the Athenians intervened, at Eurydice's invitation, in favor of the succession of Eurydice's sons and in opposition to an invasion by another Argead claimant and then the Thebans intervened in Macedonia, for a second time, and Pelopidas supported the succession of Perdiccas III and limited Ptolemy to the regency. Some scholars place the Athenian intervention before the death of Alexander II, rather than after it, and before the second Theban intervention.

As we have seen, Diodorus considered Ptolemy king after Alexander II's murder (as do the *Marmor Parium* [*FGrH* 239A 74] and other chronologies) and allotted him a three-year reign (Diod. 15.71.1). It is not certain, however, that Ptolemy was ever king and, even if he were, he cannot have been king long since no coins of the period bear Ptolemy's name. Aeschines (2.29) refers to him as *epitropos* (on the meaning of this term, see discussion in Chapter 1) in a context that appears to refer to the period after Athenian intervention. The scholiast for Aeschines 2.29 terms Ptolemy an *epitropos* for Perdiccas and Philip and says that he ruled three years. Plutarch (*Pel.* 27.2–3) says that Ptolemy had seized control of rule, though whether he means that Ptolemy had become king is difficult to say.[19] Doubtless Ptolemy had killed Alexander II hoping to be recognized as king and was supported in that ambition by a faction, whereas Eurydice and her sons believed that Perdiccas, her second son, was now king, though he was probably not yet an adult. Both candidates may have been acclaimed by different groups, and the news of Alexander II's murder—let alone any subsequent events—may have been slow to spread.

An incident mentioned by three ancient sources is relevant to the issue of whether Ptolemy became king after the death of Alexander II, but its chronology is problematic. Aeschines (2.26–27), in a speech delivered many years after the death of Alexander II and reported yet more years later to the Athenian assembly, describes events surrounding a threat to the succession of the sons of Eurydice, but not one originating with Ptolemy. (Aeschines cannot himself have been an eyewitness, and his source could have been Athenian, not Macedonian.) According to Aeschines, a certain Pausanias, having been in exile (*Suda* s.v. "Karanos" says he'd been exiled by Amyntas III[20]), returned for the sake of *arche* (rule) and was favored by the situation and by the support of many. Pausanias had a Greek force and took Anthemus, Therme, Strepsa, and other places (*Suda* s.v. "Karanos" says he actually took over rule). Aeschines claims that the majority of Macedonians favored Pausanias, though not all. The implication of Aeschines' remarks is certainly that Pausanias was an Argead, possibly one with more clout than Ptolemy.[21] Diodorus (16.2.6), for what it is worth, says that Pausanias was "related to the royal house." According to Aeschines (2.29), Eurydice salvaged the situation by persuading the Athenian admiral Iphicrates to give aid. The *Suda* (s.v. "Karanos") says that Eurydice and an Athenian general (presumably Iphicrates) formed an alliance and drove Pausanias out. Ptolemy, at the time of this incident, is clearly not king and probably not regent, since he is not mentioned by any source.

When did Iphicrates save the day? The text of Aeschines explicitly places Iphicrates' salvage operation after the deaths of both Amyntas III and Alexander II, names Perdiccas and Philip, and says they were still under age. It is significant that, in Aeschines, Eurydice asked Iphicrates to protect kingship for her sons, and no mention is made of Ptolemy in connection to the Iphicrates episode, though immediately after, Aeschines blames Ptolemy, whom he explains had been made *epitropos*, for his anti-Athenian policy about Amphipolis and alliance with Thebes. Aeschines follows up with a similar complaint about Perdiccas III's Amphipolis policy, once he had come to rule. In other words, Aeschines seems to picture an order of events in which at first, after the murder of Alexander II, given that the obvious heir is a minor, no one is clearly king or regent and Iphicrates is thus called upon to protect Eurydice's sons' claim on the throne against Pausanias. Then, given the order of the speech, Ptolemy is regent, and then yet later Perdiccas III becomes king in his own right. Cornelius Nepos (*Iphic.* 3.2), though vaguer, implies that the incident occurred after the death of Alexander II, since he mentions only two sons (naming Perdiccas and Philip) as the ones who were driven out. The only other ancient source that mentions Iphicrates' intervention does not clearly place the incident after the death of Alexander II. The *Suda* says that the incident happened after the death of Amyntas but does not mention the death of Alexander II, and it says that the sons of Amyntas (names unspecified) had been driven out by Pausanias. This would mean, if the incident happened while Alexander II still lived, that he had been driven out of his kingdom. On the whole, it seems most likely that Pausanias's incursion and Iphicrates' response happened soon after Alexander II's murder. We should prize the testimony of the fourth-century source over the much later (and vaguer) ones. I see no reason to do the reverse and significantly emend the text of Aeschines.[22] (See further discussion in Chapter 4.)

According to Plutarch (*Pel.* 27.2–3), after Alexander II's death the friends of the dead king called upon Pelopidas (who had already returned to Thessaly to deal with a recurrence of troubles there) for help.[23] If my order of events is accepted, then renewed Theban interest in Macedonia could have been triggered, in part, by Athenian intervention, not simply by the appeal of Alexander II's friends after Ptolemy's murder of Alexander II. Pelopidas would, in other words, have been motivated not simply by the desire to maintain the position Thebes had initially asserted in the north but also by great power rivalry with Athens for domination of the north.[24] Pelopidas, who had brought no soldiers with him to Thessaly since he had originally set off on a diplomatic mission, once he had hired some mercenaries, immediately went from Thessaly to Macedonia and marched against Ptolemy. When Pelopidas approached, Ptolemy persuaded Pelopidas' mercenaries to change sides by bribing them. However, fearful of Pelopidas's name and repute, Ptolemy acknowledged him as the stronger. When he met with Pelopidas, he welcomed him, asked for favor, agreed to preserve the realm for the brothers of the dead man, and to have the same friends and enemies as the Thebans.[25] In addition, he gave Pelopidas his son Philoxenus and fifty *hetairoi* as hostages.[26] Unlike Pelopidas' first attempted settlement, this second one clearly favored Eurydice's sons over Ptolemy and punished Ptolemy: his son was now a hostage and the number of hostages was greater, even though this time the hostages may have belonged to only one faction (Ptolemy's) as opposed to two, as in the earlier episode.[27] Despite Pelopidas's short-term vulnerability because he lacked immediate access to his own troops, Ptolemy's actions obviously signal his recognition of the greater power of Thebes.

Pelopidas, as a statesman and power broker, despite Plutarch's rather rosy characterization of him, acts in pursuit of enlarging Thebes' role in northern Greece, though he does seem interested in maintaining some level of stability in Macedonia. Plutarch's narrative strongly implies that Pelopidas and the Thessalians, though initially more displeased with Alexander II than with Ptolemy, prevented Ptolemy from becoming king when Alexander II and Ptolemy first quarreled, and then, after Alexander II's assassination, preserved the throne for Alexander II's brothers. Aeschines (2.29) calls Ptolemy the *epitropos* and complains about Ptolemy's "ungrateful and unprincipled conduct" in terms of

Ptolemy's acceptance of a Theban alliance when the Athenians were disputing about Amphipolis with Thebes. Ptolemy's anti-Athenian policy in terms of Amphipolis may simply have been the result of pressure from Thebes or a return to traditional Macedonian policy in terms of Amphipolis.[28]

Thus the evidence suggests that Ptolemy tried to be king and perhaps even gained some recognition as king but, in the end, he simply served as regent (an institutional role possibly imposed on Macedonia by the Theban Pelopidas; see Chapter 1) for Eurydice's remaining sons.[29] Nothing more is known of the events of Ptolemy's brief regency. Whatever the order of events, both the Thebans and the Athenians were responsible for safeguarding Alexander II's throne and, after the murder of Alexander II, securing the throne for Eurydice's remaining sons and forcing Ptolemy to accept mere regency.[30] Eurydice's sons would not have been able to inherit or retain the throne without the external support of the two major powers of the day; they had some internal support, but that by itself was not enough. One might add that possibly the most important long-term impact of Alexander II's reign was the departure of Philip and more than eighty other elite Macedonians to Thebes; their Theban experience would have both military and political consequences for the future of Macedonia and the entire Greek peninsula.[31]

The next episode in this dynastic soap opera was somewhere between predictable and inevitable. Diodorus (16.2.2) recounts that Ptolemy was assassinated by his "brother" Perdiccas, who from then on ruled as king in his own right. The scholiast for Aeschines 2.29 specifies that Perdiccas organized a plot to eliminate Ptolemy. It is possible, though not likely, that Perdiccas III eliminated Ptolemy only after Perdiccas had taken over independent rule.[32] Perdiccas III's brother Philip returned from his years as a hostage in Thebes, probably soon after Ptolemy's death and the beginning of Perdiccas' independent rule.[33] Carystius of Pergamon claimed that Euphraeus, a student of Plato's, persuaded Perdiccas to give Philip some territory of his own, territory termed "the beginning of his *basileia*" (rule or kingdom) where Philip kept some sort of military force. After the death of Perdiccas in battle, having kept this force in readiness, Philip rushed in and took charge (Caryst. Perg. *ap.* Ath. 11.506e–f; Athenaeus inserted a comment after this, indicating his doubts about the truthfulness of this story).[34] If this testimony is correct, it recalls the territorial *archai* held by at least one and probably two of the brothers of Perdiccas II. Given the obscurity of that earlier situation, even if it is a genuine parallel, comparatively little can be deduced.[35] Certainly, there is little to show any serious trouble between the remaining sons of Eurydice.[36]

Not surprisingly, after two violent deaths within a handful of years, outside powers yet again tried to manipulate the Macedonian situation to their advantage. Perhaps influenced by Philip or simply out of self-interest, Perdiccas III apparently tried to continue the alliance with Thebes. The Thebans were preparing a fleet and so needed timber, and the Macedonians arranged for the required timber in return for support against Athenian efforts in the north, as confirmed by a decree of the Theban league c. 365 that honors a Macedonian as a Theban *proxenos* (guest friend) and *euergetes* (benefactor).[37] Perdiccas got increased revenues from the timber arrangement with Thebes and he also reorganized finances by doubling harbor fees, thanks to the influence of an Athenian exile, Callistratus.[38] Perdiccas may have used those new revenues to improve the size and quality of Macedonian military forces, though not enough, as it proved, to cope with a massive new Illyrian invasion soon to begin. [39] The Athenians continued to be active in the northern Aegean during Perdiccas III's reign, maintained bases on the Thermaic Gulf (Pydna, Methone, and Potidaea), and made alliances with some of the upland Macedonian kingdoms, Orestis and Pelagonia (Orestis, fearing Illyrian invasion, had joined the Molossian kingdom).[40] Perhaps unenthusiastically, c. 364/3, Perdiccas briefly gave assistance to the Athenian commander Timotheus against the Chalcideans, though this particular Macedonian-Athenian alliance proved ephemeral.[41] The Theban fleet was equally ephemeral: it died with Epaminondas in 362 (Diod. 15. 78.4–79.2). Even after the decline of Theban influence, Perdiccas actually helped the Amphipolitans to resist the Athenians and in the end the Athenian general Timotheus abandoned the siege of Amphipolis.

The Athenians were not, however, Perdiccas III's worst problem. His ambitions went down to sudden defeat at the hand of the Illyrians. The Illyrians had in recent years once more become a potent force, managing to do serious damage to the Molossians.[42] The size of the army Perdiccas brought to the field against the Illyrians indicates not only his improved resources but also how grave the threat of the invading army under Bardylis was.[43] The Illyrians defeated the Macedonians in a great battle: Perdiccas and four thousand other Macedonians perished, and the Macedonian army panicked and lost heart for resistance

(Diod. 16.2.4–5). In the aftermath of Perdiccas III's stunning defeat, the Paeonians began to pillage the borders, the Illyrians prepared to launch a massive invasion of the sections of Macedonia not already under their control, the Thracian king sponsored an Argead claimant to the throne (a man named Pausanias), and the Athenians supported another claimant to the throne (Argaeus), backing this effort up with a force of three thousand hoplites and a fleet, all under the general Mantias (Diod. 16.2.5–6).

Perdiccas III had reigned longer and proved considerably more competent, not to mention less rash, than his older brother.[44] Perdiccas had begun to build a more stable Macedonia than had existed in some time. His enlarged army may possibly have been created as a response to the renewed Illyrian threat, but if so, it was not enough: he was not able to survive a renewed external threat to his kingdom. That the Illyrians invaded a number of years after Perdiccas had taken the throne, whereas during the reigns of his father and brother, Illyrian peoples took more or less immediate advantage of a change in monarch, suggests both that Perdiccas, once he had eliminated Ptolemy, was less vulnerable at the start of his independent reign than his father and older brother had been at the beginning of their reigns, but also that the Illyrian attack came primarily because the Illyrians had, over the course of Perdiccas' reign, grown in power, unity, and experience, and that the invasion happened because of their growing strength and confidence, not particularly because Perdiccas III was a troubled ruler. The Illyrian attack and its success derived from Illyrian strength more than it did from Macedonian internal weakness. Nonetheless, the success of the attack immediately prompted problems in addition to those caused by the invasion itself; Illyrian success precipitated a brief return to dynastic strife.

The primary (though hardly exclusive) disruptive force in Macedonia during the fifth and early fourth centuries had been the royal house itself, with its interminable struggles for power growing out of the absence of any very clear pattern of succession and the practice of royal polygamy. But a subtle change gradually happened, something that could easily have been reversed. Indeed, as we have observed, various individuals and groups attempted reversal but did not succeed. Amyntas III ruled a long time, and in turn his eldest son by Eurydice, then his next eldest, and then finally Eurydice's youngest son would rule. Violent death remained a fact of life for Argead rulers, but gradually this particular strand in the dynasty had established legitimacy that would prove compelling, despite stressful circumstances. Even the disaster of Perdiccas' death in the midst of massive military failure did not change this. Assorted foreign powers sponsored Argead claimants, but none of these claimants generated much long-term enthusiasm from the Macedonian populace. The claimants were not of the line of Amyntas III. The kingdom of Macedonia continued for several more years yet to be the plaything of current great powers, but internally it was already more stable. Dynastic stability alone would not have saved Macedonia after the death of Perdiccas III, had not Philip II proved the greatest military leader in Macedonian history and created the greatest military institution the Greek world had seen, but he would not have been able to do that had his hold on the loyalty of his people and army not been strong enough to withstand the humiliating massacre.

### Philip II (360/59–336)

Philip's reign began with the kind of assortment of crises which had characterized Macedonian history, particularly for the previous forty years.[45] If Macedonian history were a movie, the audience would doubtless think that the plot was repetitive and predictable: the new king Philip would have to pay off some of his enemies with land or cash, try to play one great power against another, search out foreign support in order to defeat his dynastic rivals, and yet would still die violently, thanks to internal strife. Philip II's reign actually fits this familiar pattern in many respects. Although he broke the mold and managed to realize the ambitions of earlier rulers and then surpass them, to a nearly unimaginable degree, he was indeed ultimately murdered and his murder did threaten to plunge Macedonia back into its old disarray and weakness. Yet, his son succeeded him, achieved even more stunning victories, and only the lack of viable male candidates of the line of Amyntas III after the death of Alexander III led to grudging and gradual acceptance of a new ruling family. Despite his ultimate success, the first few years of Phillip's reign looked quite familiar: he was the wily Argead who switched alliances with speed and confidence, the ruler who experienced defeats but managed to survive. Philip II was both literally and figuratively a survivor. (Figure 3.1 depicts Philip II.)

Our sources differ as to whether Philip was recognized as king immediately after his brother's death in battle (so Diod. 16.1.3, 2.1) or

FIGURE 3.1 Philip II of Macedon. Marble bust, Roman-era copy of copy of fourth-century BCE original, attributed to Philip. From Ny Carlsberg Glyptotek, Copenhagen, Denmark.

Image courtesy of Bridgeman Art Library.

served as regent for his brother Perdiccas' infant son Amyntas (Just. 7.5.9; Satyr. *ap.* Ath. 13.557b).[46] We do not know that the Macedonians would have presumed that young Amyntas was automatically to be considered king. While some previous Argeads had sometimes acted as substitute rulers for young kings (as Ptolemy Alorites was apparently forced to do), generally these "regencies," if that is what they were, were typically quite brief and ended with the elimination of the child ruler and the transition of the regent to direct rule. Indeed, some historians doubt that the Macedonians had regencies (see Chapter 1). My own view is that the Macedonians, given the current military crisis, would not have recognized a child as king and that Philip probably ruled immediately as king in his own right.[47] Apparently, even early on, Philip had reason to feel confident that elements within the elite would not turn to his nephew young Amyntas. Thus, in order to begin to rule, Philip had already convinced many members of the elite that he was the best choice.[48]

Philip did not eliminate his nephew; it was his son Alexander who would do that, many years later, after the murder of Philip (Just. 12.6.14). Of course, at the time Philip took over control of the kingdom, he had no sons of his own and his young nephew was the only other male descendant of the line of Amyntas III and Eurydice. Consequently, it is not surprising that Philip did not initially eliminate his only heir, though Amyntas' continued survival implies that Philip did not feel threatened by his existence. Even years after the Illyrian crisis, though by then Philip had two sons (Arrhidaeus, later called Philip III or Philip Arrhidaeus, and Alexander III), Amyntas, since he was at least several years older than either of Philip's sons,[49] had a better chance of living to adulthood than his younger cousins. Moreover, since Philip was himself the third of three brothers to take the throne, the king had reason to keep several heirs in reserve. Indeed, that he married his daughter Cynnane to Amyntas suggests, among other things, that Amyntas was indeed, in Philip's mind, a reserve heir. Philip may or may not have been ruthless enough to murder his brother's young son, but it is more to the point to recognize that he had, for many years, good reason to keep Amyntas alive.

As noted, Philip's reign commenced with worse than usual Macedonian disarray: military disaster on an unprecedented scale (Amyntas III had been forced to flee the kingdom but he had not fallen in battle along with thousands of others as Perdiccas III did), four different foreign powers (Illyrians, Paeonians, Athenians, Thracians) jockeying for power to determine events in Macedonia, and at least two (each with foreign backing) rival claimants (Argaeus, Pausanias) to the throne. Thus our first task is to consider why Philip was able, with considerable rapidity, to defeat other Argead contenders and to establish himself securely on the throne. Philip's kingship, like that of his weaker predecessors, continued to be shaped by his dealings with the Macedonian elite, despite the fact that he would consolidate royal power and limit that of the elite as no Argead had before him and that he transformed his newly unified kingdom into the greatest power on the Greek peninsula. Thus, while one should certainly not ignore the real changes Philip effected in the relationship between king and elite, neither should one fail to note continuity with the past. Indeed, Philip himself clearly understood, judging by his actions, that to change the nature of the kingdom, he had to change or at least reshape the relationship between king and elite. Ironically, Philip's innovations did not save him from assassination by a Macedonian aristocrat. Indeed, some would argue that resentment of his innovations motivated or at least assisted the assassin.[50]

One reason for Philip's success is quite simple and has nothing to do with any action of Philip's. His father and brothers may not have been distinguished rulers in the eyes of historians, but from the contemporary Macedonian point of view, they were their most recent kings and Philip was their closest living kin, other than his nephew Amyntas. Philip would have seemed more royal than other claimants who were presumably related to monarchs more distant in time and memory (Philip's half-brothers are a somewhat different case; see following). If, a possibility we have noted, his brother Perdiccas had already allotted Philip some regional power and responsibility, this too would have contributed to his acceptance as king. The un-glamorous, scrappy quality of Amyntas III and his sons—men often defeated but never down for long—may have seemed peculiarly and endearingly Macedonian to their subjects whose collective experience was similar to that of their rulers (see Chapter 1). Had Philip experienced further grave military difficulty, he might not have retained the throne, but the crisis at the time of his accession may, if anything, made the Macedonians less eager, at least in the short term, to switch branches of the royal house.

Another reason for Philip's rapid acceptance is partly his own doing and partly his brother Perdiccas' work. The combination of horrific defeat experienced by Perdiccas and then Philip's rapid series of victories created a bond between king and people. Many Macedonians would have lost family members in the massacre in which Perdiccas III perished. Philip, like them, needed victory both for vengeance and for safety.[51] Victory certainly builds unity and loyalty but so, curiously, does defeat. One has only to think of the role of great military defeats like Thermopylae or the Alamo or Gallipoli or even Dunkirk in the formation of the national identity of those peoples who experienced them to see that such a military catastrophe could act to unify rather than divide.[52]

Apart from the Illyrian menace and the Paeonians who had also invaded, Philip had to deal immediately with the two claimants to the throne. Diodorus (16.2.6) says that the Thracian candidate Pausanias was somehow kin to the royal family. It is usually assumed that Pausanias was an Argead and probably the man of that name who had attempted to take the throne soon after the death of Alexander II, the one Iphicrates dealt with, and that the Athenian candidate Argaeus is probably the same person who, according to Diodorus, ruled Macedonia for two years while Philip's father Amyntas was in exile (Diod. 14.92.4).[53] In this sense, the beginning of Philip's reign revisited, typified, and condensed the problems his father and brothers had confronted into a brief period during which he dealt with all these difficulties in a manner that endured, though in some cases these problems had to be dealt with again, if on a much reduced scale. It was, apparently, literally déjà vu, at least in some respects.

Philip coped with the more modest threat of Pausanias by offers of peace and bribes to the Thracian king and to the Paeonians (Diod. 16.3.4). It was the sort of thing Macedonian kings had done before, but in Philip's case, he implemented these measures not as a long-term policy but only to gain time so that he could deal with each opponent one at a time, not all at once. Of course, perhaps his predecessors had shared a similar plan but failed to realize it. Philip's long-term ascendancy, in the end, depended on greater military success than any previous Macedonian ruler; he was not the first to temporize or switch sides; he was the first to put these strategies to lasting and effective use. Argaeus was a more difficult problem than the other contender, not so much in his own right but because of the importance of his Athenian sponsorship (Lib. 15.42, 20.23).[54] Despite Philip's voluntary withdrawal from Amphipolis, the Athenian general Mantias, although he himself stayed at Methone where he had landed, sent Argaeus with mercenaries to Aegae. Argaeus failed abysmally: first the citizens of Aegae[55] refused to support his bid for the kingship and so he was forced to turn back to Methone, and then Philip appeared, attacked, and killed many though he released the survivors, except for Macedonian exiles (Diod. 16.3.5–6). Philip had to make further concessions to the Athenians about Amphipolis, but no more is heard of their candidate.[56] Subsequent events demonstrate that these concessions to the Athenians were, once more, simply temporizing measures.

When one considers why Philip succeeded so quickly in repelling other claimants to the throne, the most obvious answer is that the two contenders he dealt with had already been driven from power, along with their factions and supporters, by his father or by one of his brothers. His predecessors had already demonstrated that these claimants were losers. The importance of these two men derived from the support of external powers, not from any internal Macedonian enthusiasm for them, as the response of the people of Aegae made particularly clear. Sponsorship by hostile foreign powers likely helped to discredit them with the Macedonian people. That Philip immediately defeated Argaeus only confirmed his own legitimacy and reconfirmed Argaeus as a treacherous failure. Still, it is worth recalling that Amyntas III (see Chapter 2) had returned to power at least once and probably twice through the support of foreign powers. Consequently, one might conclude that the previous failures of these two claimants may have had more impact than their outside support.

While the Argead pretenders by themselves did not present any serious danger to Philip's rule, had he not won broad support from the mass of the population and the elite by military victory and clever diplomacy, the kingdom itself might have disappeared and with it Argead kingship. In his willingness to use bribes to stave off immediate military threats,[57] Philip may have reminded his subjects of his father, but his victories were unprecedented. Here Philip was oddly fortunate in having a crisis to seize upon and he proved adept at finding the advantage in apparent disadvantage. Although Diodorus claimed that Philip reformed the Macedonian army, almost overnight, into a disciplined fighting force of a very different sort from previous Macedonian armies (Diod. 16.1–3), it is more likely the reforms happened over many years.[58] As we have seen, he rebuilt confidence and unity by a series of speeches (Diod. 16.3.1), forming an army of national unity, in part, by the force of his personality and by his compelling words. Since most of Upper Macedonia was in Illyrian hands, Philip's subsequent victory against the Illyrians meant that, rather than having to divest control of that region from the princelings who had not previously been under consistent Argead control, they gave up their former independence in return for regaining their territory.[59] Better yet, it made the Illyrians, not Philip, the villains who robbed the princes of their independence. Doubtless Philip's new central authority did not happen without any resentment at all, but the circumstances in which he acquired it tended to minimize public resentment among the former princely houses. His early marriage policy (aided, perhaps, by his own partly Lyncestian heritage[60]) consolidated this situation.[61]

A third claimant to the throne did appear during Philip's reign, but the timing of his attempt remains uncertain. At least one of

Amyntas III's sons by Gygaea either contended with Philip for the throne or was believed to have done so (or to be about to) by Philip. Justin (8.3.10–11), speaking of the destruction of Olynthus in 349/8, says that Philip attacked and destroyed the city because the Olynthians were sheltering two of his half-brothers after he had slaughtered their brother. Justin asserts that Philip wanted them dead as would-be claimants to rule. Exactly when Gygaea's son, probably the oldest, Archelaus,[62] made his attempt on the throne is not clear. Unlike the other Argead claimants, he could proclaim that he was Amyntas' son, but Philip, of course, was more closely related to the former rulers, his full brothers, than Archelaus could claim to be. While Archelaus' attempt is not datable in any precise way, it probably did not come at the time of Philip's accession, given that our sources mention other claimants and do not speak of the sons of Gygaea, and may have occurred not long before Philip's pursuit of the brothers to Olynthus.[63] It seems curious that Archelaus did not assert his claim early in Philip's reign, when Philip was more vulnerable. On the face of it, a son of Amyntas would appear to have offered more attractions to the Athenians than did Argaeus, the descendant of some long-dead Argeads, a man who had already once been driven out of the kingdom. The failure of the sons of Gygaea to present any claim at the time of Philip's accession strongly suggests, as I have already argued, that they were too young to do so (see Chapter 2).[64] Philip's murder of one brother and the flight of the other two probably happened when they reached adulthood, either because they were actually trying to overthrow him or because Philip feared that they were about to do so. Two generations later, both of Alexander the Great's sons would be eliminated at about the point of adulthood, for similar reasons. In any event, the enduring claims of the sons of Gygaea doubtless contributed to the apparent prominence of Eurydice during the reign of Philip, particularly the early part (see Chapter 5).

Once Philip had thoroughly established himself on the throne, having dealt with foreign threats and domestic ones posed by yet more members of the royal house, and having begun to centralize Macedonia to a degree and on a scale not previously known, the forces of disruption and disunity in Macedonia derived, primarily, from elite groups resisting royal authority and only secondarily and occasionally from within the royal house. This remained the pattern until the disappearance of the Argead house at the end of the fourth century.

Having dealt with all these crises and begun the military revolution that helped to turn Macedonia into a great power, Philip II moved rapidly to unify his chronically divided kingdom. Possibly, he had already married at least once before he became king, but by 357 he may have had as many as five of his ultimately seven wives. The scale of his polygamy reflects the scale of his ambitions, constituting a kind of imperialist marriage policy. Rapidly, Philip turned from the defensive to the offensive, refusing to give up Amphipolis, facing war with the Athenians, and beginning to acquire new territory. As early as 358 he began to intervene in Thessaly (a policy, in the light of family history, in which he doubtless took considerable pleasure). Though he met with the occasional defeat (e.g., his loss to Onomarchus of Phocis in 353), Philip kept going and gradually the external powers that had so often in the past troubled Macedonia were incorporated into Philip's realm or subordinated to him; he involved himself in central Greece both diplomatically and politically. Philip also campaigned in Thrace and took over more territory there, despite Thracian and Athenian cooperation. In 357 he conquered Amphipolis, thus removing the threat that had caused so much trouble to so many of his predecessors. He granted out newly conquered lands to ordinary men as well as *hetairoi* and moved whole populations in order to consolidate his internal control. Having battled the Athenians on several occasions and also having made peace with the Athenians on several occasions, Philip defeated the alliance of Thebes and Athens at Chaeronea in 338. At this point, Philip had become, for all practical purposes, supreme on the Greek peninsula; he planned to invade the Persian Empire, but his own assassination in 336 by (a disgruntled lover) meant that his son Alexander led the joint Graeco-Macedonian expedition instead.

Thus, by 349/8 at the latest, Philip had consolidated the male royal line: the Argeads were now the descendants of Amyntas III and Eurydice. Moreover, he had already produced two sons of his own, as well as at least two daughters. Archaeological evidence, much of it discovered in the last forty years, has also demonstrated that Eurydice played a conspicuous public role in the Argead kingdom. The short and troubled reigns of her two elder sons are unlikely to have produced the expensive and conspicuous monuments associated with her. Amyntas

III may have highlighted Eurydice,[65] but I will argue that it was primarily Philip who put her to the fore. Only in the reign of Philip did Macedonia become rich and stable enough to generate the wealth to pay for these monuments, and only in the reign of Philip did the king and royal family begin to stand out conspicuously from the rest of the elite, thanks largely to Philip's royal stage craft (see Chapters 5 and 6).

# 4

# *Eurydice and Her Sons*

Eurydice is the first royal woman in Macedonia known to have taken an active role in public events. Literary sources preserve a handful of names of kings' wives and daughters before her, but they are mere names (indeed, sometimes they are not named), mentioned because of whom they married or mothered.[1] Some of these women may, in fact, have played a role, unknown to us, in public affairs, but in the case of Eurydice, we know that she did.

As I suggested earlier (see Chapter 1), some of our knowledge about Eurydice derives from the chance survival or preservation of material relating to her, but literary references to her existed not out of chance but because she was the mother of Philip II (and, to a lesser degree, because of her two other royal sons). These references were preserved and even augmented because Philip II remained a well-known and controversial historical figure throughout the ancient period. Some passages about his mother in ancient sources depict her as equally controversial, in ways that compromised Philip's reputation and that of his family. Still, as we have already observed, other authors report that Philip was able to play an important role in Greek history because, at a critical moment, his mother acted to ensure that her two younger sons would be able to rule. Moreover, apart from Eurydice's actions, monuments and inscriptions of the period (some of these the result of her own patronage, some that of her sons—most likely of Philip II) all confirm that in her own day she had a public profile, part of the developing image-making program of the Argead clan, particularly under Philip. The picture of Eurydice I have just sketched—defender of her sons' futures and respectable royal matron and patron, an image supported by a variety of sources—contradicts that preserved in at least three written sources

(Justin 7.4.7–8; 5.4–9; the scholiast for Aeschines 2.29; and the *Suda* s.v. "Karanos") which portray Eurydice as adulterous and/or murderous in respect to her husband and those very same sons.

Indeed, our extant sources are full of contradictions and obscurities about Eurydice's career. I will assess the available evidence connected to a series of questions relating to her public career and actions. Was she an adulterer? Was she the murderer (or would be murderer) of her husband and any of her sons? Who was the man named Ptolemy who played such an important part in her life and that of her sons? Did she marry Ptolemy? If she married him, when did she do so, in relation to what events? The chapter concludes with a discussion of the nature, likely origin, and credibility of our extant sources and with a reflection on the role of fourth-century propaganda in what our extant sources say about Eurydice and an examination of Eurydice's role as a political actor and faction leader during the 360s.

### Was Eurydice an Adulteress?

Justin (7.4.7–8) provides the most salacious (and memorable) account of Eurydice's adultery and her supposed murders. Anyone who has seen one of the various film versions of *The Postman Always Rings Twice* or read the James M. Cain novel on which the films are based will recognize Justin's plotline about Eurydice: a married woman conspires with her lover to kill her husband and take over his business. In this case, the business is running an entire kingdom.

Justin, in effect, fashioned a Macedonian noir narrative, but his narrative is even more lurid and considerably more implausible than typical noir movies. Justin claims that Eurydice plotted with her lover and son-in-law (unnamed by Justin) to kill Amyntas III, marry her lover, and pass rule on to him. Eurydice's daughter Eurynoe, the woman wronged, foiled this evil plan by revealing the affair and plot to her father. According to Justin, Amyntas nonetheless spared Eurydice because of their shared children. Having escaped these dangers, Amyntas died old, of natural causes, passing rule to his son Alexander II. The *Suda* s.v. "Karanos" notes that there are writers who claim that Eurydice's sons were spurious, though it does not itself seem to embrace this view. These are the only ancient sources that mention Eurydice's adultery, and only one of them actually takes the allegation seriously.

There seems little reason to do so. Many elements in Justin's account are simply not believable: Amyntas' implausible willingness to forgive Eurydice and her apparent continued presence at court even after her supposed adultery and her murders of Alexander II and Perdiccas III (see further discussion later in this chapter).[2] Justin's narrative, which seems to begin toward the end of the reign of Amyntas III, does not actually throw any doubt on the legitimacy of her sons (Eurydice's lover is married to her daughter, so her daughter must be old enough to be married, and thus her children's legitimacy is not really challenged, even implicitly, by Justin). Justin's statements constitute an attack on Eurydice, but not on her sons. Athenian charges of bastardy belong to a long history of conflating political antipathy and with actual illegitimacy. We need not take these charges literally, particularly since they also relate to ethnic prejudice (see Chapter 2).[3] Justin's account and the stories the *Suda* refers to doubtless related to fourth-century propaganda against Eurydice and her sons, as we will discuss later in this chapter, but they do not provide real evidence about adultery.

### Did Eurydice Murder Alexander II or Perdiccas III?

While little suggests that we should take charges of adultery seriously, Eurydice's possible involvement in murder plots requires more serious discussion, not just because of Justin's statements. Amyntas' supposed forgiveness of Eurydice not only for her adultery but also for plotting to kill him does not seem believable, but the really over-the-top part of Justin's narrative comes after the death of Amyntas III. Justin then asserts that Eurydice arranged the deaths of her eldest son, Alexander II, and later of her next eldest, Perdiccas III, even though Perdiccas had a little son of his own (Justin seems particularly upset by Eurydice's ungrandmotherly behavior). Justin does not mention Eurydice's son-in-law after his initial reference to her adultery, but the narrative seems to imply that Eurydice continued to be driven by lust for this unnamed man and by her desire to put him on the throne (though Justin does not explicitly say so, his story also seems to assume that Amyntas spared the son-in-law as well).

It cannot be true that Eurydice killed Perdiccas III. Diodorus (16.2.4) reports that Perdiccas III died in battle against the Illyrians, not at his mother's hands, and many events, including Philip II's accession and remodeling of the army (see Chapter 3) depend on Perdiccas III's death in the midst of military disaster.[4]

The possible involvement of Eurydice in the murder of Alexander II, however, is not so easily dismissed because of the apparently supporting testimony of the scholiast for Aeschines 2.29, though this scholiast is anonymous and wrote at an uncertain date. Unlike Justin, the scholiast does not accuse Eurydice of an implausible series of murder plots. Instead, he charges her only with complicity with Ptolemy in the murder of Alexander II and he also proclaims that Eurydice married Ptolemy (the order of his narrative seems to imply that this marriage happened at some point after the murder of Alexander II and possibly before Ptolemy was made *epitropos* for Perdiccas III and Philip and then ruled for three years).

Quite apart from the problem of whether and, if so, when Eurydice married Ptolemy (see further discussion in this chapter) is the notion that she and he were somehow allied and together murdered Alexander II. Here we should bear in mind that only two sources refer to their murderous collaboration—Aeschines' scholiast and Justin (if, that is, we assume that Ptolemy is the unnamed lover in Justin's narrative). The scholiast says that Eurydice took part in the murder with Ptolemy (the verb the scholiast employed is "συλλαμβάνω"). Whereas Justin casts Eurydice as the lead murderer (if the lover takes part in her crimes, Justin does not mention it), the scholiast makes Ptolemy the main actor and Eurydice simply his collaborator.

How one would know that she had collaborated is unclear, particularly since the other accounts of Alexander II's murder (see Chapter 3) make it a public crime involving Ptolemy and other males. Diodorus (15.71.1), Marsyas (*ap.* Ath. 14.629d), and Plutarch (*Pel.* 27.2) all attribute Alexander II's death to Ptolemy and do not mention Eurydice, let alone blame her. Demosthenes (19.195–196) tells a story about the daughters of one of Alexander II's assassins; the story does not mention Ptolemy one way or the other, though it does make clear that Alexander II died at the hands of a group of assassins. Quite possibly, believing in the marriage between Eurydice and Ptolemy, whether he believed it happened before or after the death of Alexander II, the scholiast simply assumed that she was involved in the assassination.[5]

Other evidence, in terms of the Iphicrates episode we shall discuss shortly, pictures Eurydice as an advocate for her remaining sons (Aeschin. 2.28.29; Cornel. Nep. *Iph.* 3.2), and an essay actually holds her up as a model parent (Plut. *Mor.* 14b–c; see further Chapter 5).[6] Eurydice's patronage at Aegae, Philip II's apparent publicity about her before and after her death, and her great-granddaughter's decision to change her name to Eurydice's (see Chapters 5 and 6) all make it highly unlikely that Eurydice, directly or indirectly, took part.

With any murder, motivation is a fundamental issue, and the two sources that assign her some role in the death of Alexander II provide none, or at least nothing convincing. Justin's only explanation for Eurydice's supposed multiple murders is lust, whereas the scholiast offers none at all. Given the obvious factual errors in Justin, the scholiast's statements are the only ones that deserve serious attention. Knowing who is really involved in a conspiracy is always difficult; the scholiast may reflect speculation about Eurydice's involvement, though he provides no motivation for either the murder or her alliance with Ptolemy. It is difficult to see why she would have wanted her son dead, even if she didn't like him or disapproved of his adventurous and disastrous policy in Thessaly, whether or not she was married to Ptolemy at the time of the murder. As we shall see, she certainly went out of her way to protect her remaining sons. We can imagine a kind of *Sophie's Choice* scenario in which she sacrificed one son to preserve the other two,[7] but, apart from lack of evidence, that does not explain why she would have believed that Ptolemy would not then kill her remaining sons as well.[8] Eurydice may have married Ptolemy, but she is unlikely to have collaborated in the murder of her son Alexander II.

It is the supposed objects of Eurydice's murderous plots that makes such allegations unbelievable: whether or not the publicized affection for her sons was simply a matter of image, killing them for the sake of a man who had at least one other son and by whom she had none makes no sense. Royal women typically also had more power during their sons' reigns than during their husbands', so Eurydice's incentive for these repeated attempts at murder (and presumably remarriage) is not obvious. Moreover, in the 360s she could have been reaching the close of her child-bearing years (if she were born around 405; see Chapter 6) and so was less likely to produce a son by a new husband. She had more to lose than to gain by the deaths of any of her sons.

Moreover, as we shall see, the relationship between an adult son and his widowed mother was often idealized; that would make the murder of such a son by his mother especially shocking. Cross-culturally, worries about the sexuality of widows and about the children they had or might have and about inheritance (political, symbolic, or financial) attached or belonging to them could and did create conflict. Justin's Eurydice exemplifies fears about the sexuality and loyalty of widows (worries that they would change their allegiance to the new husband or for the prospect of one), and his version of events also demonstrates the vulnerability of widows to innuendo.[9] Indeed, the prolonged acceptance of his narrative speaks to the endurance of these issues.

For many years, scholars largely accepted the most hostile parts of the tradition about Eurydice and yet at the same time downplayed her importance. Macurdy raised the first serious doubts about Justin's testimony in 1927, but she pictured Eurydice, primarily, as the victim of circumstance, forced to marry her son's murderer, but without "political power" and dependent on "an indomitable will or the charm of beauty, or . . . both."[10] In other words, Macurdy rejected the notion of Eurydice as a villain but also deemphasized her power and agency. Macurdy correctly argued that there was no evidence for institutionalized female royal power in the Argead era but failed to recognize—like many historians of her era—that political power is not necessarily defined by office holding and is certainly not limited to it, particularly in the context of hereditary monarchy. Macurdy's analysis focused on Eurydice's presumed victimization, personality, and her (entirely unattested) beauty.

In any event, subsequent scholars largely ignored Macurdy and either did not mention Eurydice at all and instead spoke of Ptolemy (whom they presumed to be her husband; see further in this chapter), even when the ancient source named Eurydice and not Ptolemy,[11] and/or they wholeheartedly embraced Justin's villainous anti-heroine.[12] In 1988 Greenwalt rejected Justin's testimony, and in 1992 Mortensen made a lengthier case for abandoning Justin's "bad" Eurydice.[13] In recent years, this view has largely prevailed; few any longer consider Justin's mélange of adultery and murder historical, though scholarly opinion varies about how much agency and clout Eurydice actually had.[14]

### Ptolemy Who?

In order to assess the likelihood that Eurydice married Ptolemy, we must first consider the confusing evidence about his identity.[15] Who was this mysterious Ptolemy? (On this point, see also Chapters 3 and 4.) Justin's reference to Eurydice's alleged but unnamed lover has often been combined with other evidence about the actions of persons called Ptolemy, yet these various pieces of evidence do not necessarily all refer to the same person. As we have seen, Eurydice's unnamed lover in the Justin narrative may or may not be the Ptolemy who appears on an Athenian inscription from late in the reign of Amyntas III as a prominent signatory of the treaty.[16] Someone named Ptolemy contested with Alexander II after the failure of his Thessalian expedition and ultimately murdered him; again, this may or may not be the unnamed man in Justin's narrative or Eurydice's reputed lover.

Diodorus twice (15.71.1, 16.2.4) refers to the assassin of Alexander II as "Ptolemy Alorites" (from Alorus) and to Alexander II as his brother (*adelphos*), and he also (15.71.1) calls him the son of Amyntas. "Amyntas" was unfortunately a common name in Macedonia but, since Diodorus called this particular man Alexander II's brother, one must consider the possibility that he actually was. Amyntas III was not a young man when he became king, and Gygaea's sons, as I have suggested, were if anything younger than Eurydice's (see Chapter 2). Ptolemy could have been a son of Amyntas III by an otherwise unknown wife (i.e., neither Eurydice nor Gygaea).[17] If, however, he were a son, apparently an older one, of Amyntas III and also the man whose name appears on the Athenian treaty, it is remarkable that he was not a candidate for kingship until, apparently, Alexander II's policy failed so dramatically. This could imply that he was not in fact a son of Amyntas III. One would also wonder why Pelopidas would not prefer him to younger brothers. Instead, Pelopidas kept Alexander II on the throne after his actions in Thessaly and punished Ptolemy after the murder of Alexander II, forcing him to be merely *epitropos*, not king, thus preferring Perdiccas III, despite the fact that he was still too young to rule on his own.

Even if he was probably not a son of Amyntas III, Ptolemy was, however, likely an Argead, although his Argead identity is never explicitly stated in an ancient source. Ptolemy's presence as a signatory of the treaty (assuming it is the same Ptolemy), his ability to contest Alexander II's power with some success so soon after the death of Amyntas III, his treatment by Pelopidas at the time of Pelopidas' first visit to Macedonia (see Chapter 3), and his recognition as regent all tend to support the conclusion that he was a member of the Argead dynasty.[18] Ptolemy could well have been a member of another branch of the dynasty. A lot of ink has been spilled on assorted hypothetical Argead genealogical tables constructed to provide Ptolemy with a specific Argead ancestry.

Typically, all go back to some reconstruction of the line of Alexander I and his sons and/or brothers (not an unreasonable assumption, but there were, presumably, other Argeads too). Since an Amyntas other than Amyntas III (Amyntas II or Amyntas "the little") was or briefly tried to be king in the early fourth century (see Chapter 2), another possibility seems to be to link Ptolemy to him.[19]

More puzzling yet is the tendency in our sources to refer to Ptolemy as "Alorites"—by his town of origin—rather than by a patronymic.[20] Perhaps authors refer to him by his geographic origin to distinguish him from others with the same personal name and possibly the same patronymic; after all, being called the son of an Amyntas unfortunately would not, in practice, distinguish him from many others. There may have been more than one Ptolemy at court; all the Ptolemies we have encountered, as I have observed, were not necessarily one and the same.[21]

What seems most likely is that Ptolemy was an Argead who was well enough connected to have a faction at court but not well enough connected to become king on the death of Amyntas III; only the embarrassment of Alexander II's failure in Thessaly (and, some would say, Eurydice's advocacy of Ptolemy) made Ptolemy somewhat viable and even then, as it proved, not successfully viable. He could have been one of the *philoi* (friends) Aeschines (2.26) says betrayed Eurydice and her sons and so likely someone who had originally supported the succession of Alexander II (but, if so, the notion that he, at any point, became Eurydice's husband becomes less likely). Let us turn to the problem of a possible second marriage for Eurydice, to the man who had murdered her eldest son.

### Eurydice's Possible Marriage to Ptolemy

Let me begin by putting consideration of the possible marriage of Eurydice and Ptolemy in a much broader context: marriage in the Greek world generally and more particularly in the context of royal marriages, especially the marriages of royal widows. In the Hellenic world, marriages were arranged, typically by males, for practical (not romantic) reasons, to create legitimate children and to advantage family interests in various practical ways. In a royal dynasty, those practical reasons often had to do with politics. Generally speaking, women—royal or not—would not expect to have a say in whom they married, especially not if they were first-time brides. Widows of the upper classes of child-bearing age typically remarried quickly, and their remarriages often meant that they did not live in the same household with the children of their first marriage. Widows could be vulnerable legally and financially, but they could also sometimes manipulate their circumstances to their personal advantage.[22] In some parts of Greece, including Macedonia in all likelihood, widows could control property, at least until a son came of age.[23] Much depended on a widow's relationship with her son, a relationship that was idealized in a manner often helpful to the widow, but in a way that would make a widow's murder of her own son particularly heinous and notorious.[24]

Most information we have about royal Macedonian widows comes from the period after the death of Philip II; it is in fact largely Hellenistic, and much of it involves dynasties other than the Argeads. Thus it is difficult to determine to what degree Eurydice followed a pattern and to what degree she created one. Though royal sons and brothers arranged some marriages,[25] other widowed Argead women later in the fourth century did exercise or attempt to exercise control over the choice of a new spouse or they chose not to remarry at all and generally acted quite independently of their sons or brothers.[26]

An additional consideration must be borne in mind when assessing the likelihood of a marriage between Eurydice and Ptolemy: our extant literary sources sometimes romanticize and eroticize royal marriages, whether in a positive way or a negative one. Even though in reality royal marriage for a man or woman was rarely a personal choice or based on personal preference, ancient authors sometimes provide narratives that insist that it was. Philip II is said first to have fallen in love with Olympias (Plut. *Alex.* 2.2) and later Cleopatra (Plut. *Alex* 9.4), and Alexander the Great with Roxane (Arr. 4.19.5; Plut. *Alex.* 47.4, *Mor.* 332c, 338d; Curt. 8.4.24–26), even though all were marriages that served a variety of political purposes. On the other hand, narratives exist that villainize and negatively eroticize women involved in royal marriages, offering up treacherous mothers and lustful wives, as in Justin's stories about Eurydice or in some of accounts of Arsinoë's period in Macedon as wife of Lysimachus (Paus. 1.10.3.; see discussion later in this chapter). The truth is usually less colorful.

Bearing these general considerations in mind, let us reflect on the relative probability that Eurydice married Ptolemy Alorites. Only one piece of direct evidence supports the existence of such a marriage, the testimony of the scholiast for Aeschines for the marriage. Certainly, Aeschines' own references to Eurydice and to Ptolemy in no way indicate or imply a marriage. Aeschines could have repressed mention of the marriage in his original speech to Philip out of fear of offending Philip (Ptolemy had, after all, murdered the king's brother). Other authors might have done the same. However, as we have noted, the scholiast also associates Eurydice with the murder of Alexander II. This alone makes the scholiast's entire comment less than credible, though it certainly plays to fears that a remarried widow would abandon the interests of the children of her first marriage in favor of the interests of her new husband.[27] That only one extant source (not a contemporary one) mentions the marriage does not argue for its existence, particularly since Eurydice was the mother of so well known a figure as Philip and the grandmother of an even more famous one. Many in southern and central Greece resented Macedonian domination. It is hard to believe that Demosthenes, in particular, could have resisted using such an excellent opportunity for invective, had Ptolemy married her. If Eurydice had had a choice, self-interest did not lie with acquiring a new husband who had at least one son by another woman and none by Eurydice.[28]

On the other hand, the existence of such a marriage would not have been particularly surprising, especially since Eurydice may not, indeed, have had a choice, particularly if Ptolemy himself wanted the marriage.[29] Ogden has argued that marriage to the widow of a ruler's immediate predecessor—a type of marriage he originally termed "levirate"—conveyed a special kind of legitimization; naturally he sees the Eurydice/Ptolemy marriage as an example of this phenomenon, one he considers widespread in the dynasty.[30] I am less sure that this pattern is so marked, though marriage to a royal widow might well have made it more likely that the new ruler became the guardian of any minor sons of the widow. In the case of the widowed wife of Archelaus, such access may have led to the murder of her son (Pl. *Grg.* 471c; Arist. *Pol.* 1311b), and one could imagine, if the marriage happened soon after Amyntas III's death, that Ptolemy took similar advantage. The circumstances of the assassination of Alexander II, however (see Chapter 3), were public and did not require special familial access to the king as might have been the case if, as apparently was the case with Cleopatra's child, the stepson was quite young. At the time of his brother's murder, Perdiccas III was not yet an adult, so one could imagine Ptolemy wanting access to him for sinister purposes, but the reality is that, in the end, Perdiccas III killed Ptolemy, not the reverse. (See further in this chapter.)

Indeed, the date of this possible marriage (not so much the absolute date as its timing in terms of other critical events of the period) directly relates to its purpose and significance and to the likelihood that it happened at all. Ptolemy, as I have just noted, could have married Eurydice almost immediately after Amyntas III's death. If we believe that Ptolemy was initially one of Alexander II's *philoi*, then one could suppose that Alexander II himself arranged the marriage. Given, however, that Alexander II was old enough to rule on his own, no compelling advantage for Alexander to such a marriage occurs. Possibly he might have wanted to please or placate Ptolemy, but we don't know that he needed to, at the time he took the throne.

Another possible time for such a marriage, as I have just suggested, would have been immediately after Alexander II's murder (the scholiast for Aeschines 2.29 seems to imply such timing) but before Pelopidas' return for a second intervention. We do not know where the assassination of Alexander II happened or if Eurydice was in the same place as her son when he was killed, but it must have been a perilous moment.[31] If she did not participate in the murder, then not only her children but she herself could have been in physical danger, much as Arsinoë and her sons were after the death of Lysimachus. Just as Cassander married Alexander's half-sister Thessalonice, after a siege and the arrest and the killing of Olympias (Just. 14.6.13; Diod. 19.52.1–2; Heidel. Epit. *FGrH* 155, F 2.4), Eurydice may have been forced to marry Ptolemy after her son's assassination. Alternatively, she could have married Ptolemy after the murder of Alexander II in hopes of protecting the succession of her remaining sons, though knowing there were no guarantees.[32] Whether before or after Alexander II's assassination, this marriage could have happened as part of an attempt by Eurydice herself or her *philoi* to end the strife between the two warring factions within the kingdom. However, if Ptolemy planned to rule himself and did not plan to serve as regent for Perdiccas, no clear benefit for him in marrying Eurydice at this point appears.[33] Archelaus may well have married his predecessor's widow, possibly to gain access to her son whom he then murdered, but if Ptolemy married Eurydice before the arrival of Pelopidas, he had already murdered Alexander II, and he certainly did not take the marriage as an opportunity to murder Perdiccas.

The most plausible date for this marriage, if it happened, would be the time after Pelopidas compelled Ptolemy to accept a role as regent; indeed, it is possible that Pelopidas could have insisted on this marriage arrangement as part of his settlement.[34] Such a marriage would have, at least formally, united the warring factions. Again, Eurydice's personal preference (even the personal antipathy of a mother toward the murderer of her son) would have had little or nothing to do with it, given that Pelopidas was the one currently guaranteeing her sons' succession.

The murder/adultery saga that dominates Justin's narrative, makes a partial appearance in the scholiast, and some version of which was known to the author of the *Suda*, could have been inspired by the actual existence of the marriage. Given the absence of other evidence for the marriage, perhaps the best argument in its favor is that its existence could explain the origin of the "Black Legend" (see further in this chapter) about Eurydice. The marriage of a mother to the murderer of her son would have been shocking, even when her lack of choice was self-evident and even if the marriage happened after the death of Alexander, under pressure from Pelopidas. Certainly, the marriage would have seemed more shocking after her son's murder than before. Such a marriage would have been rich soil for the growth of propaganda against Eurydice and her sons, not simply at the time it happened but for years after. No one should simply assume that the marriage is fact, but it is a possibility.

### Eurydice and the Assistance of Iphicrates

Married or not, Eurydice acted in concert with the Athenian admiral Iphicrates to resolve a succession crisis in favor of her sons—a crisis precipitated by the arrival in Macedonia of Pausanias, a new claimant to the Argead throne, who had invaded and threatened to seize power.[35] Aeschines, the major source for this incident, does not indicate that Ptolemy was already regent when Pausanias appeared (indeed, he does not mention Ptolemy at all until after the problem of Pausanias had been resolved), and his subsequent reference to Ptolemy might be read to indicate that he was not (Aeschines 2.26–29). I have already argued (see Chapter 3) that this incident happened after the assassination of Alexander II, rather than prior to it, but before Pelopidas forced Ptolemy to accept being regent and, to guarantee the arrangement, took his son and many others hostage.[36] The succession of a Macedonian king, particularly a succession following an assassination, was the ideal moment for a claimant to the throne to arrive; that is surely what Aeschines (2.27) means when he notes that Pausanias' return in strength happened at an opportune moment.

Three ancient sources describe, with varying amounts of detail, what happened next. At the time of Pausanias' arrival and initial success, Eurydice took action that prevented Pausanias from establishing himself as king and cutting Eurydice's sons out of what they doubtless considered their birthright. The earliest and most detailed account of this episode (Aeschin. 2.27–29) appears in a speech of the Athenian orator Aeschines, delivered in front of the Athenian assembly in 343, supposedly summarizing a speech he had given, as part of an Athenian embassy, to Philip in 346, but referring to events in Macedonia c. 368, after the murder of Alexander II (see Chapter 3).[37] Aeschines says he began by reminding Philip (in detail) of Athens' previous good will and good works for Philip's father Amyntas III. Next he recalled those things which Philip had himself both witnessed and received as a benefit from the Athenians. Soon after the deaths of Amyntas and Alexander II, while Perdiccas and Philip were still children, their mother Eurydice was betrayed by those who seemed to be *philoi* (friends). Pausanias, who'd been in exile, returned to rule. The situation favored him: he had many supporters and a force of Greek soldiers. He took Anthemus, Therma, and Strepsa, as well as some other places. Aeschines comments that while not all Macedonians supported Pausanias, the majority approved of him. At this point, the Athenians elected Iphicrates general, assigning him to attack Amphipolis. Iphicrates arrived in the region with a few ships, intending to investigate the situation and not yet lay siege to Amphipolis. Eurydice summoned Iphicrates and successfully persuaded him to lend military support to her remaining sons, so that they could live to rule.

Aeschines then begins to quote his own speech to Philip in 346, citing the testimony of all who were present at the meeting between Eurydice and Iphicrates (whether Athenians accompanying Iphicrates or Macedonians with Eurydice or both he does not specify). Aeschines says that Eurydice put Perdiccas into Iphicrates' arms (hands) and Philip onto his knees (commenting that Philip was a little child) and that Eurydice said, "Amyntas, the father of these children, when he lived, made you a son and treated the city of the Athenians like family. As a consequence, you, as a private person, have become the brother of these boys and, as a public person, a friend to us." After that, Aeschines tells Philip, Eurydice began to make powerful pleas for their sake (that is for the sake of the two brothers) and her own sake and for the kingdom's, and generally for their survival (safety). Iphicrates, he says, gave heed to this and drove Pausanias out of Macedonia and preserved rule for Philip.

Aeschines explains that next he spoke concerning Ptolemy, who had been established as *epitropos* of affairs, about how he had conducted himself in an ungrateful and terrible way, first by working against Athens in terms of Amphipolis and then by making an alliance with the Thebans when the Athenians and Thebans were in a dispute. (In Aeschines it is not clear whether Ptolemy's role was established before or after the Iphicrates scene just described, since Ptolemy is not mentioned until after the narration of the Iphicrates incident, but the implication, I believe, is that he was not *epitropos* at the time Iphicrates appeared).[38] Aeschines then goes on to complain about how Perdiccas III, once king, also warred with Athens over Amphipolis. In other words, his speech seems to treat the policy of Argead rulers/regents in chronological order.

The *Suda* (s.v. "Karanos") also omits any mention of Ptolemy in terms of the Iphicrates episode. It is vaguer (and probably less factually correct). It says that after the death of Amyntas III, Pausanias, who'd earlier been exiled by him, had seized power, overpowered Amyntas' sons, and had taken over rule. But Eurydice, the *Suda* says, made an alliance with an Athenian general active in the region of Macedonia, and he drove out Pausanias. The Roman biographer Cornelius Nepos, in his brief life of Iphicrates, says that after the death of Amyntas, Eurydice, fearing for her two sons, fled to Iphicrates, who defended them with his forces (Nepos, *Iph.* 3.2). Nepos, too, fails to mention Ptolemy in regard to the Iphicrates saga.

Several aspects of this episode are problematic. We do not know the physical location of Eurydice and her sons at the time of the Pausanias crisis. Aeschines has Iphicrates come to Eurydice, but the location of this encounter is not specified. The *Suda* may imply that she and her sons had been driven out of Macedonia, and Nepos certainly says that they fled to Iphicrates. In all three accounts of the Iphicrates episode, Eurydice seems to be in charge of her sons. Aeschines' account, the most detailed, cannot be literally true in all respects: the sons Eurydice puts into Iphicrates' hands and lap were adolescents at this point, not "lap babies," and Philip cannot have been physically present in Macedonia since Pelopidas' first trip to Macedonia (while Alexander II was still alive) had ended with Philip's departure to Thebes as a hostage. Nonetheless, Aeschines' account is generally accepted as historical, albeit with some rhetorical exaggeration and a very self-interested portrayal of Aeschines, who was after all defending himself, and with an Athenocentric point of view.[39] Aeschines clearly expects Philip to be pleased by his recital and to be proud of his mother. Speaking roughly twenty years later, Aeschines could easily have omitted Eurydice from this narrative, no matter how important she had been originally, and simply focused on the critical aid Iphicrates gave Amyntas' sons; surely he would have done so had Eurydice, at the time of Iphicrates' appearance, either recently been involved in her older son's murder or (as some would have it) was about to be so involved. Aeschines' theme, after all, was Athenian good works for the Argeads. Eurydice was icing on the cake, but only if she was appropriate dynastic "decoration," something she would not have been had she murdered or helped to murder Alexander II.

*Fourth-Century Propaganda and Our Extant Sources on Eurydice*

None of our literary sources is in itself an eyewitness account of events of this period. The only Macedonian source of whom even a fragment remains relevant to this period, Marsyas of Pella, has nothing to say about Eurydice (see Chapter 3). Many Greeks visited the Macedonian court—Iphicrates, as we have seen (c. 368), Aeschines and Demosthenes (both in 346, as part of an Athenian embassy), Theopompus the historian (in Macedonia c. 342),[40] and Anaximenes of Lampsacus[41] and many others wrote about it in the fourth century, and others much later. These visitors would have come away with different impressions, having talked to a variety of individuals, and perhaps would have unknowingly repeated highly partisan and possibly contradictory accounts of Macedonian events, reflecting a generation's worth of changing views by different court groups on Eurydice, who was probably recently dead at the time of the visits of Aeschines, Theopompus, and Anaximenes. Moreover, much of what happened at the Macedonian court was not necessarily public, and speculation must always have played a part in accounts of secret conspiracies, even close to the time of these events.

The written tradition was probably significantly Athenocentric to begin with, and then the passage of centuries, if anything, intensified this bias. The values of the Second Sophistic and Roman imperial period doubtless shape what we know as well. In some cases these much later sources may have had access to primary sources, and in others, what they read may already have been third- or fifth-hand. I am reluctant, unless specific evidence survives, to assume that fourth-century writers were prone to outright invention and Roman ones were not.[42] Moralizing was a goal of virtually all sources, and this concern led to selective versions of the past and, particularly in terms of women, highly colored ones.

Fourth-century politics and propaganda may well be the ultimate source of Justin's narrative about Eurydice, but Pompeius Trogus and certainly Justin himself have their own agendas—particularly concerning royal women—ones that may have shaped the accounts to an unknown degree.[43] Justin liked lurid narratives generally and especially those about high-profile women and their supposed sexual and criminal exploits.[44] Politically active women in Justin tend to be foreign, indeed barbarous; powerful royal women seem to emasculate royal men.[45] Connections between royal Macedonian women and Roman political concerns in the early imperial period are doubtless present.[46]

As his depictions of later Macedonian royal women (for instance, Olympias, mother of Alexander the Great, and Arsinoë, daughter of Ptolemy I and wife [serially] of Lysimachus, Ptolemy Ceraunus, and Ptolemy II), demonstrate, consistency of characterization or motivation is not always Justin's concern. Justin's Arsinoë, for example, is initially the would-be poisoner of her stepson but later in Justin's narrative she becomes a pathetic victim and melodramatic but grieving mother (17.1.1–12, 17.2.6–8; 24.2.1–3.10).[47]

By contrast, Justin's treatment of Eurydice is more consistent: she is always bad, always a woman who betrays her duties as wife and mother. Justin employs the same word, *insidiae*, about Eurydice's bad actions three times (7.4.7, 7.5.4, 7.5.7). The word can refer to ambushes or surprise attacks, traps, or plots. In other words, Justin's Eurydice is all about betrayal, but in a tricky, underhanded way. But Justin's version of Eurydice's actions also plays into gender stereotypes not uniquely his or uniquely Roman, as I noted at the beginning of this chapter. For instance, Pausanias (1.10.3), a Greek writer of the Second Sophistic period, gives a version of an episode in Arsinoë's life that somewhat resembles Justin's adulterous Eurydice story: a wife plots her husband's death because of her (would-be) relationship with another man, her husband's son.

The *Suda*, an encyclopedic work written in Byzantine times, used a variety of ancient sources, as the "Karanos" entry we have discussed makes clear. The Roman Cornelius Nepos lived in the first century BCE and wrote biographies, apparently short ones, judging by those that have survived. His brief sketch on Iphicrates is largely about his military accomplishments, but the episode with Eurydice and her children is mentioned to show Iphicrates' uprightness and dependability. Eurydice is referred to only to demonstrate Iphicrates' character, so it is difficult to know whether her apparent passivity in Nepos is a consequence of Roman coloring or simply her unimportance in the narrative. Nepos does refer to Theopompus in his biography of Iphicrates (3.2), so he obviously used him as a source.[48]

Despite individual agendas and Roman coloring, it remains likely that the hostile version of Eurydice as a murderous plotter had its origin in fourth-century Macedonian court gossip, often filtered through the lens of the historian Theopompus (generally supposed to be Pompeius Trogus' main source for Justin's Book 7). Theopompus understood Macedonian court life as extravagant and barbaric (*FGrH* 115 F 224–225 a–b).[49] We should not assume, however, that Theopompus was uniformly hostile to Philip or his ancestors. The ultimate source of this court gossip could certainly have been Gygaea and her sons, at least one of whom was a contender for the throne during the reign of Philip II, and their remaining supporters, part of a general attempt to denigrate Eurydice and her sons (see Chapters 1 and 2).[50] But other court groups at one point or another hostile to her and/or her sons (e.g., surviving followers of Ptolemy Alorites) may also have played a part.

Lane Fox refers to Justin's account of Eurydice's murderous and would-be murderous activities as the "Black Legend."[51] I suspect that he intends this as an allusion (and a parallel) to the "Black Legend" about Catherine de Medici, another foreign royal widow; the "Legend" blamed the St. Bartholomew's Day Massacre primarily on Catherine and depicted it as premeditated. Significantly, this "Legend" originated within French court circles, though it was later implemented (and expanded) by Huguenot writers and has proved, true or not, to have enduring popularity. As one scholar observed, "Propaganda is seldom more effective than when it blames a single individual for all the ills of the world," also noting that, in sixteenth-century France, the queen provided a "perfect target for xenophobia, social snobbery and misogyny."[52] Similarly, Justin's story makes Eurydice, almost alone, responsible for the continuing upsets of the 370s and 360s, and trades in broad stereotypes about scheming and violent royal women (Clytemnestra, for instance). One should also note that, true or not, Justin's and the scholiast's accounts must have depended, ultimately, on people who claimed to know the truth about events whose truth may, in fact, never have been clear in any absolute way. How, for instance, could one be sure that Eurydice, even if married to Ptolemy, plotted against her son? It seems unlikely that she would have announced it.

Another indication of the influence of the fourth century on our extant sources is also present in Justin. In contrast to his portrayal of Eurydice, Justin's treatment of Amyntas III, though quite brief, is a remarkably flattering portrayal of a man who possibly murdered his way to the throne and who hardly covered himself with military glory. Justin (7.4.3–4) refers to Amyntas as having succeeded to the throne (the implication is that he was simply next in line, rather than that he murdered another claimant) and describes Amyntas as distinguished for his energy and equipped with all the virtues of a general. Justin adds that Amyntas waged difficult wars against the Illyrians and Olynthians (7.4.6).

This characterization of Amyntas III is one that a faction championing his other set of sons (those by Gygaea) might well have embraced since it puts the best possible light on Amyntas III's limited military success and generally rocky reign. It is difficult to think what other group might have pictured Amyntas III in so positive a way and Eurydice in so negative a one. It is interesting that Justin's narrative does not "bastardize" Eurydice's sons, but instead focuses on Eurydice's supposed murderous actions. This too may reflect the point of view of Gygaea's sons and their supporters.

Despite widespread rejection of Justin's account of Eurydice, other elements in Justin's narrative—the name of Amyntas III's other wife, Gygaea, the names of his sons by her, the name of Amyntas III's daughter by Eurydice (actually her existence itself), and the failed attempt by one of Gygaea's sons to take the throne—are taken seriously and without question by most scholars, though these bits of information are found only in Justin.[53] None of these elements, viewed separately, is particularly unbelievable, but given the apparent falsity and hostility of the broader Eurydice narrative, one could wonder if we should continue to treat this uniquely provided information as unquestioned fact. Alternatively, we can simply conclude that these "facts," like a lot of the hostile treatment of Eurydice, came to Justin from a fourth-century source supportive of Gygaea's sons.

### The Picture of Eurydice in Our Extant Sources

There are a number of fascinating things about all the ancient accounts that refer to Eurydice, but particularly about the most important of them, Aeschines' speech. In all three accounts of the Iphicrates episode, Eurydice serves as a succession advocate for her sons and negotiates with males to do so. As would later be the case with Olympias (for instance, Aeschin. 3.223; Hypereid. *Eux.* 19), Eurydice is referred to by personal name in front of the Athenian assembly (Aeschin. 2.26), something that would never happen to a respectable Athenian citizen woman.[54] Yet Aeschines' description of Eurydice's action is somewhere between admiring and sentimental; naming her is not intended as an insult, but rather happens because he treats Eurydice as a public figure.

There were reasons for this perception that have to do with how the Greek world looked at both internal and external political relationships. In the Hellenic world, internal political associations as well as relations between foreign powers were understood in terms of kinship and *philia* (friendship); this view was particularly pronounced in terms of hereditary monarchy.[55] Diplomacy was highly individualized, and personal— not necessarily public—relationships often defined those designated to conduct international dealings. The world of the family, as demonstrated by the adoption of Iphicrates by Amyntas III, inspired many terms used in international relations.[56] *Philia* relationships could involve women (Arist. *Nic. Eth.* 1: 1157b–1158a) and given the central importance of reciprocity in *philia*, women part of such relationships expected to receive and convey benefits.[57]

Aeschines employs the vocabulary of *philia* to describe Eurydice's dealings at court (that is to say internally) and also with the Athenians. Aeschines says that she has been betrayed by those who seemed to be her/their *philoi* (Aeschin. 2.26).[58] She summons the Athenian general, reminds him that Amyntas made him his son and thus, in his private role, a brother of her boys and in a public one a *philos* "to us" (that is, to Eurydice and her sons; Aeschin. 2.28).[59] Thus, she entreats him on her own behalf as well as that of her sons and the kingdom. In Aeschines' account, since there are witnesses, this scene plays out in some sort of public arena. What Eurydice does works, doubtless because it was in Iphicrates' and Athens' interest to act as she requested, but her activist role as he recounts the episode is striking. Aeschines (2.27) pictures her as part of the network of *philia* that bound individual members of Greek elites and entire states together. Amyntas III's adoption of Iphicrates (probably in return for aid provided[60]) is another element in this kind of international relationship, one Eurydice could and did use to advantage.[61] According to him, she was both injured and benefited by these relationships. The *Suda* refers to her *symmachia* (formal alliance) with Iphicrates (and presumably Athens). Even Nepos' Romanizing account, with its more passive and desperate Eurydice, implies that her actions brought the restoration of her sons.

The *philia* relationships mentioned refer, in part, to competing elements within the Macedonian elite. In the troubled years after the death of Amyntas III, the political involvement of various elite groups is apparent. On his first visit to Macedon (Plut. *Pel.* 26.3–5), Pelopidas returned exiles to Macedonia but also took hostages (including Alexander II's brother Philip) back to Thebes with them; it is likely the returnees were friendly to Ptolemy and the hostages Pelopidas took were probably from both factions, but most likely more came from Alexander's supporters. After Alexander II's murder, more references to these factions occur, membership defined by allegiance (or lack of same) to powerful individuals. We hear of others acting with Ptolemy in the assassination (see Chapter 3); it would have done Ptolemy no good to kill Alexander II if he did not have supporters ready to help him take advantage of the murder; they help to explain why Pelopidas, was not more severe with Ptolemy, Alexander II's murderer; Pelopidas, it will be recalled, had only a small (and, as it turned out, not loyal) mercenary force with him. As we have noted, Aeschines (2.26) comments that Eurydice, after Alexander II's assassination, had been deserted by those who had seemed to be *philoi*, clearly suggesting that some members (perhaps Ptolemy himself) of the elite who had once supported Alexander had now changed sides. Eurydice then turned to Iphicrates, the adoptive "son" of Amyntas (Aeschin. 2.28). Plutarch (*Pel.* 27.2) reports that the *philoi* of the dead king persuaded Pelopidas to return to Macedonia and force Ptolemy to accept only the regency and not claim to be king.[62] In the end, more than eighty members of the Macedonian elite were held hostage there in Thebes, presumably representatives of both elite factions. The scholiast for Aeschines 2.29 claimed that Perdiccas, like Ptolemy before him, organized a plot to kill his enemy, in this case Ptolemy. Once more an Argead's path to power depended on a group of elite supporters, often termed *philoi* by our much later sources but almost certainly *hetairoi*. The evidence available tells us that Macedonian factions sought the support the great powers of the day to win internal victories but also that these great powers, Thebes and Athens, tried to manipulate Macedonian affairs and groups to serve their own self-interests. We could understand Ptolemy as more connected to the Thebans and Eurydice and her sons to the Athenians, in this period, but this would be to mistake convenience (Macedonian, Theban, and Athenian) for principle or long term policy.

While our sources tend to refer to *philoi*, as I have noted, in English we usually speak of factions in the Macedonian court, as I have just done. These groups seem focused on individuals, but their "membership" must have fluctuated constantly; there were probably more factions than we realize. Some *philoi* were foreign, others domestic. Aeschines tells us that some who had been supporters of Alexander II ceased to be, probably having shifted support to Ptolemy instead. The claimants we hear of like Pausanias and Argaeus (see Chapter 3) must have had friends in Macedonia and Amyntas' other set of sons, those of Gygaea, doubtless had adherents as well. Some may have clustered around a particular son of Eurydice, whereas others may have been more tied to Eurydice than one of her young sons.

Our sources, as we have seen, likely ultimately depend on writers who visited the Macedonian court in the mid-fourth century, more than a generation after the events on which this chapter focuses, and they presumably talked to assorted court figures who, even if they had been at court in the early 360s, may or may not have remained connected to the factions of that period. For others, too young to have been present, there would have been family memories, though often doubtless colored by current interests. Philip II had his own view, one (see Chapters 5 and 6) he promoted. Even if we had eyewitness accounts, the private, conspiratorial and yet collaborative nature of many of these events would make it difficult to know in some absolute way what happened (see also Chapter 1).

Despite the ways in which Aeschines, in particular, embedded Eurydice's actions in *philia* networks and described her ability to manipulate them (as well as to be threatened by them), scholars have sometimes discounted or trivialized Eurydice's role in preserving rule for her sons and thus in making the reigns of Philip II and his son Alexander the Great possible. Though none of the ancient accounts gives Ptolemy a role in the Iphicrates episode, some have assumed that he not only had such a role but that he was the real agent, not Eurydice. Indeed, some scholars mention his name in terms of this incident and omit any reference to Eurydice, though the ancient sources do the reverse.[63] We know of no precedent for Eurydice's action by a Macedonian royal woman, but this is hardly proof that it had not happened before and, in any case, Eurydice may simply have done the unprecedented.[64] It is particularly significant that her appeal seems to have been couched in the diplomatic language of kinship; this was something Ptolemy, if he were not a son of Amyntas III, could not have done.

The presumption that Ptolemy was the main actor in this incident seems to assume an Athenian gender/political norm not in evidence for Macedonian monarchy, to prize what some think should have happened over the only actual relatively contemporary evidence we have, Aeschines' account.[65] While it is possible that Aeschines repressed any mention of Ptolemy in terms of the Iphicrates episode because of his role in the death of Alexander II, this seems unlikely given that the very next section of the speech (2.29) refers to Ptolemy, and unfavorably. Neither of the other ancient accounts of the incident mentions him either. Moreover, those who assume he was involved in the encounter with Iphicrates do so, at least in part, because they believe that he was already regent, and we do not know that he was. If he wasn't, it is hardly surprising that he played no part in an attempt to safeguard the throne for Eurydice's remaining sons. Doubtless he too wanted Pausanias out of the picture, but for his own benefit. It is unlikely that he could have pursued the path that Eurydice successfully followed.

Even if we assume that Aeschines enhanced and romanticized Eurydice's role, little attention has been paid to what an unusual construction—a fictional construction, some would say—this role is, in terms of its original Macedonian audience (particularly Philip) and in terms of the audience of the Athenian assembly. Aeschines' speech assumes that Philip will approve it and that his Athenian audience will be sympathetic as well. Indeed, in Aeschines' account, Eurydice seems to have staged the scene, doubtless to gain sympathy for her situation and that of her sons (see further Chapter 5). The ahistorical juvenalization of Philip and his older brother Perdiccas (whether part of Aeschines' original speech or added in 343), so as to enable Eurydice to put them into Iphicrates' hands and lap, is clearly a play for sympathy, but it depends on not only Philip but the Athenian audience seeing Eurydice's actions in a favorable light, definitely not seeing her as a woman acting inappropriately. Eurydice appears as a super-mother and as a manipulator and participant in international diplomacy. All three accounts of Iphicrates' intervention more or less matter-of-factly assume that Eurydice would be knowledgeable about both internal factions and Greek politics and that Iphicrates accepted her advocacy. It is frustrating that we cannot be certain whether Ptolemy was as yet *epitropos* or whether he was as yet or ever Eurydice's husband. Nonetheless, it is difficult to escape the conclusion that Eurydice was acting in a role conceived of as her responsibility. Aeschines makes her appealing, but he does not suggest that she is confounding expectations or acting against any assumed norms; if anything, he does the reverse.

Significantly, both Justin's hostile narrative and the far more sympathetic account of Eurydice found in Aeschines picture Eurydice as an aggressive figure, an actor in events. Justin makes her the dominant figure in the series of plots (certainly it is not the unnamed lover who appears in Justin's narrative), and it is particularly telling that Justin pictures her as the leader of a faction, just as Aeschines seems to do. Even the scholiast for Aeschines 2.29, though putting primary emphasis on Ptolemy, has her collaborating with him, apparently before she had married him. Despite the many uncertainties of our accounts, whether for her own interests or out of affection and loyalty to her sons, Eurydice led her surviving sons and their supporters until Perdiccas III was old enough to do the "right thing" by Macedonian standards, that being to kill Ptolemy and rule in his own right.

The episode with Iphicrates, apparently dating to c. 368, is the last reference to specific actions of Eurydice. Several dedicatory inscriptions indicate that Eurydice survived into the reigns of Perdiccas III and Philip (see Chapter 5). We do not know when she died; if the tomb ascribed to her by Andronikos and others does indeed belong to her (see Chapter 6), then she died as an old woman, in the 340s, well into the increasingly successful reign of her youngest son.

# 5

# *Eurydice's Public Image during Her Lifetime*

We now turn from discussion of Eurydice's intervention with Iphicrates and its consequences to the broader topic of her public image during her lifetime. Greenwalt suggests that she had a "well defined public presence" not only because of her marriage and production of heirs to the throne, but also because she wanted and was able to acquire a "public role" at court.[1] We have no way to determine how much of this public image of Eurydice's was self-generated and how much was due to the effort of her male kin, particularly Philip II. But Eurydice certainly presented an image to the public, one constructed both by her actions as reported in literary sources (e.g., the dramatic and somewhat staged Iphicrates episode) as well as by dedications, monuments, and physical images, attested by inscriptions.

Inscriptional evidence indicates that Eurydice made at least three dedications during her lifetime, about whose nature (and therefore expense) we have limited knowledge. Uncertainty about the independent agency of women often surfaces in discussion of women's dedications, patronage, and euergetism (acts for the communal good, typically funded by members of elites) in the ancient world. Subsequent Argead women apparently controlled income of their own;[2] Eurydice may well have done so too, though it is possible that her dedications were entirely underwritten by one of her sons.[3]

More complicated, if partly unanswerable, is to what extent these dedications reflected Eurydice's own ideas and initiatives and to what degree they reflected those of her sons. One should note, however, that Eurydice and her sons may not have understood such a distinction as a meaningful one.[4] In either case, Eurydice's actions and dedications likely related to communal values too; so often elite images reflected those of the wider community at the same time as they embodied them. Neither of Eurydice's surviving sons was old enough to have contributed to the public posture she assumed in calling upon Iphicrates' help (Philip, in fact, was probably not present), and yet the picture she generated of herself in that incident accords well with the public presence indicated by the dedications I will discuss. Her action in summoning Iphicrates and convincing him to be an advocate for her sons generated a distinctive public persona, focused on her as the exemplary (and certainly respectable) mother of royal sons, as a woman able to manipulate *philia* networks (Iphicrates' adoptive relationship to her dead husband and to her son, as well as that of the Athenians to her family) to protect her sons, and as a woman willing to act in public in front of men to do so (thus Aeschines' reference in his speech to those present who could confirm the truth of the incident; Aeschin. 2.28). She was aggressive, but in support of her role as mother, specifically a royal mother. Eurydice's dedications confirmed the persona her actions with Iphicrates initially generated.

Nonetheless, although these individual dedications conformed to and buttressed the broader public image of her family, the only family member other than herself specifically named in these dedications is Eurydice's father, the mysterious Sirras, who appears in her patronymic; in fact, all four inscriptions (three dedications and a fourth, non-dedicatory inscription) focus on Eurydice. They do not name her sons or husband; even if her sons in effect paid the "bill," a choice was made to name only Eurydice.

This pattern conforms to a common one concerning Argead women and Hellenistic royal women. Apart from the four Eurydice inscriptions, only a few others relating to royal women survive from the Argead period, and none of these are from Macedonia itself. Like the Eurydice inscriptions, none of these refer to the husbands or sons of the royal women.[5] Change apparently began after the death of Alexander the Great in 323. Roxane, who had married Alexander III (the Great), made a dedication to Athena in Athens, one in which she is referred to as the wife of Alexander. The date of the dedication is, however, more likely after Alexander's death, in the period 319–316, rather than before it. In other words, it is likely that the inscription refers to her as the wife of a man even though she was probably by this point, his widow.[6] Naturally, none of the Argead period inscriptions refer to royal women by title, since there was no title for royal women in that period: based on current evidence, in about 306 the wives (and sometimes daughters) of the Successors began to appear in inscriptions with the title *basilissa*.[7]

Intriguingly, even once royal women in Macedonia and elsewhere in the Hellenistic world had a title, in addition to the title, in inscriptions they (or those generating the inscription) sometimes referred to fathers as well as husbands, and there are a number of inscriptions that include only a royal woman's name, title, and patronymic.[8] Some of these inscriptions might date from a time when the woman in question was not yet married or was already a widow, but a fragmentary dedication (from a much larger inscription) to a male god from the "Eucleia sanctuary" at Aegae (see discussion in this chapter) by Laodice, wife of the last king of Macedonia, Perseus, is unlikely to be from the period before she was married since she was a Seleucid and so not a resident in Macedonia prior to her marriage, and it cannot have been from her widowhood since the monarchy was abolished and she returned to her Seleucid homeland.[9] This dedication has only a title and a patronymic.[10] In addition, a statue base from Veria has an inscription that gives a woman's name (largely destroyed) and a patronymic; given the patronymic, it is probably the base for a statue of Stratonice, wife of the male founder of the Antigonid dynasty, and likely dates to the third or second century.[11] The Laodice inscription seems to parallel the Eurydice inscriptions, apart from the fact that both Laodice and her father Seleucus are referred to by royal titles. Very few documents mention ordinary Macedonian women during any period, but the surviving small collection suggests that women were sometimes called by personal name, sometimes by reference only to the husband, avoiding use of the woman's personal name, as in Athens (see Chapter 4), and sometimes with a patronymic. In any event, it is difficult to say whether typical practice is relevant to royal women.[12]

Thus the Eurydice inscriptions seem to follow a common, though hardly universal, pattern. Moreover, if all the inscriptions date from the period in which Eurydice was a widow, as I believe (see further discussion in this chapter), the absence of reference to her husband is even less remarkable. Given that, whoever exactly Sirras, Eurydice's father, was (Lyncestian, Illyrian, or some combination of the two; see Chapter 2), Amyntas III had almost certainly married her because of who her father was (i.e., the marriage was a part of an alliance), it is unsurprising that she used the patronymic throughout her life. The patronymic certainly does not tell us, one way or the other, whether her father was partly Illyrian; using it was simply ordinary practice and not somehow a flaunting of her ethnic background, whatever that was.[13]

It is more interesting (but not surprising) that the inscriptions do not refer to her sons as co-dedicators, particularly if they helped to fund her dedications. Olympias' dedication at Delphi, however, although quite possibly funded by plunder from Alexander's Asian conquests (since we know he sent her plunder), does not mention him;[14] Olympias and Cleopatra (the sister of Alexander the Great) appear on Cyrene grain lists without reference to him either, even though they may have been donating in concert with his policy and possibly with his funding.[15] In all these cases, the documents focus on the royal woman and treat them as independent actors, whether or not they actually were. In Eurydice's case, this focus parallels the concentration on her (not on her sons or male *philoi*) in Justin's negative narrative and in Aeschines' very positive reference to her in his speech (see Chapter 4); her dedications do publicize the Argeads, but indirectly, whereas they publicize Eurydice herself very directly indeed. The dedications may indicate her importance in her family faction or signify that they were intended to work against the negative propaganda of her enemies, but even the inscription that specifically relates to her role as mother does not name her sons.

An essay—"On the Education of Children"—in the corpus of Plutarch's works, though possibly not written by Plutarch himself,[16] holds Eurydice up as a model in terms of the education of her children and includes a dedicatory inscription of hers that the author quotes in full (Plut. *Mor.* 14b–c).[17] "Plutarch" begins by saying that the reader should emulate Eurydice who, though she was an Illyrian and three times over a barbarian (see Chapter 2 for discussion of the literal truth of this description of her ethnicity), nonetheless took up education well after the prime of life, for the sake of her children's instruction. He comments that the epigram she dedicated to the Muses fully demonstrates her love for her children. In fact "Plutarch" may have misunderstood the dedication (probably because a dedication to the Muses would have been a conventional choice); a convincing emendation of the text means that her dedication was not to the Muses but to female citizens.[18] Rejecting this part of the emendation, however, some scholars continue to believe that Eurydice did dedicate to the Muses and that she called herself a female citizen.[19] I prefer the former version of the epigram and give this translation, while still attempting to recognize the ambiguity inherent even in the emendation.[20]

Εὐρυδίκη Σίρρα πολιήτισι τόνδ᾽ ἀνέθηκε
‹ἐμ›Μούσαις εὐκτὸν ψυχῇ ἑλοῦσα πόθον.
Γράμματα γὰρ μνημεῖα λόγων μήτηρ γεγαυῖα
παίδων ἡβώντων ἐξεπόνησε μαθεῖν

Eurydice, daughter of Sirras, dedicated this for/to citizen women, having gained the desire (*pothos*) of her soul, through the Muses. She, already the mother of sons who had reached adolescence, labored to learn letters, which are the memory of words.

Since this inscription is not physically preserved, we do not know what she dedicated or where or when she did it. The dedication could simply have been a votive tablet, but given the nature of her other known dedications, as we shall shortly see, a statue of some sort seems more likely. Saatsoglou-Paliadeli has suggested that Eurydice dedicated an image of *Pothos* (desire) itself, the desire that motivated Eurydice's educational accomplishment.[21] Personifications of this concept appeared in Greek art during the fifth century, often in relationship to women.[22] Ancient authors often connect Alexander the Great and a *pothos* for various kinds of knowledge. Whether this similarity in diction derives from some specific and Macedonian connection or, more likely, relates to a common heroic code (here understood in terms of royal women) is debatable.[23] Given the reference to the Muses, whether or not this was an actual dedication to them, the inscription could have been placed in a sanctuary to them, whether in Aegae where Eurydice's other dedications have been found, or perhaps at Dion (at the foot of Mt. Olympus),[24] where a sanctuary to Zeus and the Muses existed. Archelaus celebrated a festival to them there, to honor Greek intellectual and artistic life (Diod. 17.16.3–4), and perhaps to recall Hesiod's story about the birth of the Muses near Olympus (Hes. *Theog.* 51–62). Thus the cult of the Muses had royal patronage prior to Eurydice's day.[25] Konishi has argued that the Muses were originally associated not with music but with literacy, an association this inscription seems to confirm.[26] Eurydice's dedication has a public quality, whether her dedication was to citizen women generally or if, instead, Eurydice describes herself as one. In either case, she identifies herself with the other women of the community and, by implication, with their roles, at the same time as she serves as a model for them. Consequently, the agora of a city might well have been where it was placed.

Given that Philip, the youngest of Eurydice's sons, was born c. 382 and so would have reached adolescence about the time of his father's death in 370, the assumption has been that this dedication was made in the 360s.[27] If this is correct, since Eurydice's son Alexander II's reign was so short and fraught (see Chapter 3), Eurydice probably did not make this dedication then. I would suggest a date sometime after the elimination of Ptolemy, during the independent reign of Perdiccas III (365–360/59), as the most likely timing for the dedication and inscription. Perdiccas III's court was known for its intellectual rigor and so Eurydice's unusual effort and desire to commemorate that effort would suit the court climate.[28] We know very little about the education of elite Macedonian women at any period, though royal women seem to have become better educated by the Hellenistic period.[29] There is no reason to think Eurydice's earlier lack of literacy was distinctive or due to her possible Illyrian background; thus her new literacy would have been distinctive and worth celebrating.[30] One wonders if Eurydice composed the epigram herself, although she much more likely commissioned it.

Despite the continuing uncertainty about some aspects of the text of the inscription, it is a fascinating piece of evidence about Eurydice and the Macedonian court and Macedonia itself in the period. Whether, as some would have it, Eurydice refers to herself as a female citizen, or, as I believe, she makes a dedication to or on behalf of her fellow female citizens, the epigram associates this particular royal woman with the other women of the community. She implies that other women—perhaps particularly other mothers—can or perhaps should emulate Eurydice's behavior; that is the reason why Eurydice makes the dedication in a way that involves them.[31] She holds herself up as a model and yet makes herself part of the wider community of women. Female patronage often focused on women in the community or paralleled traditional duties of women (e.g., food provision), and Eurydice's dedication seems to fit this pattern; indeed, it may be a model for subsequent royal women.[32]

Although she pictures herself as part of a female community, Eurydice also elevates and idealizes herself and, by implication, her family, in keeping with the developing practices of her husband and sons. Amyntas III manipulated the royal image on coins to his own ends, combining the traditional with the new.[33] Greenwalt has suggested that Amyntas III, for rather specific reasons, promoted Eurydice and her sons and that this promotion, in turn—more or less accidentally—transformed into "a dynastic tradition" that developed an understanding of lineage as "based upon the lines of both parents."[34] Certainly during the reign of Philip II, but possibly also during Perdiccas III's reign, the royal family consciously enlarged and glamorized itself.[35] Philip was really, as the complex of theater and palace at Aegae reveals, a master of royal stagecraft (as we shall shortly see). All of Eurydice's dedications tended to elevate her and by implication the family as well, but this particular dedication does something different from the practice of her male kin: it idealizes Eurydice's motherly qualities, Eurydice as the mother of the very sons a hostile tradition (and doubtless faction) claimed she had killed or tried to kill—ones to whom she was anything but faithful (see Chapter 4). This dedication is the poetic equivalent of the story Aeschines tells about her: both sentimentalize her as the loyal mother of sons, and both present a mirror image to that of Justin's evil and murderous mother. The dedication generates an image of Eurydice that advantages her sons and conjures up the picture of a conventionally close family, as does the scene with Iphicrates.

Moreover, the epigram has a distinctive, personal quality, in addition to its adherence to themes we know would have been attractive to her sons and to their supporters. The inscription also celebrates the fact that Eurydice has done what other women have not and has done it later in life; she is proud of her exceptionalism and wants to flaunt her achievement. The epigram has something of the same quality as the dedication of the Spartan king's daughter, Cynisca, at Olympia, an inscription that boasted that she, Cynisca, was the only woman who had won an Olympic victory.[36] Eurydice's inscription does not single her out from other women in the exactly the same way—if anything, it suggests or implies that others should follow her example—but there is much the same pride in her accomplishment and desire to publicize that accomplishment.

### Eurydice and the "Eucleia Sanctuary" at Vergina/Aegae

Whereas the absence of a physical context for Eurydice's epigram about her late acquisition of education leaves a number of issues about it unresolved, the very presence of a considerable quantity of evidence about the context of the two dedications Eurydice made at Aegae/Vergina complicates any reading of their significance. Since Aegae, the burial place of the Argead kings and the first capital of Macedonia, was located on the relatively steep hillside of Mt. Pieria, the city was built on a series of terraces: at the top was the palace, and below that the theater. About eighty meters further down the hill from the theater, in what seems to be the area of the agora, a sanctuary usually attributed to Eucleia (based on the two inscriptions commemorating Eurydice's dedications to Eucleia, we will discuss shortly) was first excavated in 1982, and excavation continues.[37] Chrysoula Saatsoglou-Paliadeli was long the principal excavator of this sanctuary. The sanctuary included a Doric temple, oriented east-to-west, a stoa annex to the south of this temple, a building with a central court, and to the east of the sanctuary there were an altar and (originally) three rectangular marble bases for dedications, one of which was found in situ, with a dedicatory inscription to Eucleia by Eurydice. (See Figure 5.1 for a ground plan of the main terrace of the Eucleia sanctuary.)

All the Eucleia sanctuary structures mentioned were erected in the fourth century, though some additions and alterations to the sanctuary appeared in the following centuries.[38] Not only the dating of the

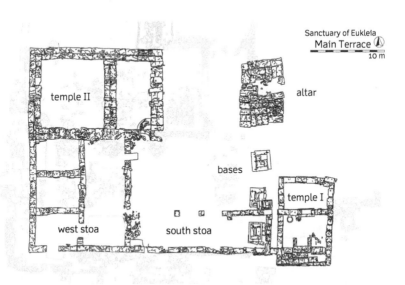

FIGURE 5.1 Ground plan of the main terrace of the Eucleia sanctuary. From Kyriakou and Tourtas 2015: fig. 13.2 (drawing A. Tourtas, after N. Haddad in Saatsoglou-Paliadeli 1993, p. 53).

Image courtesy of the Aristotle University of Thessaloniki, Vergina excavation archive.

sanctuary itself but the fact that it shared the same orientation (north-south) as the closely connected palace-theater complex indicates that it was part of the urban plan of Philip's day.[39] The palace, theater, and most of the sanctuary played a part in Philip II's developing royal stagecraft.[40] The sanctuary complex was heavily damaged in the second century, apparently at the time of the Roman conquest, though use of the site in some form may have persisted into the first century CE.[41]

Four deposit pits were found in the area of the sanctuary. One pit, just outside the northeastern corner of the temple (Pit 1990), contained the body of a slightly larger-than-life-size peplophorus (peplos wearing) female statue (Figure 5.2 shows the statue body in the pit), the separately constructed head and neck of the same statue, two more statue heads,

FIGURE 5.2 The peplophoros statue body from the 1990 pit at the Eucleia sanctuary. From Kyriakou and Tourtas 2015: fig. 13.10. The female statue within the "statuary pit." *Αρχαιολογία. Μακεδονία και Θράκη*, Melissa Publishing House, Athens 2017: fig. 385.

Image courtesy of the Aristotle University of Thessaloniki, Vergina excavation archive.

an inscribed statue base, as well as much pottery and other materials.[42] Another pit, in the southeast corner of the antechamber (Pit 1991) held, again among other items, a very large marble snake (1.8 meters high).[43] Two more pits were found as well, one in 1993 (with architectural fragments) and the other in 2003 (containing two porous blocks and potsherds).[44]

Recently (2008, 2009), two late fourth-century burials were found within the sanctuary area. Features of these burials resemble the royal burials found under the Great Tumulus at Vergina and so suggest that these too were royal burials, if atypical ones.[45] A royal identity for these burials would tend to confirm the close association between the sanctuary and the royal family.

Let us consider the two statue podia (as noted, the first was found in situ, in 1982, and the second in 1990, in the 1990 pit), each with an inscription: "Eurydice, daughter of Sirras, to Eucleia." The first base lacks moldings on the top and bottom edges,[46] and the excavator concluded that the base was reconstructed in the Hellenistic period.[47] It is missing the marble block on the top upon which a dedication would have rested.[48] The dedication text, inscribed on the long side of the rectangular front, is well preserved and appears within an area shaped like a band, even down to the realistic details of strings at each end. This band could be connected to the cult of Eucleia.[49] Andronikos dated the inscription on the base to the second half of the fourth century, based on the lettering.[50] Saatsoglou-Paliadeli believed that the inscription couldn't be later than 350–325; she did not exclude a date between 375 and 350, but the more recent dating of the Eucleia sanctuary buildings already mentioned implies that the dedicatory inscriptions, too, date roughly to mid-century.[51] In terms of the inscription itself, letter shape alone would seem to preclude a dedication during Amyntas III's reign (since he died in 370/69) and also probably that of Eurydice's eldest son, Alexander II (370/68–368/7) and her possible marriage to Ptolemy (since Ptolemy was killed by 365).[52] Thus the dedications, like the palace, theater, and sanctuary, were probably erected around 350.

The second inscribed marble statue base, found in the 1990 deposit ditch, has the same inscription and lettering as the first (though the text was not inscribed within a band), and so the excavator dated it to the same period as the first. (See Figure 5.3.)[53] This base is better preserved with upper and lower moldings still in place. The top surface indicates that it originally supported a large marble statue.[54]

FIGURE 5.3 The statue base found in the 1990 pit at the Eucleia sanctuary, inscribed with a dedication by Eurydice daughter of Sirras to Eucleia. From *Αρχαιολογία. Μακεδονία και Θράκη*, Melissa Publishing House, Athens 2017: fig. 382.

Image courtesy of the Aristotle University of Thessaloniki, Vergina excavation archive.

Saatsoglou-Paliadeli originally thought that the peplophorus body and the detached head and neck, all made of Pentelic marble, a stone originating in Attica, and all found in the same pit with the base, were the parts of a single dedication of Eurydice's. (See Figure 5.4.)[55]

Subsequent investigation led her to doubt that the statue fitted into the base with which it was found.[56] Palagia has suggested that the 1982 base, unlike the one found in the same ditch with the statue, is large enough to support the peplophorus statue.[57] The peplos, an "Argive" form of dress, often shown worn over a chiton, essentially an archaic style, was characteristic of many fourth-century statues of goddesses, and this particular statue type appears to be dependent on Cephisodotus' statue of Eirene (Peace) holding the infant Ploutos (c. 370) and may also be the work of an Athenian artist.

Inscriptional evidence indicates that women, about the middle of the fourth century, began to be honored much more regularly with portrait statues.[58] These images, typically in prominent positions like Eurydice's dedication, kept up a "perpetual public presence" for the family of the woman.[59] In Greek art, distinguishing between mortal and

FIGURE 5.4 The peplophorus statue body from the Eucleia sanctuary standing upright.

Image courtesy of the Aristotle University of Thessaloniki, Vergina excavation archive.

divine females is always difficult,[60] but given that images of priestesses often replicated or imitated the archaic garb of goddesses, like the peplos worn by the statue in the Eucleia sanctuary,[61] this statue, whether or not a match for the second statue base, could be a portrait of Eurydice, possibly as a priestess of Eucleia.[62] Some believe that there was an alteration, possibly a replacement, of a portion of the head of the statue with one that was more human-looking, showing signs of aging, and that the statue may originally have been conceived of as an image of the goddess Eucleia and then later changed to become a portrait, possibly of Eurydice.[63] Palagia, however, has argued that the fact that Eurydice's name is in the nominative in the inscription, rather than the accusative, works against understanding the dedication as a portrait and, rejecting the notion that the head has been altered, concludes that the statue was conceived of as an image of the goddess Eucleia.[64]

A fragmentary inscription, from the area of the same sanctuary,[65] apparently recording a dedication made by Laodice, wife of Perseus, the last king of Macedonia, as we have already discussed, implies that the sanctuary continued to appeal to the ruling dynasty (by this point no longer Argead but Antigonid) and particularly to its female members. Laodice's inscription, however, is a dedication to an unnamed male deity,[66] not to the female deity Eucleia. The excavator has suggested that the large sculpture of a snake found in pit 1991 represented Zeus Meilichius (Zeus the gentle or kindly), a deity sometimes depicted in snake form, sometimes in human form with an accompanying snake. In other Greek cities, he was worshipped as a protector and guarantor of fertility (agricultural and human) and wealth.[67] Some dedicatory reliefs to him seem to show family groups, and a striking number of dedications to Zeus Meilichius were made by women.[68] The snake sculpture may well have been a cult statue from the cella of the sanctuary.[69] Thus, though the sanctuary is conventionally known as the sanctuary of Eucleia, it could possibly have been primarily focused on another deity, and only secondarily on Eucleia.[70] However, around the Greek world, comparatively few temples and cult images of Zeus Meilichius are known, and his cult often shared sanctuary space with that of other deities.[71] What we do know, however, is that the focus of Eurydice's dedication was Eucleia and that her dedications were prominently displayed, in a place people walking by would have seen.

Who was Eucleia, and what was her cult about? Her name means "good repute" or "good fame": she was a deity but also a personification of good repute and could represent the qualities that brought it about. Though, as we have seen, the sanctuary buildings at Vergina that I have discussed date to the fourth century, her cult in Macedonia could have been older. Euripides wrote *Archelaus* under the patronage of Archelaus, the Macedonian king. The play was probably performed in Macedonia, possibly at Aegae, and featured a re-write of the dynastic foundation myth with a man named "Archelaus" as the hero. Though only about a hundred more or less intact verses of the play survive, "*eucleia*" is mentioned four times, in the context of renown acquired by military success. Thus a possibility exists that the cult existed in Macedonia in the late fifth century and was even, early on, promoted by the ruling family.[72] Eucleia's cult took various forms around the Greek world; discussion of the nature of the cult at Aegae has been complicated by the assumption that it must have been like that of another city, even though her cults differed to some degree from city to city. Cults of gods, even those of the Olympians, varied from place to place and sometimes over time. Consideration of possible occasions for Eurydice's dedication has been colored by knowledge of the nature of other cults.

A temple to Eucleia was built in Athens after Athenian victories in the Persian war (Paus. 1.14.5); thus in Athens, Eucleia was associated with military victory, an association going back to Homer[73] and present, as we have noted, in Euripides' play. Andronikos suggested, on the assumption of parallelism with the Athenian cult, that Eurydice's dedication came after Philip II's decisive victory at Chaeronea in 338, apparently assuming that the sanctuary and the dedication were of that same date.[74] Given that Eurydice was born sometime around 410 or a few years after (see Chapters 2 and 6), she was unlikely to have been alive in 338 (or after) and even more unlikely to be the one, rather than her son, commemorating a military victory.[75] Saatsoglou-Paliadeli has proposed that the dedication commemorated Eurydice's successful effort to have Iphicrates intervene in Macedonian affairs on behalf of her sons, arguing that this occasion suits the notion of Eucleia as a protectress of the glory that comes from an individual's deed with a public benefit. She concludes that the dedication happened comparatively soon after the event, in the 360s.[76]

Although the Athenian cult was dedicated to Eucleia alone,[77] there was a Theban cult to Artemis Eucleia (Paus. 9.17.1), and versions similar to this existed elsewhere. Plutarch (*Aristid.* 20.5–6) not only refers to a fifth-century Theban cult to Artemis Eucleia, but volunteers that most people think Eucleia is Artemis and adds that some consider her the daughter of Heracles and Myrto, and that she died a virgin and then received cult honors. He observes that she has an altar and an image in every agora and that she gets sacrifices from males and females about to be married. Borza tentatively suggested that the Macedonian cult might have been more like that of Artemis Eucleia in Boeotia. He noted the strong Theban influence on Macedonia in the mid-fourth century (see Chapters 3 and 4), the tradition that Eucleia was a daughter of Heracles and so an appropriate choice for veneration by the Heraclid Macedonian royal family, and the fact that in Boeotia and Locria (where the cult was also popular), pre-marriage sacrifices happened at her altars.[78] Mortensen suggested a connection to the Artemis Eucleia cult at Corinth, given Eurydice's Lyncestian and thus Bacchiad roots. In addition, she observed that Artemis was often associated with childbirth and fertility, so Eurydice, the mother of four, could have found this appropriate.[79] Eurydice's dedications, however, refer only to Eucleia,[80] not to Artemis Eucleia, and so indicate veneration of the independent deity, not the Artemis cult, although admittedly at the same shrines, by-names or epithets for deities were sometimes used and sometimes not.[81] Given known differences between the Eucleia cult at Athens and those of Artemis Eucleia elsewhere, it seems best to focus on the deity named in the dedication.

I do not think, however, that the dedications happened in the 360s, before the reign of Philip, even if they were indeed inspired by the Iphicrates episode.[82] The dedication might have had a less incident-specific context: the general good reputation of Eurydice and her family. A date sometime in the 350s seems more likely for Eurydice's dedications, not only because this was the era of the broader building project in the western part of Aegae but also because Eurydice's reputation (and thus that of her sons) seems to have been challenged in that period, presumably by the sons of Gygaea and their supporters (see Chapters 3 and 4), thus contributing to the "bad" Eurydice stories.[83] A woman's *kleos* was much affected by her sexual reputation, and Eurydice's had been questioned or compromised. Moreover, if she was at any point married to Ptolemy, her son's murderer, her public image would have been even more affected. Eurydice and thus her sons (whose legitimacy depended on her sexual faithfulness) had a *kleos* problem,[84] and the dedications were intended to solve that problem by demonstrating that she had the right kind of *kleos* and that she venerated the goddess who brought it.[85] If the statue was indeed modified to make it more portrait-like, then at some subsequent point, she not only dedicated it to good repute, but actually embodied it, in effect personifying the personification. I continue, however, to doubt that the statue was intended as a portrait. Whether or not the statue was conceived of as a portrait, Eucleia's cult at Aegae had a political edge.[86]

Do Eurydice's two dedications to Eucleia relate to a broader role than that of statue dedicant, however splendid her individual dedications? Did Eurydice fund not only the two dedications, but the sanctuary itself and/or the cult of Eucleia at Aegae?[87] Whether or not she herself founded the sanctuary and cult, the apparent date of the initial structures suggests it might have been a royal foundation, if not that of Eurydice, then that of Philip II. It could be mere chance that the extant dedicatory inscriptions from this sanctuary were all made by royal women;

Philip himself certainly had reasons to celebrate his fame and his military victories. If the main cult celebrated in the sanctuary was actually that of Zeus Meilichius, then the issue becomes even more complicated, not to mention speculative.

Religious ritual and festivals were very much the business of women in the Greek world, and elite women tended to play a particularly prominent part, sometimes as patrons, sometimes as priestesses.[88] The Eucleia inscriptions are the first clear evidence of an Argead woman fulfilling the role of patron,[89] but it is not unlikely that Argead royal women played a conspicuous role in cult prior to Eurydice and Olympias certainly did soon after Eurydice. Indeed, there may have been a dynastic cult in which Olympias (and presumably other Argead women) had a part.[90] A group of late sixth-and early fifth-century female burials at Aegae have been interpreted as those of royal women and one, at least, has been understood by the excavator as the burial of a priestess.[91] Eurydice could have been a priestess of Eucleia,[92] but unless more direct evidence that she held this office surfaces, we should not assume that she was. There is, however, nothing implausible in the notion that she was a priestess. Priesthoods were often hereditary, and holding one enhanced the reputation of the entire family.[93] Statue base inscriptions, however, usually mentioned priesthoods if they existed,[94] and Eurydice's inscriptions mention no priesthood. Patronage by royal women would develop considerably in the Hellenistic period. As with both of Eurydice's dedications, royal women's efforts usually emphasized qualities tied to traditional female roles within the family but had a public aspect and gave the possibility of acquiring public praise and appreciation.[95]

If this sanctuary was a royal foundation relating to a cult closely associated with the royal family, the mysterious late fourth-century burials on the edge of the sanctuary may be explained or at least given a context. They, of course, would have happened long after the death of Eurydice, so we shall return to them for discussion in the last chapter, when we discuss Eurydice's posthumous reputation.

The dedicatory inscriptions by two royal women found in the area of the sanctuary (Eurydice's two and that of Laodice, wife of Perseus) confirm, as does the general building program, that the switch of the administrative capital from Aegae to Pella didn't cause a decline in importance of Aegae for members of the Argead and Antigonid dynasties; the palace, theater, agora, and cemetery remained in use until the Roman conquest, and some reuse persisted for another century or two. Indeed, extensive destruction at Aegae at the time of the initial Roman conquest and subsequent quashing of the revolt of the pretender Andriscus suggest the opposite: the Romans understood that it was a site of importance to Macedonian monarchy.[96] The cult or cults connected to the sanctuary was apparently centered in the agora of Aegae and yet, surrounded as the sanctuary was by the palace and theater complex and royal tombs, this civic cult elided into one that seems quasi-royal.[97]

### Palatitsia Statue Base

We do not know when Eurydice died. The last references to her are the various accounts of the Iphicrates episode, yet, as I have just suggested, the Eucleia dedications strongly suggest that, minimally, she lived into the 350s. I will argue that she likely died at some point in the 340s (see Chapter 6) and was almost certainly dead by the time, after his great victory at Chaeronea, her son Philip ordered the construction a building at Olympia, the Philippeum, which contained god-like images of himself, Olympias and Alexander, and Amyntas III and Eurydice (that structure and the significance of the fact that her image was one of those included are discussed in the next chapter). I mention the Philippeum here because of its possible connection (or lack of same) to another inscription.

A third inscription relating to Eurydice was found near Aegae, about 2 kilometers away, in the village of Palatitsia. This inscription also appeared on a statue base; the statue base was subsequently altered for re-use as a column base in the early Christian basilica at Palatitsia.[98] Because of this alteration, the inscription is only partially preserved (see Figure 5.5).[99] Unlike the other two Eurydice inscriptions from Aegae, this one simply names Eurydice and lists her patronymic, so it is not a dedication; it must, instead, have been a label for a portrait statue of Eurydice. The base on which the inscription appears is very similar in dimension and shape to the statue base found in the Eucleia sanctuary (the one in the 1990 pit) but it differs in the location of the inscription on the base (on the left-hand lateral side), making it likely that this statue base constituted one element, on the far right, in a larger statuary group. The excavator concluded that it must have been part of a statue group of more than three (see Figure 5.6).[100]

Given that Eurydice's image was similarly placed on the far right in the Philippeum (see Chapter 6), the excavator concluded that this base

FIGURE 5.5 Saatsoglou-Paliadeli's reconstruction of the statue base from Palatitsia, inscribed with Eurydice's name and patronymic. The reconstruction shows the unusual placement of the inscription on the base. From X. Σαατσόγλου-Παλιαδέλη, Σκέψεις με αφορμή ένα εύρημα από τα Παλατίτσια, Ancient Macedonia V. Papers read at the fifth International Symposium held in Thessaloniki, October 10–15, 1989, Thessaloniki 1993: 1339–1371.

Image courtesy of the Aristotle University of Thessaloniki, Vergina excavation archive.

and its accompanying statue was originally part of a grouping similar to that in the Philippeum and might thus have constituted part of a more or less simultaneous double dedication in two locations, as was the case with the Daochus groups dedicated at both Delphi and Pharsalus.[101] She believes that the statue it once supported must have been as large as the peplophorus statue found in the ditch next to the Eucleia sanctuary.[102] The Palatitsia inscription itself is quite damaged and so dating is difficult, perhaps not possible. The excavator has suggested that, if it is related to the Philippeum group, it should be dated in the third quarter of the fourth century and after 336.[103]

While there is nothing implausible about the suggestion of a double or duplicate statue grouping, as happened with the Daochus statue groups, neither is there any necessity to make such an assumption of synchrony and identical composition, though it remains a possibility.[104]

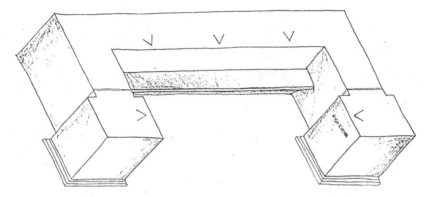

FIGURE 5.6 Saatsoglou-Paliadeli's reconstruction of statue group from Vergina area (Palatitsia) including statue base with Eurydice's name and patronymic. From X. Σαατσόγλου-Παλιαδέλη, Σκέψεις με αφορμή ένα εύρημα από τα Παλατίτσια, Ancient Macedonia V. Papers read at the fifth International Symposium held in Thessaloniki, October 10–15, 1989, Thessaloniki 1993: 1339–1371.

Image courtesy of the Aristotle University of Thessaloniki, Vergina excavation archive.

Moreover, the base for the statue group from Macedonia, as Saatsoglou-Paliadeli has convincingly reconstructed it, was rectilinear, whereas the Philippeum's base was semi-circular. Semi-circular positioning unifies a statue group and, especially when placed within a *tholos* like the Philippeum, it creates a theater-like space, whereas linear groups generate more of narrative-like viewing experience, possibly a chronological one.[105] While Eurydice's position in both the Philippeum group and the Palatitsia monument was literally peripheral, the Palatitsia base's apparent structure, which put the image of Eurydice at a right angle from whatever images took up the center, creates greater separation. If, as in the Philippeum, another woman's image was placed on the other end, then we could see a kind of sexual segregation and categorization, but that is not the only possibility.

Alternatively, one can imagine a royal statue group at Palatitsia constituted at a somewhat earlier period, a group not necessarily identical in "population" to that of the Philippeum. The Palatitsia statue group could have been created in Eurydice's lifetime, particularly given her apparent long-standing association with Aegae, or soon after her death and well before Chaeronea and the Philippeum. One could, for instance, envision a group that showed Philip with his parents and brothers: that three full brothers all became kings was a rather distinctive achievement and would have had particular appeal for a Macedonian audience. In such a grouping, Eurydice's figure might have been paralleled with one of Amyntas, also at right angles to the central figures. It is worth noting that, yet again, in this inscription Eurydice appears with a patronymic, but with no reference to her husband or to her sons. The presumption was, apparently, that she was so well known that this would not have been a problem; in addition, her appearance in some sort of grouping, almost certainly a family grouping, would have reinforced her public identity. Whether or not she took up residence at Aegae, the amount of commemoration of her in the environs of that site is striking.

In terms of the public image of Eurydice during her lifetime, the focus, directly and indirectly, seems to have been on motherhood. Idealized motherhood is self-evidently central to her public appeal to Iphicrates and to her dedication in reference to her late-acquired education, but it is indirectly involved in the Eucleia dedications as well. Her *kleos* was important because she was the mother of kings; it had been called into question and her dedications demonstrated her possession of the right kind of repute. If she were indeed a priestess of Eucleia and/or the founder of the sanctuary, then these associations, as well, could have confirmed her role as an appropriate and fitting mother for royal sons. The base from Palatitsia, presumably from a family group, would have honored her as the mother of kings or perhaps simply as the mother of Philip. Motherhood, in the ancient world, crossed the line from public to private life and consequently, particularly for a royal woman, could be the source of danger and opprobrium but also of praise and admiration.[106] At different times, being the mother of royal sons was both for Eurydice, sometimes even at the same time. Yet her lifetime monuments and dedications imply that she served as a model mother (and perhaps as a patron of mothers) for the kingdom.

# 6

# Eurydice's Public Image
# after Her Death

This is a chapter about the remembrance of the life of Eurydice in Macedonia and elsewhere in Greece. My focus is on her public memory, though much of what became public experience originated in private, within Eurydice's family group, among those who knew her, and among her descendants. Almost certainly, initially, her son Philip crafted her posthumous public image, but gradually other members of the family had a role and, as the specifics of her life grew dimmer with the passage of time and the end of the Argead dynasty, Eurydice became part of a remembered greater Macedonian past.

Whatever the original intent of the statue that she had dedicated in front of the Eucleia sanctuary (see Chapter 5), the passing of time may well have transformed it, in the public mind, into an image of Eurydice herself; ordinary people, many not literate, may not have made much distinction between the actual portrait statue whose base was found at Palatitsia and the image from the Eucleia sanctuary. Sometime after the Roman defeat of Macedonia and the end of the kingdom, people at Vergina buried, with great care, the statue and others from the sanctuary Eurydice had patronized (see Chapter 5). In addition, another image, this one certainly a portrait statue of Eurydice (the one in the Philippeum at Olympia), has a history of its own; this statue traveled, if not very far. Personal names have much to do with memory; this is particularly so in the case of Eurydice. Being named after someone (or in this particular case, naming yourself after someone) powerfully recalls and reanimates their memory. Eurydice's young great-granddaughter chose, as an adult, to rename herself after Eurydice. In a peculiar way, the choice of the famous archaeologist Manolis Andronikos to attribute an idiosyncratic tomb at Vergina to Eurydice has generated another, a modern sort of public image and memory of Eurydice. I suspect the name of the tomb will endure even if a time comes when we know in some fairly absolute way that it cannot have been hers. The tomb suits our reconstructed memory of Eurydice, whoever actually was the original occupant of the tomb.

No written source tells us when Eurydice died or specifically speaks of her death, but a collection of factors imply that she was dead by 346 or 343 at the latest. She likely made her Eucleia dedications in the 350s (see Chapter 5), and we know of no other later public action or gesture of hers apart from those dedications (though, of course, there may have been many, given the limited nature of our information). As I have noted, Eurydice's birth date probably fell in the last decade of the fifth century, so a death in the 340s would mean she had lived a long life by ancient standards. She was probably dead by the time Aeschines, participating in an embassy to the Macedonian court, delivered his speech to Philip in 346 and even more likely by the time of Aeschines' trial in 343, when he gave the Athenian assembly an account of his earlier speech to Philip (it is the version from 343 that is the source of our current text; see Chapter 4).

In the speech as we have it from that occasion, when Aeschines mentions Eurydice's summoning of Iphicrates, he observes that many of those who were present on this occasion can attest to the truth of this episode (Aeschin. 2.28), but he does not say that Eurydice herself can verify his account. It is conceivable that he did, in fact, suggest that she could affirm his statements when he actually spoke to Philip in 346, but that she was dead by the time he spoke to the assembly in 343 and so he edited out this reference as inappropriate in this altered circumstance. Such an alteration would make it just possible that the tomb Andronikos attributed to her, with its Panathenaic vases datable to 344/ 43 (as we shall see) did indeed belong to her. Obviously, the absence of reference to Eurydice as a possible living witness is not absolute proof that she was dead no later than 343, but it implies that this was the case.[1]

Presumably, the first posthumous commemoration of Eurydice was her funeral and her tomb. No literary text mentions her funeral and no inscription refers to her tomb. By the middle of the fourth century, Philip II had accumulated great power, acquired much wealth, and demonstrated considerable desire to display both, at Aegae and elsewhere. Royal and elite Macedonians had long filled their tombs with rich funerary goods. Thus one would expect that Philip II would have arranged an impressive funeral and tomb for his mother, a woman critical to his own career, one who had, during her lifetime, played a role in dynastic display.

Indeed, Manolis Andronikos attributed a distinctive tomb at Vergina to her, a tomb, as I've noted, conventionally known as the "Tomb of Eurydice" and that he first excavated in 1987. He dated the tomb to about 340.[2] (I will employ the tomb name without quotation marks hereafter because to do otherwise would be to ignore the power of the initial naming; the conventional name has helped to convince people that the tomb belonged to her.) No inscription, however, connects Eurydice to this particular tomb, and fragments of three Panathenaic vases found in the pyre associated with the tomb preserve the name of the eponymous archon of 344/3.[3] This archon date does not absolutely eliminate the possibility that this tomb belonged to the mother of Philip, but it makes such an attribution difficult, given the implications of the passage from Aeschines that I have just discussed.

Other factors further complicate this attribution, most notably our own expectations about what sort of burial Eurydice should have had, just as readings of the identities of the occupants of Tomb II at Vergina have been colored by our presumptions about would have been appropriate for a great king like Philip II as opposed to what we deem appropriate for his mentally limited son, Philip Arrhidaeus (as we will discuss shortly).[4] It is easy for such expectations to create circular arguments, particularly if our expectations are shaped by burials that may, in many cases, have happened twenty or thirty years later than the ones under consideration. Another complicating factor is that the Tomb of Eurydice was, as we shall see, quite thoroughly looted, a fact that tends to focus attention on its enduring structures (architecture, decoration, and fittings of stone or plaster) and makes comparison with the un-looted Tomb II or Tomb III complicated by lack of parallelism in our knowledge of these structures and their contents. We need to imagine Tombs II and III (as they are today) bare of all the distinctive items that filled them until forty years ago and, at the same time, picture the Tomb of Eurydice's main chamber stacked with goods and crowded with funerary impedimenta.

These problems with the vanished contexts of the tombs are important because, since its discovery in 1987, the date of the Eurydice tomb has played an important role in the controversy about the identity of those buried in the Great Tumulus at Vergina and the date of Tomb II, even though the Eurydice tomb, although located at Vergina, is far removed from the Great Tumulus. The dispute has centered on whether Philip II or Philip Arrhidaeus (III), his son, Alexander the Great's half-brother, was buried in Tomb II under the Great Tumulus. (Philip II died and was buried in 336, whereas Philip Arrhidaeus died in 317 and was buried in 316 or 315.) From the beginning of the controversy, one of most important issues has been when the barrel vault first appeared in Greece: Tomb II has a barrel vault and so does the Eurydice tomb. Those who believe that Philip II's remains and those of one of his wives were placed in Tomb II therefore concluded that the vault's appearance pre-dated Alexander's invasions and was likely a homegrown innovation,[5] whereas those who oppose the identification of Philip II have often argued that the barrel vault was imported after Alexander's campaigns.[6] The dating of the tomb attributed to Eurydice, because of its vault, has played a critical role in the debate, whether understood to support the connection of Philip II to Tomb II or to deny it.

This controversy has caused uncertainty not only about the identity of the occupants of Tomb II but also about the general chronology of the development of the Macedonian-type tombs (large barrel vaulted underground tombs; hereafter the term "Macedonian tomb" refers only to these vaulted tombs).[7] The Eurydice tomb has often been read as a very early Macedonian tomb, perhaps the earliest. It lacks some of what seem otherwise fairly common (though not universal) characteristics of these Macedonian tombs (most particularly a decorated façade[8]) and possesses some idiosyncratic features.[9] The burial associated with the Eurydice tomb resembles, in some respects, that of Tomb II. As we have seen, the Panathenaic vases associated with the burial predate the death of Philip and certainly predate Alexander's invasion. Thus, if these vases are understood to date the entire tomb and burial, then it becomes dif-ficult to sustain the argument that the barrel vault is a post-Philip phe-nomenon, but, as we shall see, not everyone thinks the vases provide anything more than the upper limit of the date of the burial.

In considering the Eurydice tomb, we will begin by discussing the nature of the tomb and burial, review the factors that had led some to believe that this was the burial of a royal woman, next address the ques-tion of whether connecting it to Eurydice makes sense (quite apart from the question of when the barrel vault first appeared), and only then (and briefly) reflect on where this tomb might fit in the development of Macedonian-type tombs. I see no reason to think certainty can be reached on any of these issues in the near future, but the tomb is an eerie and fascinating construct, worthy of discussion and attention no matter to whom it belonged. It remains unpublished and there has been no lengthy discussion of it in English since 1994; preliminary though this consideration is, I hope it will function as a useful update.[10]

The Eurydice tomb lies about 4 meters east of the Rhomaios tomb (another Macedonian tomb),[11] near the northwestern gate of the city of Aegae, in the general area of a cluster of late archaic, early classical female burials—burials often interpreted as belonging to members of the royal dynasty, possibly royal women who performed some priestly function.[12] While most Macedonian tombs had a mound (tumulus) constructed over them individually or over them and some neighboring tombs as well, neither the Eurydice tomb nor the nearby Rhomaios tomb has a covering mound.[13] Though the Eurydice tomb has a barrel vault, the vault was not originally visible because the entire tomb was encased in a roughly rectangular structure; from the outside it looked like a traditional cist (box) tomb. Like other Macedonian tombs, this one is constructed of blocks of porous limestone, though the walls of this tomb are much thicker than other (and probably later) Macedonian tombs.[14] The tomb is quite a large structure (10.60–10.70 m. by 7.50–7.95 m.).[15] It contains an antechamber and a burial chamber and two sets of two-leafed marble doors, one in the front of the tomb and a second set opening from the antechamber into the main chamber. This floor plan is replicated in many other large Macedonian tombs. Rough plaster covered the south-facing façade of this tomb. A separate wall of stone was constructed in front of the tomb, presumably to guard against unwelcome entry; it has not yet been removed.[16]

Remnants of the funerary pyre were found in front of the tomb (in the *dromos* or entry area) and around the roof.[17] As with the pyre from Tomb II, this pyre was not a simple stack of wood but a house-like structure complete with a doorknocker and other metal fittings; the door alone is estimated to have been about a meter across.[18] The body, placed on a *kline* (couch), was accompanied by various objects and vases, including the three Panathenaic vases,[19] perhaps filled with oil to help the fire burn.[20] While the practice of cremation had spread to the Macedonian elite, and female cremations are known in Macedonia from the fifth century,[21] the house pyres of the Eurydice tomb and that of

Tomb II at Vergina are archaeologically unprecedented in Macedonia,[22] though they do resemble descriptions of the funerary pyre Alexander had constructed for Hephaestion, his friend and probable lover, in 324. They also seem to mimic heroic burials described in Homer.[23] Even modest cremation burials were expensive, and these distinctive ones must have been especially so. Kottaridi has connected cremation burials, at least elaborate ones, to heroization and possibly to Argead claims of descent from Heracles (who had himself burned on a pyre and is sometimes considered to have become a god).[24]

The antechamber is 4.48 meters wide and 2.5 meters deep. The interior height is 5.8 meters. The plastered walls imitate isodomic masonry, but those of the main chamber do not.[25] Iron nails, hammered in a pi pattern, covered the vault of the antechamber. Despite the heavy front barrier wall, thieves gained entry to the tomb in antiquity by drilling into the antechamber through the blocks at the top of the front wall of the tomb. Because of the effects of the robbers' opening, the plaster on the walls of the antechamber had largely fallen to the floor by the time excavators entered the tomb. The excavators found two skeletons in the tomb area: one on the roof level of the tomb and another sprawled on its stomach on the floor of the antechamber, near the eastern wall, covered by fill from the entry point. The excavator believed that these were the remains of tomb robbers who had, perhaps, quarreled over the loot. Future analysis may confirm or reject that supposition.[26] The open position of the doors connecting the antechamber to the main chamber suggests—since the metal hinges still functioned at the time the robbers broke in—that the robbers entered the tomb comparatively soon after the burial.[27] A fragment of metal, possibly from a helmet, was also found in the antechamber. The helmet—if that was indeed the source of the fragment—could have belonged to someone interred in the main chamber[28] or it could have fallen into the antechamber through the opening left by the robbers.[29] It is true that the royal tombs at Vergina were looted by Pyrrhus' Gallic mercenaries c. 274 (Plut. *Pyrrh.* 26.6), but even soldiers plundering a tomb would not likely wear their helmets while doing so.[30]

The burial or main chamber (4.48 m. by 5.51 m.) was once, on three of its four walls, covered by polished white plaster that would have been difficult to distinguish from the actual marble of the doors. Though the ceiling of the chamber was vaulted, Kottaridi believes that a false ceiling of blue painted wood once existed, covering the vault.[31] The fabrication of the fourth wall of the chamber is unique: though the exterior of the tomb lacks the palace-like façade that many of the larger Macedonian tombs have, the fourth wall of the main chamber is itself a convincing Ionic façade that resembles an actual marble façade. There are four half-columns, two windows and a door, and an elaborately decorated and brilliantly (and expensively) painted entablature.[32] The appearance of this false entryway was so convincing that the robbers tried to break through the "doorway" with an iron bar (whose mark remains). The very thick back wall has preserved the plaster and original brilliant colors of the "façade" to a remarkable degree.[33]

Despite the thorough looting of the content of the tomb, some significant items survive in the main chamber. On the left (northwestern) corner, fragments of a gold and ivory *kline* were found.[34] To the right, in the northeastern corner of the tomb, was a monumental (2.01 m. high and 2 m. wide at front and 1.18 m. deep) "throne," covered with elaborate decoration, and in front of it a matching footstool, also of marble and similarly decorated. These items seem to have been constructed of Parian marble whose slightly yellowish tint resembles that of ivory; presumably the chair and stool were intended to mimic the chryselephantine couches and furniture found in elite burials (for instance, in the couches in both chambers of Tomb II) and apparently used in life. The brightly colored and gilded decorative scheme of this marble furniture also resembles that of chryselephantine *klinai* (couches).[35] Apparently, the cremated remains of the dead had been placed in a marble *larnax* (box) on the seat of the throne; the remains, like those in the chamber and antechamber of Tomb II, had been wrapped in purple fabric (judging by the traces of purple on the sides of the *larnax* and its lid). When the robbers entered the tomb, they unceremoniously dumped the contents of the *larnax* on the floor, leaving the *larnax* on its side on the floor and the lid of the *larnax* at an angle on the seat of the throne, propped up against one armrest.

But the most remarkable feature of the Eurydice tomb apart from its ghostly "façade" is the painting on the back of this throne.[36] Hades and Persephone, not enthroned but riding in a four-horse chariot, appear, shown frontally. The composition of this painting is not, as one might at first expect, equally balanced between the two deities; Hades is slightly off-center to the left and Persephone (highlighted by a special flower in the decoration of the "frame" of the painting) is actually at the center.[37] The cremated bones of the dead could be read as an offering placed in front of Persephone.[38] Hades and Persephone appear to have arrived to guide the dead person to the afterlife themselves.[39] A connection seems to exist between the illusionary door to the afterlife and the underworld deities depicted on the throne.[40] Reddish staining around the figure of Hades and the arms of the chair suggest that purple cloth had been draped there as well, possibly part of some sort of baldaquin.[41] Though the ancient robbers looted the apparently costly funerary offerings, in the main chamber fragments of gold jewelry and of alabaster and terracotta vases survive.[42] Two squat *lekythoi* (oil flasks), attributed to the Eleusinian painter, have been reassembled from some of those fragments. The west wall of the chamber shows traces of the chests that were once stacked against it.

The plundering of the Eurydice tomb did not end in antiquity. Between August and September of 2001, someone robbed the tomb of Eurydice again. The robbers removed six or seven of the small figurines (of sphinxes and women) in two rows that supported the base and sides of the chair, some of which had already been robbed in antiquity.[43] No trace of the figurines taken in the recent robbery has been found.

Was this the burial of a woman? As yet, no analysis of any human remains from the tomb has been published. Andronikos believed that it was the burial of one particular woman, Eurydice.[44] We shall discuss reasons for that specific attribution shortly, but first we need to reflect on the simple issue of the gender of the person commemorated. Some scholars have associated thrones with female burials, but that view is less common now, though the significance of these funerary thrones remains ambiguous, as we shall see.[45] Given that one Macedonian tomb at Vergina (Tomb II in the Bella Tumulus) contains a throne, if a far less impressive one, and it appears to have been a male burial and that the gender of the person buried in the nearby Rhomaios tomb (which contains a marble throne somewhat more similar to the Eurydice one) is unknown, it seems clear that the throne cannot prove or disprove the gender of the occupant.[46] Moreover, even if we could be certain that royal or elite Macedonian women banqueted sitting down—as opposed to being represented in funerary circumstances as doing so—reading tomb interiors as banqueting rooms, though attractive, seems simplistic.[47] Many funerary items and decorations do not indicate gender construction one way or another.[48] The fragments of the three Panathenaic vases found in the pyre could have belonged to a male victor, but Panathenaic vases were objects of trade and also were retained as heirlooms.[49] A recently discovered burial demonstrates that silver versions of these vases might be used in the interment of people who did not themselves compete at the games and may even suggest some specific connection between the Argeads and such Panathenaic vases. In 2009, two late fourth-century burials, one of an adult and the other of a child, were discovered in a ditch in the Eucleia sanctuary at Aegae (see Chapter 5). These burials, like the ones found the year before in the same ditch, are widely considered to be royal. The child's remains were placed in a silver Panathenaic vase. These new discoveries will continue to feed speculation, but a young child (sex not determined) could not have won the vase himself or herself.[50]

Other aspects of the burial more specifically indicate that a woman was interred in the tomb. This tomb was part of a small cluster of rich individual female burials, apart from the Rhomaios tomb, though the others date significantly earlier.[51] The fact that excavators uncovered fragments of gold jewelry in the chamber means that a woman must have been interred in this tomb,[52] though the *kline*, the possible helmet fragment, and the Panathenaic vases (if won by male athletes, but that, as I have noted, is hardly guaranteed) could mean that both a man and a woman were buried in the tomb together (as was not uncommon in Macedonia).[53] Still, on the basis of current information, this idea of dual interment seems considerably less likely than that this tomb contained a single female burial.

Was this woman royal? It has not been easy to determine which burials at Vergina were royal and which simply belonged to members of the elite.[54] (Those who reject the identification of Vergina with Aegae naturally do not consider this or other tombs at Vergina royal, since Aegae was the site where the Argeads were interred.) The Argeads were not pharaohs and dined, drank, and fought along with their *hetairoi*. Some burials that no one has ever suggested were royal—the Derveni tombs, for instance—contained goods very similar to those found in Tombs II and III from Vergina.[55] Still, these goods are not identical; where vessels at Derveni are silver, those from Vergina II and III are gold.[56] One must also note that the quality of the Persephone painting in Tomb I at Vergina so far lacks comparison at other Macedonian sites. The three tombs once covered by the Great Tumulus have seemed particularly likely to be royal because of the size of the tumulus and because it was created after the end of the Argead dynasty; it is usually assumed that Antigonus Gonatas ordered it built, to recover the tombs, some of which were disturbed by Pyrrhus' mercenaries, and as a kind of commemorative. Kottaridi believes that the women buried in the cluster of tombs around the Eurydice tomb served some priestly function; she may be right (elite women did often serve as priests), but the evidence, currently, is tenuous.[57] But, if she is correct, then one still wants to know why they are buried by themselves and who they were—king's daughters, royal widows, or royal wives? Yet not only the Eurydice tomb itself but the distinctive throne and the nearly unique pyre "house" imply a person of considerable importance. Thrones do not seem peculiarly female, but they do seem to suggest prestige, possibly royal and even heroic status; they are monumental and in Macedonia appear in Macedonian-type tombs.[58]

Whether Eurydice was in fact entombed in the tomb of Eurydice remains the most difficult issue associated with the tomb, even if we assume the occupant was a royal woman who was placed in the tomb within a few years of 344/43, let alone if we take the date of the tomb down into the beginning of the post-Alexander era. Apart from the general issue of the dating of barrel vaults, given that most of the contents of the tomb were looted, surviving material from the tomb offers comparatively little specific information on the date of the burial. The Panathenaic vases tell us that the burial came after the games of 344/3, but, as we have already noted, we cannot assume that the presence of these amphorae means that the burial happened soon after the Panathenaic games of that year. The vase fragments found in the chamber attributed to the Eleusinian painter might also come from around 340, but might also date later.[59] If it proves true that ordinary pottery from the tomb suggests a date around 340 (this material has not yet been published),[60] then one might conclude that a compelling case had been made for a pre-Alexander date, but this is not yet certain.[61]

Even if we assume that the tomb dates to about 340, problems with assigning the tomb to Eurydice remain. Andronikos concluded that the tomb belonged to Eurydice because of the great size of the tomb (the largest known at the time), the throne, the apparent wealth behind its construction and outfitting, Eurydice's dedications at Aegae, and—somewhat mysteriously—chronological considerations.[62] As we have noted, the Aeschines passage and the Panathenaic vases' date actually make it harder, not easier, to attribute the tomb to Eurydice. The tomb is visually compelling and seems fitting for a remarkable woman whose son had become the most powerful man in the Greek world. But we cannot assume that tombs match our judgments of which royal woman was most important. Philip had seven wives, and only Olympias (who lived until 316 or 315) can plausibly be excluded from consideration as an occupant of this tomb;[63] even if we assume one of these wives was buried with Philip in Tomb II, at least five others remain unaccounted for. There is also the wife of Perdiccas III; we know he had one, the mother of his son Amyntas, but have no specific information about her, not even her name.[64] Today these other women seem obscure, but they were probably quite well known at court in their own day and might well have had very nice tombs. Eurydice could have been buried in this tomb, but it is anything but certain and perhaps not even likely, attractive though the idea remains.[65]

Let me turn to consideration of how this particular tomb fits into the general issue of the chronology of Macedonian tombs. As we have seen, the dispute about the chronological development of Macedonian-type tombs (and the identity of the occupants of Tomb II) depends on whether the barrel vault developed locally in Macedonia by the middle of the fourth century or whether it began after Alexander's conquests, under the influence of tombs and structures seen in the former Persian Empire. Given that Macedonia was, for a time in the late sixth and early fifth centuries, under Persian dominance and that there were various subsequent but pre-Alexander kinds of contact, direct and indirect, with Persian court culture (including people) prior to the reign of Alexander, it is conceivable that the development/implementation of this tomb form was indeed influenced by Asian practice, but before Alexander.

Moreover, it is quite unclear how linear—if at all—the evolution of these Macedonian tombs was; each one was somewhat different.[66] Some think that, once the dead were interred and the mound created, these tombs were not visible and so attribute the great degree of variation among them to that fact,[67] whereas others think that some or all were visible.[68] Obviously tombs used over generations must have been somehow accessible to allow subsequent burials, though this does not guarantee that they were always visible. It is intriguing that the rise and fall of Macedonian tombs seems to mirror the rise and fall of Macedonian monarchy.[69] In any event, royal tombs, even if subsequently not visible, must have been viewed by many at the time of a funeral and interment. Still, one wonders if the appearance of tombs with decorative facades does not signify a desire for the tomb to have a public face. These facades, resembling that of the propylon of a palace or, as some would see it, a temple, do have a theatrical element.[70] The desire to give the tomb a public aspect is not, however, apparent in the Eurydice tomb, even apart from the wall constructed to hide the front door. Indeed, the odd encasement of the vault of this tomb could have been intended to hide the vault in order make the tomb look like a cist tomb.

This brings us to the usual explanation given for the development of chamber tombs as the preferred tomb form for the elite: the need to find secure roofing (able to bear the weight of a tumulus) for larger tombs, on the presumption that the larger size was attractive because of the increasing quantity of grave goods.[71] One thinks, for instance, of Tomb Alpha, a very crowded cist tomb, at Derveni.[72] Even in Archaic times, Macedonians had long tended to put more objects into their burials than other Greeks,[73] possibly reflecting a more specific and vivid picture of the afterlife than many other Greeks.[74] Certainly, with the reign of Philip II, more Macedonians could afford to put more and more expensive objects into their tombs. Vaults could indeed carry more weight and cover a larger surface.

But should we assume that only these practical, more or less technological motives developed simply because of greater disposable wealth and that they explain the appearance of this tomb type? The change in the structure of elite tombs seems related to changes in belief and values and thus in the function of the tomb, but tying down what those beliefs and values were is difficult; it is easy to be simplistic in analyzing ideas about the afterlife and thus the function of these tombs.[75] The current appearance of surviving tombs encourages a kind of stereotyping: unlooted cist tombs look like storage areas for the offerings for the dead, whereas Macedonian tombs, particularly if they have been looted, look like houses with empty rooms. Though those with facades do resembles temples in some ways, the façades primarily reference domestic but royal buildings (palaces), reflecting the centrality of monarchy to the culture of the elite.[76]

Macedonians in the fourth century were increasingly interested in Orphic and other beliefs that posited a happy afterlife for those who believed, were initiated, and knew the correct ritual. The vault of Macedonian tombs may have had religious significance by alluding to the vault of heaven (Plato *Phaedr.* 347b–c), as well as practical utility.[77] Hatzopoulos has argued that Macedonian chamber tombs were not intended as houses for the dead, however much they might have resembled houses or palaces, but rather as places for commemoration and perhaps where the initiated dead made a transition from the land of the living to the land of the dead, paying particular attention to Persephone.[78] The Eurydice tomb seems both quite relevant to Hatzopoulos' view—the back wall of the tomb is surely to be read as the entrance into the underworld and the epiphany of Persephone and Hades painted on the back of the funerary throne also indicates belief in an afterlife somehow guaranteed by Persephone[79]—and yet is exceptional, compared to other tombs.[80]

Notably, no other tomb has anything like Eurydice's final, interior "façade." It seems to refer to common religious beliefs, yet it differs from Tombs II and III at Vergina and their impressive facades. Though the Persephone-Hades throne painting of the Eurydice tomb highlights Persephone as the queen of the underworld and the fresco of Tomb I at Vergina deals with Persephone as the maiden seized by the ruler of the underworld, both have an overt religious aspect that refers to the afterlife and that is not directly readable in the frieze of Tomb II.[81] Attempting to delineate belief from funerary practice is admittedly dubious at best, but the Eurydice tomb—whoever was actually placed in it—remains compelling and evocative. It invites us to step from the land of the living to that of the dead and it validates and empowers the person for whom the throne was intended. I rather wish that this person was Eurydice and it may have been, but more likely it was a somewhat later person, probably a royal woman, important in her own day but whose importance is lost to us.

Philip II commemorated his mother in other ways, not simply in her tomb, wherever and whichever that might be. After the battle of Chaeronea in 338, Philip II arranged for the creation of a distinctive building at the Panhellenic shrine of Zeus at Olympia, a building known as the Philippeum.[82] We know about the Philippeum because of two descriptive passages in the works of the Roman-era writer Pausanias (5.17.4, 5.20.10) and because of surviving remains of the building and their recent reexamination and partial reconstruction.[83] The Philippeum was a circular roofed structure (a *tholos*) placed within the sacred space at Olympia, near the sanctuary of Zeus, the supposed ancestor of Philip and his Argead dynasty. Inside the Philippeum five large statues stood on a high semi-circular base. Pausanias said they were made of ivory and gold, as were many statues of divinities and few or none of human beings. The remains of the Philippeum's statue base (the statues themselves are long since gone), however, demonstrate, as Schultz has shown, that the statues were, in fact, marble, though they must have looked chrysele-phantine and so misled the ancient observer.[84] Pausanias explains that the images in the Philippeum were of Philip, Amyntas III, Alexander, Olympias, and Eurydice (Paus. 5.20.10). Schultz's reexamination of the base concluded that the statue of Philip stood in the center (visible from the door) and that images of his father and son were on either side of him and that the two women's statues were placed at either end of the group.[85]

Thanks to the corruption of the text of Pausanias 5.17.4, some questions about the identity of the "Eurydice" in the Philippeum have arisen.[86] The mother of Philip II was not the only royal Macedonian Eurydice; there was certainly at least one more royal woman of that name, and some think there were several more, including Philip II's last wife, a woman generally called Cleopatra but who may also have been called "Eurydice." I will discuss this issue at greater length shortly. For the moment, it is enough to say that whether or not Philip's final bride was ever called "Eurydice," she cannot have been the woman memorialized as part of the group in the Philippeum.[87] Her inclusion in the grouping of statues makes no sense, given that the Philippeum was a carefully constructed dynastic monument intended for a sacred precinct, not the latest update on which woman/wife was in favor with Philip. Moreover, Philip probably did not marry Cleopatra until after Chaeronea,[88] and the physical remains indicate no change in the original statue program and building.[89] Perhaps more important, Philip had not yet had a child by Cleopatra, let alone a son. Until she did, Cleopatra/Eurydice was not relevant to the construct. The group is a lineage, constructed at the time the king was planning the invasion of the Persian Empire: Philip chose to portray himself, his father, his apparent heir, and the mother of his heir. Olympias is there because she was Alexander's mother, not necessarily because Philip favored her. Court tensions between Philip and his son Alexander and his son's mother Olympias became so noto-rious subsequent to his marriage to Cleopatra that Philip had to make a public reconciliation with Alexander and Olympias (Plut. *Alex.* 9.3–6), but, if the marriage had not yet happened, the tensions were probably not yet apparent. The Eurydice in the Philippeum was Philip's mother. (The probable group monument at Vergina/Aegae that included a statue of Eurydice daughter of Sirras may have pre- or post-dated that of the Philippeum [see Chapter 5], but its existence does tend to suggest that it was the same Eurydice in both monuments, the daughter of Sirras.)

The Philippeum was an important monument: it was Philip's construction of his dynastic image for the wider world, after his victory at Chaeronea had confirmed his domination of the Greek peninsula. It was part of the lead-up to the invasion of the Persian Empire that he planned but died too soon to accomplish.[90] The placement of the monument alludes to his Heraclid origins and it locates him and his family in proximity to the gods.[91] Philip, in the procession he arranged for his daughter's marriage, had images of himself processed with those of the twelve Olympians (Diod. 16.92.5). This gesture did not necessarily mean that he believed he was a god, but it did seem to equate him with the gods. The Philippeum extends this equation to his parents and probable heir to the throne and his heir's mother.[92] That all the statues appeared to be chryselephantine contributed to this, since statues of that fabrication usually represented gods.

As with the Eurydice inscriptions at Vergina, the inclusion of Eurydice and Olympias in the group meant that women played an important part in the presentation of the dynasty, particularly in the presentation of the royal lineage. Dynastic monuments including multiple members of the family had become fairly common by the second half of the fourth century and would become yet more common in the Hellenistic period, but only some of these groups included female members of the dynasty. Their inclusion was not simply a matter of course.[93] Philip chose to include the two women, despite the fact that both were, in various ways, controversial figures. Eurydice, as we have seen, had very negative stories told about her and endured, along with her sons, some humiliating experiences, but was portrayed by herself and here by Philip as a heroic figure. Olympias, the mother of Alexander, had a distinguished lineage (her dynasty traced its origins to Achilles and thus to Zeus) and had become the most prominent of Philip's wives primarily because she was the mother of his apparent heir, but court intrigue and quarrels after Philip's last marriage were notorious, and our sources preserve an extremely negative picture of her and her actions.[94] Neither woman suited the expectation for the appropriate behavior of women as seen in central and southern Greece, yet Philip chose to include them in this very conspicuous monument. His inclusion of, by the standards of the rest of Greece, his less-than-glorious parents who had lived during a far less glamorous and successful period in Macedonian history, is important. This statue group, whether or not identical with the possible group at Vergina (see Chapter 5), seems similar in ideology.

Rather than being apologetic about his origins, Philip advertised them, feeling, apparently, no need to include more well-known ancestors like Alexander I. He constructed a lineage and a line of descent, but it was a narrow one. In effect, it suggested that he ruled because he was the son of Amyntas and Eurydice and that his son Alexander would rule because he was the son of Philip and Olympias.

Intriguingly, the statue of Eurydice (and that of Olympias) did not stay put in the Philippeum. Pausanias (5.17.4) reports that by his own day (mid-second century CE), their statues had been moved from the Philippeum to the nearby Heraeum. Pausanias says nothing about who moved the images of the royal women, when, or why. The fact that each statue stood at one end of the semi-circular base made it easier to move them, whatever the motivation. One can imagine why the image of Olympias might have been moved during the era of the Successors, particularly since Cassander, who had opposed Olympias and had had her murdered, exercised considerable control over the Peloponnese. It is difficult, however, to conceive of why anyone in that period would have been hostile to Eurydice (or, for that matter, to Philip's last wife). Obviously, had general hostility to the Argeads motivated whomever removed the statues, that person would have removed them all. It is far more likely that the two statues were moved at the same time and that the motivation had to do with gender issues and the ways in which the Philippeum included royal women in a display of power; this is particularly likely since the women's statues were moved to the temple of Hera, queen of the gods.[95]

Perhaps the most intriguing evidence for the continuation of the memory and significance of Eurydice, daughter of Sirras, relates to her personal name and its re-use by one of the last Argeads. "Eurydice" means "wide justice," it would be a particularly appropriate choice for a woman from an elite or royal family, as Eurydice, daughter of Sirras, apparently was. Various characters in Greek literature were named Eurydice,[96] and the name may have been more common in Macedonia.[97] Given the known interest in Orphism in Macedonia, it seems natural to think that the daughter of Sirras' name choice related to the variant of the Orpheus myth that gave Orpheus a wife named Eurydice, one whom he, depending on the version, did or did not successfully retrieve from the underworld. The problem is, however, that, even in versions that tell this story, Orpheus' wife has another name; the earliest account that calls her "Eurydice" is second-century BCE.[98] Of course, it is possible that a

Eurydice variant of the story existed earlier though we lack written evidence. Alternatively, the name may have appeared in poetry because of the many royal women, starting with the daughter of Sirras, who carried the name, possibly because a particular Eurydice was an enthusiastic participant in Orphic rites.[99] Given that the origins of Eurydice daughter of Sirras were at least partly Lyncestian, the name choice is unsurprising and appropriately aristocratic.

In the absence of titles for royal women, certain names may have acquired dynastic significance. Of course, we see the repetition of names of royal males as well. It is possible that such names, male and female, had an almost title-like significance, particularly when the name repeated was not simply the traditional replication of the name of a grandparent. Another Argead naming practice assigned personal names to royal women related to their father's successes. Philip II gave two of his daughters names—Thessalonice and Europa—that referred to his victories (Ath. 13.557d; Steph. Byz. s.v. "Thessalonice").[100]

It seems certain that at least two royal women (and one royal man) changed their names or were known by more than one name because they or others wanted to commemorate an alteration in status or accomplishment by a change in personal name.[101] The woman we know as Olympias, one of Philip II's wives and the mother of Alexander III (the Great), may well have had three other names, at different points in her life (Plut. *Mor.* 401a–b; Just. 9.7.13).[102] Alexander's half-brother changed his name (or had it changed) either when he became king (soon co-king with Alexander IV), or in the process of becoming king (Arr. *FGrH* 156, F 1.1; Diod. 18.2.4; Curt. 10.7.2–7).[103] Adea, Philip II's granddaughter by his daughter Cynnane, changed her name to Eurydice. Arrian seems to associate her name change with her marriage to the co-king Philip Arrhidaeus (Arr. *FGrH* 156, F 9.23). (For clarity's sake, I will refer to these two as Adea Eurydice and Philip Arrhidaeus.) Obviously, the timing of the name change of Cynnane's daughter suggests that her new name had some special significance, though it is possible that these dual royal name changes showed the influence of Persian court practice as well.[104]

Before we turn to consideration of what that significance might have been, two other possible name changes by royal women to the name "Eurydice" need to be considered. Though Athenaeus (13.557c) called Adea Eurydice's Illyrian grandmother "Audata," a fragment of Arrian (*FGrH* 156, F 9.22) terms this same woman "Eurydice." Calling the grandmother of Adea Eurydice "Eurydice" could easily be a mistake made either by Arrian himself or Photius (who summarized Arrian's work and is the source of this fragment). The fact that we have the same person called by two different names in two different sources is, in itself, not evidence that she held two names at different points in her life; the extant evidence is that she was called one or the other, not both. While it is possible that Philip chose to rename his Illyrian wife with his mother's name, the evidence is hardly compelling,[105] particularly since Philip's mother was very likely alive at the time Philip married Audata.[106] Nor is there reason to think that Philip felt the need to change his wife's name because of her (and the name's) Illyrian identity; this notion would imply that he was embarrassed by a helpful foreign alliance that the marriage commemorated, one quite possibly initiated at the time of the successful conclusion of the war that had killed his brother.[107]

Philip II's last married wife, otherwise known as "Cleopatra," is uniquely referred to as "Eurydice" by Arrian (3.6.5) in a narrative "flash-back." As with Audata, this woman could have changed her name to that of Philip's mother,[108] but this reference, too, is more likely an error. Again, that different sources refer to the same woman by different names is not particularly good evidence that she was known by both.[109] Even if we conclude that Arrian's reference is not in error, we cannot really tell if "Eurydice" was the name the young woman had from the start or one she took upon marriage, or even that she was Eurydice to begin with and became Cleopatra (the name of an earlier Argead royal woman).

The whole issue of the name "Eurydice" and royal women is further complicated by its possible association with Illyrian culture. It is certain that Audata was Illyrian, likely that her daughter's name "Cynnane" was Illyrian,[110] and significant that a military tradition was maintained by these three generations of women, one apparently deriving from elite Illyrian practice. Given the controversy about the ethnicity of Philip's mother and her possible partial Illyrian background (see Chapter 2), this is a particularly complex problem. Significantly, there is no evidence at all that Philip's mother was ever called anything other than "Eurydice."[111]

Thus, though several royal women other than Eurydice's great-granddaughter might have changed their names to "Eurydice," the evidence is slight and probably the consequence of error. Certainly there is no reason to think that "Eurydice" became in some general way a dynastic name[112] or a "throne name."[113] Given the number of royal women in the same period with different names (including all of Philip's daughters),[114] it was certainly not the case that "Eurydice" was "the established name for a Macedonian queen."[115] Even more unlikely is a connection between the personal name and Illyrian roots.[116] Many discussions of the problem seem somewhat old-fashioned now in that they assume that there was one "queen" and that her status was determined at the time of her marriage.

In my view, Adea-Eurydice's assumption of the name was distinctive and suggestive, particularly because we know, roughly, when she changed it: when she married Philip Arrhidaeus. The first Eurydice, the daughter of Sirras, was, after all, twice over her great-grandmother. Adea Eurydice was an unusual young woman, with a distinctive history.[117] She was herself, by birth, doubly Argead (her mother was the daughter of Philip II and her father was Philip's nephew Amyntas, son of Perdiccas III). She married another Argead, a marriage her mother Cynnane lost her life to achieve; after Cynnane's murder, the army seems to have forced Alexander's generals to accept the marriage. Adea Eurydice's husband, co-king with Alexander III's infant son Alexander IV, was somehow mentally or intellectually disabled. Philip Arrhidaeus was always under the guardianship of some Macedonian general, but Adea Eurydice, despite her extreme youth at the time of her marriage, seemed to try to take control of the army, primarily by giving speeches to the troops, and at times throughout her brief but dashing career she seems to have made decisions for her husband, acting as though she were a regent (Just. 14.5.3; Diod. 19.11.1). Whether or not she actually fought in battle as her mother supposedly had, she faced an opposing Macedonian army dressed in military garb and was killed by Olympias as part of the deadly game of musical chairs that played out as the dynasty came to an end (Diod. 19.11.2–7; Duris *ap.* Ath. 13.560f).

Her chosen new name, like her husband's new name, stressed her Argead and Macedonian identity[118] and implies that she held up her great-grandmother as a model; her name choice surely alludes to the aggressive role Eurydice, mother of Philip II, took at a critical period in the history of the kingdom.[119] Given that her mother, Cynnane, had been murdered by the time Adea Eurydice married Philip Arrhidaeus, it is unlikely that her mother chose the name (though possibly her mother had conceived of the idea and Adea Eurydice implemented it); certainly it was not the choice of Perdiccas whose agents had brought about Cynnane's death and agreed to the marriage only because the army forced compliance.[120] This new name was not merely a personal choice but was clearly intended to allude to someone Macedonians would associate with the past; choosing this name speaks directly to Eurydice's posthumous memory and image, specifically her image with the Macedonian army and her memory within the Argead dynasty.

It may also suggest that this young woman, like her great-grandmother, understood the role she was taking on as at least partly a public one. While her birth name was probably not Illyrian in origin, as her mother's likely was,[121] the name change should be understood as positive choice made to recall Philip's mother, rather than as an attempt to reject or cloak her partly Illyrian ancestry.[122] While Adea Eurydice came to oppose Olympias and was ultimately killed (or, from another point of view, executed) by her, it is not likely that opposition to Olympias explains Adea Eurydice's name change.[123] Instead the change was a clever piece of memory politics, perhaps aimed more at the Macedonian elite than the general soldiery (they had, after all, already forced Perdiccas' faction to accept the marriage),[124] but also one that echoed her husband's name change. Given Adea Eurydice's aggressive actions with the Macedonian army and her apparent efforts to speak for her husband, this parallelism was probably conscious and certainly seems suggestive. In the course of her short life, Adea Eurydice proved even more assertive than her great-grandmother but apparently had chosen her as a model.

Eurydice, daughter of Sirras, lived through parlous times, yet these were the same times during which Macedonia was transformed from a political backwater into the greatest power in the Greek peninsula, and its kings—no longer men who struggled to survive and to enable their kingdom to do so as well—emerged as astonishingly successful generals and leaders who came to control, if only briefly, a remarkable portion of the ancient world. Because Eurydice long outlived her husband, Amyntas III, and yet her three sons were quite young at the time of his death, she was able (one might say almost compelled by circumstance) to play a critical role at the moment when their future rule was gravely threatened. Partly through her own patronage and partly through the efforts of her youngest son, Philip II, she became part of the public face of the dynasty, in Macedonia and outside of it.

The seemingly endless rounds of failed and successful assassinations, claimants to the throne, manipulations by great powers, and invasions can make Macedonian history seem risible if entertaining. All this Macedonian melodrama has obscured an important point: the kingdom survived and ultimately thrived because of enduring loyalty to the

Argead dynasty among the people and, most importantly, the elite. The wily resilience of Amyntas III and the brilliance of Philip II as a politician and general did much to generate and then sustain that loyalty, but so did the actions of Eurydice. While "monarchy" literally means one person rule, in fact hereditary monarchy has often survived and sometimes prospered because multiple members of an entire family, often several generations, worked hard to keep a dynasty afloat. Those dynastic "workers" were not infrequently women.

I have argued that Amyntas III and other Argead rulers were somewhat Odyssean figures—wily and much enduring but also much contriving. Odysseus and his wife Penelope, of course, shared a number of characteristics, despite the much more circumscribed role allotted to Penelope: both deceive and are deceived, test, contrive, and are less than trusting.[125] Reflecting on the character of Penelope in the *Odyssey* can be helpful in understanding the historical figure of Eurydice. There were, indeed, similarities between the general situation of royal Macedonian women and that of royal women as depicted in Homer and there are a number of aspects of royal and elite Macedonian culture that imitate (or perhaps perpetuate) the world of Homer, but that is not my point.[126]

The circumstances of Eurydice and Penelope were hardly identical. Eurydice was an actual widow, whereas Penelope feared that she had been widowed; Alexander II actually became king, though only on the threshold of maturity, whereas Telemachus, though of roughly the same age, had not yet become king; Eurydice's sexual fidelity was brought into question, as we have seen, whereas Penelope's was not, ultimately, jeopardized. Eurydice and Penelope are, however, similar enough to be illuminating. Penelope moves between the world of women and the male court; she dares to confront her male enemies publicly (16.409–434) but is impressed when her son tells her to return to her quarters, thus asserting his male adulthood (1.356–364). Her dealings with her son are complicated exactly because Telemachus is not quite a man yet no longer a boy and Penelope had promised Odysseus that she would not remarry until her son had reached some sort of adulthood (18.269–270). Penelope does and does not want to remarry (e.g., 19.524–534) and her sexuality is often the focus of the narrative (18.158–168), yet her faithfulness to her husband and to her son's future helped to preserve Telemachus' inheritance and Odysseus' household, despite the serious depredations of the suitors. She improvised her way, often by trickery and with some ambiguity, through a prolonged period of instability. Thinking about Penelope helps us to understand Eurydice's role in the events of her day: she was both a public and a private figure, powerful and yet passive, manipulative and manipulated, her reputation called into question and yet ultimately celebrated.

# *Notes*

*Chapter 1*

1. See references in De Shong Meador 2001, 2010.

2. Boatwright 1991.

3. Howe 2018 contains a useful discussion of the relationship between extant sources and fourth-century ones, though I am not convinced by a number of his arguments. His portrayal of the character of Ephorus' and Theopompus' work is heavily shaped by Pownall 2004.

4. Howe 2018 makes this important point.

5. The *Suda* s.v. "Antipatros" = *FGrH* 114 T 1 says that Antipater left behind a two-book collection of letters and a history, "The Illyrian Deeds of Perdiccas." No fragments of either have been identified. A letter of Speusippus also refers to a *Hellenica* of Antipater, written at about the same time as Theopompus' *Hellenica* (see Flower 1994: 19–20; Natoli 2004).

6. For narrative histories of Macedonia, see Hammond 1979; Errington 1990; Borza 1992; Müller 2016. See also Roisman and Worthington 2010 and Lane Fox 2011e. Saripanidi 2017 argues that a dramatic change in funerary habits observable at various Macedonian sites c. 675–650 speaks to political change and consolidation of central power. Hatzopoulos 1996 generally argues for earlier urbanization of significant areas of Macedonia than in some other historians of Macedonia.

7. See Müller 2016: 105–140 for a recent discussion of his reign.

8. Hammond 1979: 99.

9. Few scholars consider the story historical; some believe that it is Herodotus' invention while others believe it originated in the Macedonian court, quite possibly with Alexander I himself. See Sprawski 2010: 136, nn.19 and 20 for references. Given how flattering Herodotus' general depiction of Alexander I is (Hammond 1979: 99), we should not treat these alternatives as mutually exclusive.

10. Griffith 1979: 676 likens Philip to Odysseus, but a number of Philip's predecessors had similar qualities.

11. Cole 1974: 64 compares Perdiccas' policy to that of his father, observing that he was "a true son in his determination to run with the fox and hunt with the hounds. Such a policy may make it difficult to gain much, but also makes it hard to lose all."

12. For a recent discussion, see Müller 2016: 141–163.

13. See Müller 2016: 329, n. 168 for references to those who favor Archelaus and to those who prefer Amyntas III. See also Greenwalt 1999b and Akamatis 2011.

14. See Müller 2016: 164–193 for discussion and reference to his reign.

15. See Müller 2016: 194–199 for a discussion of the identity and order of these ephemeral rulers.

16. See Borza 1992: 23–57 and Thomas 2010 for useful overviews of the region.

17. Graninger 2010: 306–325.

18. See Archibald 2010: 326–341 and Louko(u)poulou 2011: 367–376.

19. Greenwalt 2010: 279–305.

20. See Dell 1980.

21. On the natural resources of Macedonia, particularly timber, see Borza 1995a and 1995b and Millett 2010.

22. See King 2010 and Sawada 2010 on Macedonian kingship and on relations between the king and the elite.

23. Here I favor Greenwalt 1989, Ogden 1999: xiv–xviv, and Mitchell 2007 over Hatzopoulos 1986.

24. Anson 2009 (followed by Meeus 2009) argued that child heirs were never kings and that our ancient but non-contemporary (and non-Macedonian) sources have confused guardianship with regency and that the guardians were in fact kings unless they were non-Argeads (he considers Ptolemy Alorites such an exception and a "true regent"; I am, however, inclined to think Ptolemy was probably an Argead; see Chapter 4). Still, since Pelopidas apparently imposed this role on Ptolemy (see Chapters 3 and 4), it is possible that Pelopidas imposed a non-Macedonian situation on the kingdom. Anson 2009: 383 also believes that our much later sources wrongly use the term *epitropos* to refer to the men who ruled for the two incompetent kings (Alexander IV and Philip Arrhidaeus) after the death of Alexander III and that the correct Macedonian term was *prostates* (he believes the latter term ultimately derives from the contemporary historian Hieronymus). I doubt both that our sources allow us to be certain in this matter of terminology and that practice was as consistent as he seems to believe (Carney 1995: 271–275; Heckel 2002: 87). Consequently, I shall treat succession disputes case by case.

25. Satyr. *ap.* Ath. 13.557b–e; Arr. 4.19.5; Curt. 8.4.24–26; Diod. 17.36.2; Plut. *Alex.* 77.4. On the likelihood of earlier Argead polygamy, see Greenwalt 1989: 22–28 and Carney 2000a: 23.

26. Müller 2014: 154–162 concludes that Macedonian royal polygamy was likely borrowed from Persian practice, probably in the days of Alexander I and Perdiccas II.

27. Ogden 1999: x, xix–xxi, xxvi–xxx.

28. See recent discussion of this issue in Anson 2009: 378–379. Psoma 2012 is not convincing in arguing that the king's preference in successor was systematic rather than situational, but more to the point, once the king was dead, his preference was often overturned, as we shall see. See further Chapters 2 through 4.

29. Carney 1987a: 37–38; 2000a: 23–32; 2006: 27–59; Müller 2011, 2013; Carney 2018. The fact that Olympias fled with Alexander at the time of Attalus' insult to him and that Philip reconciled with her when he reconciled with Alexander exemplifies this phenomenon (Plut. *Alex.* 10.5, *Mor.* 70b; 179c; Just. 9.7.5).

30. For instance, Ogden 1999: 13 suggests that the charge in extant sources that Eurydice, mother of Philip II, was an Illyrian is part of "an attempt to bastardise her offspring as born of an alien mother."

31. See Carney 2000a: 23–37, but see Mirón Pérez 2000: 35–52 for a somewhat different take on the role of royal women.

32. Carney 2018.

33. Le Bohec (-Bouhet) 2006 has an excellent discussion of royal Macedonian women, but it is heavily dependent on Antigonid-era inscriptions.

34. On the role of Macedonian women generally, see Le Bohec (-Bouhet) 2006 and Carney 2010b.

35. Carney 2000a: 34–35; 2010a; 2011: 197–198.

36. Carney 2010a tries to examine this question in a general way, and Chapter 4 does so in terms of Eurydice. As we'll see, she has *philoi*, seems to speak to Iphicrates in public, and knows how to manipulate kinship networks.


*Chapter 2*


1. Carney 2015 (1983): 155.

2. Zahrnt 2006, 2007, 2009: 9–11. Müller 2016: 200–216 is influenced by this view.

3. Müller 2016: 201 points out that the lack of Macedonian involvement in the wider events of the Mediterranean during this period also contributes to the source problem.

4. Borza 1992: 189.

5. March 1995: 262 makes this point, using the example of the succession of Perdiccas II.

6. See Müller 2016: 41–84 on sources for Argead Macedonia. For the period of Eurydice's lifetime, the fact that many extant literary sources date to the Roman era is critical to note, but, apart from their moralizing, particularly about elite women (see Howe 2018), I am reluctant to generalize about their agendas or to conclude that Roman-era writers generally did not invent, whereas fourth-century ones did (*contra* Pownall 2004, especially 176–182, and Howe 2018).

7. Heinrichs 2012.

8. March 1995; Zahrnt 2006 and 2007; and Lane Fox 2011a and 2011b attempted new assessments of events and chronology during this period. While not enthused by older analysis, neither am I entirely persuaded by the solutions of March and Lane Fox. I am more concerned with the order of events than with absolute dates. Generally, I will employ the dating found in Müller 2016: 320, unless otherwise stated.

9. Hammond 1979: 169–202; Errington 1990: 27–39; Borza 1992: 177–197; Ogden 1999: 3–16; Roisman 2010: 145–165; Müller 2016: 195–235; and King 2018: 49–69 give overviews of the period from the beginning of Amyntas III's reign to the beginning of Philip II's.

10. See Carney 1995: 368–376. By employing "clan" to refer to the Argeads, I do not intend to imply any sort of Macedonian primitivism but rather to indicate how broad—broader than the ordinary meaning of "family" in English—the group proved to be, as demonstrated by the possibility that Amyntas III may not even have been the great-grandson of a king.

11. Hammond 1979: 168. Aristotle (*Pol.* 1311b) says that Archelaus offered one of his daughters to a son named Amyntas in hopes of preventing differences between this son and his son by Cleopatra. Orestes is usually assumed to be the son by Cleopatra: Errington 1990: 28; Ogden 1999: 11.

12. If Aeropus were Orestes' uncle and chosen as regent for that reason, he could have been his paternal uncle, if he were another son of Perdiccas II (Hammond 1979: 134–136, 170), or he could have been his great uncle, through Perdiccas II's brother Philip

(Mattingly 1968: 474). He could even have been a maternal uncle, something more likely if Cleopatra, the presumed mother of Orestes, was an Argead. On the other hand, Cleopatra could have been Lyncestian—or, worse yet, Lyncestian and Argead—and so Aeropus could have been connected to both houses. Borza thinks he was a son of Archelaus (Borza 1992: 178). Lane Fox 2011b: 2016–2017 says that "we do not know that Aeropus was an Argead at all" but then concedes that he did seem to rule. Some have concluded Aeropus was from an upper Macedonian princely house, most likely Lyncestian (see references in Lane Fox 2011a: 215).

13. See Anson 2009: 280–281 and Chapter 1, n. 24. Lane Fox 2011a: 216 rejects this suggestion, favoring the testimony of chronographic sources.

14. Borza 1992: 181 and Müller 2016: 320 date his accession to 394/3, whereas Lane Fox's recalculation puts it at 393/2 (Lane Fox 2011a: 211–213).

15. Hammond 1979: 168 suggests that Amyntas II, Pausanias, and Amyntas III all ruled for fragments of the same year, 394/3, whereas Müller 2016: 195–199 spreads their reigns between 396/5 and 395/4. The identity of Amyntas II is even more problematic: he could be the son of Archelaus mentioned earlier (Errington 1990: 28; Ogden 1999: 11), but Hammond's reading of Aristotle (*Pol* 1311b) makes the recipient of Archelaus' daughter not Amyntas, son of Archelaus, but a son of an Amyntas whom Hammond identifies with the "little Amyntas" mentioned earlier in the Aristotle passage, a man who was assassinated by Derdas. Borza 1992: 178 speculates that Aristotle's Derdas may have been Elimiote since the name was common in that house and the Argeads had intermarried with them; he seems to consider the assassination of Amyntas a possible Elimiote plot that failed; Errington 1990: 29 suggests that this Derdas was the Elimiote ruler who married Archelaus' daughter and suggests—given that Derdas, ruler of Elimiotis, later assisted Amyntas III—that the murder of Pausanias by Amyntas III and the murder of Amyntas II by Derdas were coordinated. Hammond believes this Amyntas was the son of Alexander I's son Menelaus (Hammond 1979: 168–170, followed by Borza 1992 178 *contra* Beloch 1912–27: 3.2: 55–57; Errington 1990: 269, n. 6; Ogden 1999: 5, 11).

16. See discussion and references in Beloch 1912–27: 3.2: 66; Geyer 1930: 11; Ogden 1999: 33, n. 46. Inscriptional evidence should surely be given precedence; Beloch and Geyer (followed by Errington 1990: 269, n. 6) believe that Justin and Aelian are simply wrong; Hammond 1979: 169 implausibly resolves the conflict by concluding that Justin and Aelian refer to Amyntas II; Ogden 1999: 11 suggests various possibilities to resolve the conflict: an official adoption or charges of adultery meant to jeopardize the man who said he was Arrhidaeus' son. He suggests that the charges may have been generated by the pretender Argaeus. Ellis 1976: 38–40 accepts Aelian and Justin and considers Amyntas III a descendant of Menelaus.

17. Borza 1992: 3, 178–179 sees him as the great-grandson of Alexander I, whereas Lane Fox 2011a: 220 considers it possible that he was a descendant of a brother of Alexander I.

18. Ogden 1999: 11.

19. Hammond 1979: 172 suggests that Bardylis led the invasion. Bardylis was the Illyrian leader who, more than thirty years later, invaded Macedonia and whose forces killed Perdiccas III and ten thousand other Macedonians (see Chapter 3).

20. Which two years is debated, though the period 387–385 is more generally accepted: See discussion in Ellis 1969: 5–8, who down-dates his reign to 385–383. Borza 1992: 297 is convincing in arguing against this dating since it contradicts the only source that mentions him. See also March 1995: 261–273; Lane Fox 2011a: 223–225; and Müller 2016: 207. Müller suggests that he was never officially acclaimed, and that omission explains discrepancies.

21. See Borza 1992: 296–297; Ogden 1999: 33, n. 49 for discussion and references. Hammond 1979: 172 argues that he was a son of Archelaus, based on an implausible reading of a puzzling fragment of Theopompus (*FGrH* 115 F 29). However I am fairly certain (unlike Borza 1992: 182) that a candidate for the throne, whether that person was Argead or Lyncestian, so long as he was supported by the Illyrians, would have been useful, particularly when the invasion began.

22. Ogden 1999: 11 takes Argaeus more seriously as a historical figure than does Borza 1992: 296–297, but, though he thinks that Amyntas' reign was interrupted only once by the Illyrians (e.g., that Diodorus' narrative contains a doublet), he is reluctant to choose whether the instance happened in 393 or 387–385. My own inclination, as stated, is to the earlier date. Roisman 2010: 159 says that it is impossible to be certain; March 1995: 257–263 considers Argaeus historical but argues for a later date; Greenwalt 2010: 284 treats him as historical. Greenwalt 1988: 35 argues that both reign lengths could be correct, if it took some time for Amyntas and the Thessalians to dislodge Argaeus.

23. See Müller 2016: 202–204 for references and a recent discussion of the problem.

24. Müller 2016: 204–207 suggests that this was intended as a temporary gift, that Diodorus is confused about the nature of the arrangement. She sees this interpretation as confirmed by the first treaty between Amyntas and the Chalcidean League (Tod 1948: 2: 31). A treaty of mutual defense, it is generally regarded as dating to early in his reign, and she argues that it preceded the invasion and dates to about 393. This same stele contains a second treaty between Amyntas and the Chalcideans, dating to about 391, which is an agreement about export areas, imports and exports, and particularly about Macedonian export of timber. Bissa 2009: 114 suggests that it was intended as repayment for Chalcidean aid during the invasion, and Zahrnt 2006: 131 points out that the two contracting parties are less equal in this second treaty.

25. Parker 2003: 133–137 plausibly questions the notion that Amyntas was not the main factor here and suggests that even Xenophon's narrative supports the idea that Amyntas was already an ally.

26. Saatsoglou-Paliadeli 2011: 276 suggests that he may have fled to Aegae.

27. Parker 2003 provides a plausible reason why Xenophon's narrative focused on the two cities and not Amyntas.

28. Borza 1992: 182. Unique to Isocrates are the fortress strong-hold and the inspiration for Amyntas from a story about Dionysius; absent are the Olynthians and their gift of territory (present in both Diodoran narratives), the story of Argaeus (alternate Diodoran version one), Olynthian resistance, and the Spartan alliance (Diodorus version two). Argaeus' two-year rule during Amyntas' absence (alternate Diodoran version one) specifically contradicts the three-month interval of Isocrates. As Borza notes, even those who believe in two Illyrian invasions disagree about which one Isocrates refers to: Hammond 1979: 173 believes it is the earlier one, whereas Ellis 1969: 3–4 thinks it was the invasion of 383/2. The Isocrates passage with its dubious account of Amyntas' motivation does not inspire confidence but does seem more like Diodorus' version one, without the alternate. This, of course, matters only if there were two invasions, not one.

29. Other alternatives have been suggested: Stylianou 1998: 212 thinks the Olynthians were invading, whereas Heskel 1997: 172–173 thinks the problem was with internal Macedonian forces. Müller 2016: 202–204 suggests that it is not so much a doublet as a flashback, to remind the reader of the earlier invasion.

30. Ellis 1969: 2; Hammond 1979: 174 challenged the once commonly held view (Beloch 1912–27: 3.2: 57–58; Geyer 1930: 112–118) that the Illyrian invasions were a doublet in the narrative of Diodorus. Hammond's argument seems to deny the existence of

any doublets in Diodorus; Borza 1992: 297 rightly points out that doublets do exist in Diodorus and argues that there are more similarities than differences in the two passages and so unenthusiastically endorses the notion of two invasions. My own view is that the first part of both Diodorus passages is very similar in diction—these sections read like paraphrases with slight variations of something found in another author—and that after this, Diodorus simply includes or excludes somewhat different material from that author while, at the same time, including some material from other sources (Argaeus, clearly, did not appear in his main source).

31. Parker 2003 reaches a similar conclusion, though his focus is primarily on Spartan motivation.

32. Zahrnt 2006: 131–132.

33. For the inscription, see Tod 1948: 2:90–94. The treaty used to be read as a sign of Amyntas' weakness, whereas now it is more often read as an indication that Amyntas (and Macedonia) benefited from a resurgent Athens' need for timber; see discussion and references in Müller 2016: 211.

34. See Lane Fox 2011b: 228, n. 87 for references.

35. This involved the concession of Amphipolis to Athens by him and the rest of the Greeks. See discussion and references in Müller 2016: 212. Psoma 2012: 125 doubts that his concession of Amphipolis was genuine.

36. See references in Roisman 2010: 161, n. 52; Schol. on Dem. 1.5; Ael. Aristid. Or. 38, vol. 1 (ed. Dindorf): 715d. Lane Fox 2011a: 228–229 takes this possibility seriously and suggests some reasons why it might have happened.

37. Hammond 1979: 179 claims that Macedonia was worse off at the end of his reign than at the beginning. This seems to be an over-statement. Lane Fox 2011a: 231 thinks that Diodorus (16.2.4) and Justin (7.5.1) indicate that there was another Illyrian invasion around the time of Amyntas' death (this issue relates to the problem of Philip's years as a hostage, and I will deal with it in Chapter 3). Lane Fox generally gives Amyntas a mixed review, whereas Greenwalt 1988 and Zahrnt 2006 and 2007 offer up a positive one, more favorable than the summary I have just given.

38. Zahrnt 2006: 141.

39. Mortensen 1992: 168, though she assumes that this first wife was Gygaea, whereas I consider it more likely that there was an earlier wife, whose name we do not know.

40. Beloch 1912–27: 3.2: 66–67; Macurdy 1932: 17; Ellis 1973: 351; Badian 1982a: 104; Hatzopoulos 1986: 282; Greenwalt 1988: 37. Ogden 1999: 11 says that the evidence does not permit a decision about the order of Amyntas' wives, but then expresses doubts about the arguments in favor of Gygaea being first. Greenwalt 1989: 26–28; Carney 2000a: 47; and Lane Fox 2011a: 231 suggest that Gygaea was the younger wife.

41. Greenwalt 1989: 26–28.

42. Greenwalt 1989: 27.

43. Hatzopoulos 1986: 281 argued that only sons born to a king while he was king were eligible; if that were true, given that Eurydice's sons succeeded Amyntas, Gygaea's sons would have to have been born before Amyntas took the throne.

44. See Greenwalt 1989: 22–28; Carney 2000a: 23–27; Ogden 1999; Müller 2016: 62–64.

45. On Gygaea, see Carney 2000a: 46–47.

46. Beloch 1912–27: 3: 2: 66 suggests that she was a descendant of Menelaus; Macurdy 1927: 204–205 and 1932: 14–15, more plausibly, given the name of Gygaea's eldest son, argues that Gygaea's father was Archelaus. Ellis 1973: 351; Hatzopoulos 1986: 281; Greenwalt 1988: 43; and Mortensen 1992: 169 endorse the idea that Gygaea was an Argead. Müller 2016: 213 judges that she could have been an Argead but does not

endorse that idea. Given that epigraphic material, especially about women, is scarce until the Hellenistic period, it is difficult to assess how rare and therefore significant Gygaea's name may have been. Ogden 1999: 11 contents himself with terming her name "a traditional Macedonian one."

47. See also Saatsoglou-Paliadeli 2000 for references to the inscriptions.

48. Geyer 1930: 79–81 believed he was Elimiote. Beloch 1912-1927: 3.2: 74, 79–80 preferred an Orestian identification. Hammond 1979: 15; Oikonomedes 1983: 63; Greenwalt 1989: 37–44; and Kapetanopoulos 1994 concluded that Sirras was Lyncestian. Ogden 1999: 12–13 argues for Sirras as an upper Macedonian, probably a Lyncestian. Papazoglou: 1965: 150–151; Ellis 1976: 42, 249–250, Bosworth 1971: 93da–105; Badian 1982: 103; and Mortensen 1991: 51–55 think he was Illyrian.

49. Demosthenes (9.31) denies that Philip is a Greek, seems to imply that he was a slave and a bastard, and generally ranks Macedonians below barbarians. He, however, though he questions Philip's legitimacy (see Chapter 3), considers him a barbarian because he treats all Macedonians as barbarians, not because of Eurydice's ethnicity.

50. The essay, though found in the corpus of Plutarch's works, has not generally been considered a genuine work of Plutarch. In addition, the description of Eurydice's ethnicity is part of a contrast the author constructs: though she was Illyrian and three times barbarian, still she was a model to emulate. See Carney 2000a: 269, nn.13 and 14. Ogden 1999: 12–13 has argued that references to Eurydice as Illyrian are solely the consequence of the hostile tradition that developed about her during the reigns of her sons; my own view is that the hostile tradition most likely put a negative spin on any material about her. Hostile sources do not necessarily invent everything out of whole cloth. The author of the essay uses Eurydice as a model for educating children and clearly holds her up as a model mother; her ethnicity and specifically her "barbarity" are stressed to make his point. I do not find Ogden's arguments about Leonnatus convincing: the *Suda* s.v. "Leonnatos" says that he was a relative of Philip's mother, and Curtius 10.7.23 that he was of royal stock, but since we know Eurydice was descended from the Lyncestian princely house through her maternal grandfather, this tells us nothing definitive about her father.

51. Mortensen 1991: 52–53 argues convincingly that the "Arrhabaeus" mentioned by Thucydides, Strabo, and Aristotle is the same person, not three different ones. She concludes that the marriage of Eurydice's parents probably happened in terms of this alliance, sometime between 414 and 399. The probable date of Eurydice's own marriage makes her parents' marriage likely to date from early in the period Mortensen suggests.

52. *CIG* 1967b, line 14, though the initial sigma was mistakenly omitted; see Oikonomedes 1983: 62–64. Saatsoglou-Paliadeli 2000: 402, n. 103 refers to a fragmentary inscription from Dion. Kapetanopoulos 1994: 9 refers to a Lete inscription published in *BCH* 103 (1979) 283–284 = SEG 29, 1979 (1982) no. 608. In line 15 of this inscription, the second name is Sirras. Kapetanopoulos (1994: 10) argues that the double rho in the name is an important indication that it is a Macedonian name since he thinks there was a tendency among Macedonian names for reduplication.

53. Carney 2000a: 41; Müller 2016: 213. Ogden 1999: 12 suggests that the close associations of the Lyncestids with the Illyrians might have led to "misrepresentation" of a Lyncestian woman as an Illyrian. Molina Marín 2018: 76–77 remarks that a mixed heritage would be more likely if Lyncestis had been controlled, during part of this time, by the Illyrians.

54. Ogden 1999: 12; Worthington 2008: 178.

55. My views have evolved on this subject. Originally, I did believe that Attalus' insult was primarily about ethnicity (Carney 2015 [1992]: 171), but more recently (Carney

2006: 35) I have concluded that his insult was comparative, indicating that he saw his family as better than Olympias'.

56. See Carney 2000a: 51–81 on the marriages of Philip II.

57. Dzino 2008 and 2012; Greenwalt 2010: 279–281.

58. See Carney 2017 on Argead marriage alliances generally.

59. See discussion and references in Carney 2004: 184–188.

60. Ogden 1999: 12–13 puts the slurs about Eurydice in the context of "bastardizing" but, even if he is right, this does not mean that the ethnic slurs had no basis at all.

61. Hall 2001 is central to this discussion and I largely follow his views, though Hatzopoulos 2011b complicates the discussion of ethnicity in interesting ways. See also Engels 2010: 84, who he points out that Molossians were similarly treated but, because they never attempted "hegemony," the issue has been less fraught.

62. The available material is modest and names are debatable as evidence of ethnicity, but see Hatzopoulos 2011a: 44–45, including discussion of some recently discovered inscriptions. See also Hall 2001: 161–163 and Engels 2010: 93–95.

63. See Engels 2010: 96 for discussion.

64. Saripanidi 2017, who also argues that the Macedonians were or had become a Greek people.

65. Hatzopoulos 2011b, especially 72, argues that Macedonian ethnicity was not a problem in the rest of the peninsula until the growth of Macedonian power.

66. This approximate date has become *opinio communis*: see Greenwalt 1988: 37; C. Mortensen 1991: 53; Carney 2000a: 270, n. 16; and Müller 2016: 213, n. 101 for further references.

67. Both scholars who think she was Illyrian and those who think she was Lyncestian share this view and date the marriage, roughly, to the same period of time. See references in Carney 2000a: 270, n. 16 and Mortensen 1991: 53.

68. Greenwalt 1988: 37, for instance, understands the marriage—at the time he thought Eurydice was only Lyncestian—as intended to help Amyntas III drive the Illyrians out.

69. Greenwalt 1988: 42, n. 50 suggests that the "special status" of Eurydice and her family (here referring only to the Lyncestians) also relates to the unusual status of Alexander the Lyncestian (presumably kin of Eurydice) at the end of Alexander III's reign. On this man, see further Carney 2015 (1980) and Heckel 2006: 19.

70. See further Carney 2017.

71. Psoma 2012 argues that Argead kings systematically chose their successors and that such a practice was not a development of the era of the Successors. While her general argument is unconvincing—she assumes that a consistent system exists and then goes looking for it—her discussion of an Athenian alliance with Amyntas (Tod 1948: 2: 90–92) does suggest, if the restorations are accepted, that Amyntas had, late in his reign, begun to single out Alexander as his heir (the restoration of the inscription has the future Alexander II appears as a co-signatory with Amyntas).

72. Greenwalt 1989: 43 argues that Amyntas promoted the status of Eurydice during his reign and that this promotion held out the potential for establishing a dynastic tradition stressing the lines of descent of both parents. This is an interesting suggestion, but what we know of her prominence from both literary and epigraphic sources currently dates to the reigns of her sons. Philip II, as witnessed in the Philippeum, did stress both parents, as Greenwalt points out. For the moment, we can only say that it is possible that the promotion and prominence of Eurydice and, to some degree, of royal women in general, began with Amyntas, but it may have come only later, as a consequence of events after the death of Amyntas. Moreover, given our even poorer knowledge of Macedonia

prior to Philip II, the apparent change may be more a matter of availability of evidence than one of substantial change.

73. Molina Marín 2018: 79, suggests, on the basis of Eurydice's later dealings with Iphicrates, that she may have received visitors and ambassadors at Pella. This is possible, but as we shall see, what was critical was her knowledge of the relationship between Iphicrates and Amyntas III.

74. Greenwalt 2008: 92.

75. We can only speculate as to the factors leading to her success. Carney 2000a: 42 considers family connections, higher status, and the ages of her sons to be possible factors. Greenwalt 1988: 26–28, followed by Mirón Pérez 2000, argues that status was the determinant; even if one does not accept his belief that Eurydice was Lyncestian, Greenwalt makes a good case for the status of the mother as a major determinant in succession struggles.

76. Müller 2013.

77. See Carney 2006: 27–41. Philip's treatment of her brother Alexander of Molossia, both initially and after Philip II had quarreled with his son and Olympias had returned to her brother, suggests this. The marriage Philip arranged between Alexander of Molossia and his daughter by Olympias speaks to this same issue. Psoma 2012: 79–83 implausibly argues that royal mothers had no influence on the succession. Among other things, she conflates rule with influence and simply assumes that, at least while the king lived, if he made the decision about succession, no wife could influence it.

78. Mortensen 1992; Ogden 1999: 13, nn. 66, 68, and 16.

79. See Mortensen 1992: 156–171, followed by Borza 1992: 308; Ogden 1999: 12–13. Errington 1990: 35–36 continued to accept Justin's account. See Chapter 4 for further discussion of the reasons for the development of a very hostile tradition about Eurydice.

80. Her age is only an approximation, based primarily on the apparent age of Alexander II and on the belief that her marriage to Amyntas happened in the late 390s. This suggests that she was born no later than 404 and no earlier than 410 (see Carney 2000a: 42, n. 17).

*Chapter 3*

1. For the reign of Alexander II (and the possible reign of Ptolemy), see recent discussion and references in Müller 2016: 217–228. Hammond 179–184 thinks the murder of Alexander II happened in late 368 or even early 367; Lane Fox 2011b: 257–260 puts the death of Amyntas III in summer 369 and the murder of Alexander II in late summer 368. Zahrnt 2009: 11 dates the death of Alexander II earlier, to winter 369/8.

2. Given that his parents married sometime between 393 and 390 (Carney 2000: 41) and that Alexander II took the throne c. 370, he must have been born no later than 388, but could have been born by 392.

3. Müller 2016: 217 suggests that the wealth given Illyrians may simply have been meant to keep them quiet, not as a response to an invasion but rather as a preventative measure. Justin 7.5.1 asserts that Alexander II gave the Illyrians Philip as a hostage and then later gave him to the Thebans, whereas Diodorus (16.2.2) says that it was Amyntas III who gave him as a hostage and that the Illyrians then passed him on to the Thebans. Hammond 1979: 181 accepts Diodorus' testimony, though Griffith 1979: 204, n. 5 has doubts. Borza 1992: 189, n. 28 rejects Diodorus. March 1995: 270 follows Diodorus,

arguing that the story of Philip as an Illyrian hostage supports the notion of a second Illyrian invasion during the reign of Amyntas III (see Chapter 2). Lane Fox 2011b: 257 follows Justin on the invasion and the idea that Philip was a hostage of the Illyrians before he became one of the Thebans. See a discussion with references in Müller 2016: 217–218 for some of the problems inherent in the notion that Philip essentially spent his entire childhood as a hostage. I consider it unlikely that he was ever an Illyrian hostage.

4. Buckler 1980: 112.

5. Buckler 1980: 245–247, believing that Plutarch's diction at *Pel.* 26.2 implied a "peaceful change of authority," implausibly deduced that Alexander II, worried about his opponents in Macedonia (including Ptolemy Alorites) and so fearing to remain longer in Thessaly or maintain garrisons there, agreed to hold Larissa and Crannon only until the Thebans arrived.

6. So Müller 2016: 220.

7. Georgiados 1997: 192–193 argues that Plutarch's failure to mention Macedonian military activity in Thessaly could be the consequence of his desire to exaggerate Pelopidas' role in Thessalian affairs.

8. Many date the first incursion of Pelopidas into Thessaly and Macedonia to summer 369; see Georgiados 1997: 191 for references.

9. Borza 1992: 191 concludes that Pelopidas took these actions to prevent renewed Macedonian intervention in Thessaly. This seems an unlikely concern, given internal Macedonian strife. Georgiados 1997: 194 thinks this agreement means that Ptolemy was "temporarily" giving up a claim on the throne; we don't know, however, that he had, as yet, asserted one. See also Buckler 1980: 118–119 and Hatzopoulos 1985: 247–252.

10. Plutarch's diction (*Pel.* 26.3) is ambiguous and could refer to either outright war or simple hostility.

11. So Müller 2016: 221–222.

12. There were two Macedonian writers of this name, one from Philippi and one from Pella. The one from Pella, roughly contemporary with Alexander the Great, wrote a history of Macedonia from earliest times to his own day. I follow Heckel 1980: 453–454 in believing that this fragment comes from Marsyas of Pella and is fairly dependable information, given that the writer was born about ten years after the murder and came from a family likely to be well informed about court intrigue past and present.

13. Müller 2016: 222–223 suggests that the dance happened in a sympotic context, whereas Billows 1990: 23 pictures the dance performance happening at a festival. The fragment of Marsyas does not exclude either possibility. As Müller 2016: 223 observes, such an armed dance (like a death while hunting or in battle) provided an explanation for how it was possible to get close enough to murder someone who had bodyguards. As she notes, when we have details of the assassination of other Argeads, explanation for how the murder was accomplished is sometimes provided or implied, and sometimes the suggestion is made that the king was killed accidentally. One version of the death of Archelaus has him killed in a hunting accident (Diod. 14.37.6), but Aristotle (*Pol.* 1311b) says that he was deliberately killed. Diodorus (16.93.1–94.3) says that, on the day of his death, Philip II told his bodyguards to keep at a distance and that the man who killed him was himself part of a contingent meant to guard the king. All of these accounts may have been literary embellishments, but in a world without the many modern ways to kill from a distance, as a practical matter, assassins had to seek out occasions when they could both have access to the victim and somehow manage to be armed. On regicide, see further Carney 2015 (1983).

14. Howe 2018 takes seriously the possibility that Marsyas' account could describe an accidental death; I see no evidence supporting this view.

15. So Greenwalt 1999: 182–183; Greenwalt 2007: 94; Bosworth 2010: 99. See recent arguments *contra* in Lane Fox 2011b: 260, n. 15. Bosworth 2010: 99–100 favored the choice of Alexander II, noting that he had a chance to see the Theban army function and concluding that the new formation had not yet had time to be successful when the king was killed. Müller 2016: 223–224 does not rule Alexander II out, but prefers Alexander I.

16. Hatzopoulos 1985: 249–251 and 1989: 37–49.

17. For a recent discussion and for references, see Müller 2016: 229–235 and Chapter 4.

18. The chronology of events during this period is uncertain: Hammond 1979: 204 believed that the intervention of Iphicrates happened between the first (in the context of the quarrels of Alexander II and Ptolemy) and second interventions of Pelopidas (prompted by the murder of Alexander II). Errington 1990: 36, though he mentions the Iphicrates/Pausanias episode after the two interventions of Pelopidas, says simply that they happened at "about the same time." Borza 1992: 194 says much the same. I place the Iphicrates episode after the death of Alexander II because of Aeschines 2.26 and do not accept an emendation that would change his statement (see following and Chapter 4).

19. Hammond 1979: 183. Anson 2009: 281–283 concludes that Ptolemy was only regent and never king, not only because of the absence of coin evidence but also because the contemporary Aeschines (2.29) refers to him only as an *epitropos* (this word is often translated as "guardian"; see Chapter 1, note 24) and never as king. Aeschines, however, may be playing to Philip II's point of view (see Chapter 4). Moreover, it is not clear that this situation was static: Ptolemy may have claimed to be king and then been forced to accept mere regency. Stylianou 1998: 466 comments that the chronographers (and thus Diodorus) are wrong about the three-year reign and that Ptolemy was in fact only regent. He too cites the absence of coins. Billows 1990: 23; Georgiados 1997: 197; and Zahrnt 2009: 12 seem to consider him only regent. See Chapter 1 for a discussion of whether there was institutionalized substitute kingship, especially before the death of Alexander III, and for the general problem of the terminology for substitute kingship employed by our sources.

20. Miller 1986: 23–27 argued that Pausanias issued coins in his name while rebelling against Amyntas. Borza 1992: 194, n. 44 finds his arguments interesting but lacking in evidence.

21. Borza 1992: 193 refuses to deduce more. Hammond 1979: 184 speculates that he was a son of Archelaus and the brother-in-law of Philip, son of Amyntas II.

22. Unger 1882, followed by Hatzopoulos 1985: 250, and Lane Fox 2011b: 257, convinced that the text of Aeschines 2.26 is corrupt, would insert language that specifies that Alexander II was still alive and suggest that he was off dealing with the Illyrians and so not able to cope with Pausanias. I do not find these arguments persuasive. Bosworth 2010: 99 also puts Pausanias' invasion before the death of Alexander II and even before the first incursion of Pelopidas, but he does not discuss his reasons.

23. Zahrnt 2009: 12 dates Pelopidas' second intervention to summer 368; Roisman puts it in 367. Geyer 1930 implausibly argues that there was only one intervention of Pelopidas, not two, believing the second to be a doublet of the first; see *contra* Hammond 1979: 184–185.

24. See Georgiados 1997: 197 for discussion and references.

25. Hornblower 1991: 227 reasonably doubts that Ptolemy made the alliance for the reasons Plutarch mentions (that Ptolemy was so impressed by Pelopidas and the

Thebans). It is more likely that he saw the Thebans as a lesser evil, and less aggressive, than the Athenians.

26. Hammond 1979: 185 thinks the fifty *hetairoi* sent as hostages may have been those who betrayed their friendship to Eurydice and supported Pausanias, but they are surely far more likely to be supporters of Ptolemy, possibly some of those involved in the assassination. Of course, this could be more or less the same group.

27. Errington 1990: 36 unconvincingly deduces that they were probably mainly relatives of the first set of hostages, yet there seems no obvious reason to supplement the group of hostages already in Thebes with more from the same families.

28. Borza 1992: 194.

29. Borza 1992: 191, 194 is comparatively noncommittal, but seems to favor the idea that he was regent.

30. See Kallet 1983: 242–243 for a discussion of the possible reasons behind the interventions of both Athens and Thebes in Macedonian affairs.

31. Worthington 2008: 17.

32. Hammond 1979: 185; Borza 1992: 195.

33. Ogden 1999: 16 sees Perdiccas' vengeance for his brother's death and his retrieval of Philip from his years as hostage as typical of the solidarity of brothers born of the same mother; he tentatively treats the gift of territory to Philip as another sign of this solidarity. Worthington 2008: 19 suggests that Philip's return could have been a goodwill gesture by the Thebans, perhaps leading to the Macedonian/Theban arrangement about timber (see following).

34. Worthington 2008: 19 thinks that he ruled not "in his own right" but for his brother and speculates that the area involved went from the "gates" of the Axios to the Thermaic Gulf.

35. Hammond 1979: 188 points out the parallel, denies any hostility between the brothers (though see following), and suggests that Perdiccas III, embattled in various directions, might have appreciated the support Philip's position may have brought. Hatzopoulos, who characterized the position under Perdiccas II as the "governor generalship of the New Lands," sees the same position recreated for Philip under Perdiccas III (Hatzopoulos 1996: 178–179, 472).

36. Speusippus (*Epist. Socrat.* 30.12) implies that the brothers did quarrel. Hammond 1979: 207–208 suggests that the territory given Philip was a way, short of exile, to prevent serious strife (this seems to contradict his belief that there was no trouble between the brothers; see discussion earlier in this chapter). There is no clear evidence for public discord. Ogden 1999: 16 downplays the importance of the Speusippus passage. Natoli 2004: 17–100 argues for the letter's authenticity, but this remains a controversial point; Müller 2016: 230–232 generally doubts the idea of significant Platonic evidence and, more specifically, the story about Euphraeus persuading Perdiccas to give Philip territory.

37. Dušanić 1980: 113 argues that Perdiccas III began his reign as a Theban ally, whereas Lane Fox 2011b: 263 suggests that the pro-Theban actions of Macedonia all happened in spring 365 before the death of Ptolemy Alorites and that Perdiccas III immediately returned the kingdom to his family's usual a pro-Athenian policy. See Borza 1992: 195, especially n. 147; Worthington 2008: 19.

38. Borza 1992: 196. Müller 2016: 232 wonders if this information is to be trusted but notes that Perdiccas may have increased exports since he somehow changed the silver standard from that of his father. See Heinrichs 2012: 117, who thinks the coinage suggests

political consolidation and new political stability. He notes the absence of any known silver coins of Alexander II.

39. This is the argument of Borza 1992: 196, who points out that Perdiccas could not have lost four thousand men (Diod. 16.2.4–5) in the battle in which he fell unless he had fielded a much larger force than Macedonian monarchs had managed in many years. Polyaenus (4.10.1) seems to refer to earlier and somewhat more successful military encounters between Perdiccas' Macedonians and an Illyrian army.

40. The date is of this change in alliance is uncertain: see discussions in Hammond 1979: 185 and Errington 1990: 271, n. 6.

41. Hatzopoulos 1985: 255–256. See discussion earlier in this chapter and Errington 1990: 36–37 and Borza 1992: 195–196.

42. Greenwalt 2008: 79–106 suggests that Perdiccas III arranged the marriage of Philip II and Olympias late in his reign (rather than dating it early in Philip's own reign, the usual view), as part of a secret alliance with Molossia against the growing Illyrian threat. Müller 2016: 233 argues against this suggestion, both because she thinks that Eurydice's Illyrian roots made it unnecessary and because she finds Samothrace an improbable location for a secret alliance and betrothal. I find her second point more convincing than her first. Greenwalt's idea is interesting but speculative given the absence of reference to Perdiccas in connection to the betrothal.

43. Borza 1992: 197. On Bardylis and his possible identity (i.e., relationship to Sirras or Audata, one of the wives of Philip II), see Mortensen 1991. We should recall that the Illyrians were not, at this point, united in any long-term way; thus we cannot know if the peoples involved in this effort of Bardylis were the same or partially the same peoples who had earlier troubled Amyntas III and Alexander II.

44. Lane Fox 2011a: 262–269 offers a significantly more negative assessment of Perdiccas III's reign than is found in other accounts.

45. On the date, see Hatzopoulos 1982 and Lane Fox 2011c: 335–336. On Philip's reign see Ellis 1976; Corvisier 2002; Worthington 2008; and Fündling 2014. See also Müller 2016: 236–277 for brief recent discussion with references.

46. Grzybek 1986 imagined that Philip married Perdiccas' widow and adopted her son, an idea that Goukowsky 1993: 60 found appealing. No evidence supports this supposition (so Prandi 1998: 97, n. 35) other than the usual confusion in the sources about how two people are related to each other (e.g., Curtius 6.9.17, 10.24–25 sometimes calls Amyntas the cousin of Alexander III, sometimes the brother). Goukowsky wonders if Philip's wife Phila could have been Amyntas' mother. Such speculation seems pointless. It is certainly true that some kings married the widows of previous kings (see Ogden 1999: ix–xx and *passim*; Carney 2000a: 43), but hardly all kings did. Corvisier 2002: 76 suggests that Philip's mother Eurydice helped smooth his path to power. Such an action would suit her past policy, but we have no evidence for it and, in fact, no clear proof that she was still alive, though I believe she was (see Chapters 4 and 6). The issue is further complicated by an inscription (*SEG* 44, 414; *IG* VII 3055), of disputed date, that refers to Amyntas, son of Perdiccas as *basileus* (king). See Anson 2009: 276–277 on this inscription and its limitations.

47. It is not simply a question of whether Philip served first as regent or not, but also, if he did, how long his regency lasted. See Heckel 2006: 23 on Amyntas, nn. 44 and 45. Griffith 1979: 208–209, 702–704; Ellis 1976: 46; Cawkwell 1978: 28; and Ogden 1999: 16 favor the view that Philip immediately became king. Prestianni-Giallombardo 1973–1974 argues for a regency of four years. See Tronson 1984: 120–121 *contra*. Hatzopoulos 1982: 21ff. argues that at first Philip was not king, only regent, but that Amyntas was not

king either. Goukowsky 1993: 623, followed by Corvisier 2002: 76, suggests that both were kings early on as in the situation in 323. See Anson 2009: 276–277.

48. I do not mean to imply that the broader population had no role in Philip's accession as king (or for that matter, recognition as regent). However one wants to understand it, kings were usually acclaimed and recognized in some public situation (see Chapters 1and 2). My point is rather that movement toward another member of the dynasty, particularly a nephew too young to rule himself, would have required support from within the elite. See Anson 2009, especially 285.

49. Amyntas' exact age is unknown. Obviously, he was born no later than 359 and was old enough to have married by the time of Philip's death in 336. Berve 1926b: 30 and Heckel 2006: 23 estimate a birth date of 365. Lane Fox 2011c: 340 thinks it might have been as early as 372. I suspect that he was quite young, possibly no more than a toddler in 359 (see Carney 2000a: 278, n. 79). Alexander was born in 356. Arrhidaeus was close in age to Alexander, though whether he was slightly older or slightly younger is disputed; see Greenwalt 1984: 72–73.

50. The assassin, Pausanias, acted because he had suffered a personal injury (rape) at the hands of Attalus and Philip, Pausanias' former lover, had failed to give Pausanias redress. Alexander, however, seems to have blamed the Lyncestians and his cousin Amyntas for the assassination (though there were those who said Olympias and Alexander himself encouraged Pausanias), but the accounts of Philip's murder do seem to suggest that Pausanias hoped to survive his act and this seems to imply that more than personal honor was involved. In other words, though an offense to personal honor may have been the underlying motivation, separatist elements at court may also have been involved or, alternatively, Alexander may have taken advantage of the moment to eliminate more of these interests. On this much-discussed issue of Philip's death, see Carney 2015 (1992) for discussion.

51. Heskel 1996: 48 argued that Argaeus' attempt to seize the throne (see following) miscarried because even at that early period in his reign, Philip had already dealt with the Paeonian and Thracian threats, a considerable achievement for the king of a people who so frequently suffered invasion.

52. Bosworth 2010: 101, where he compares those who fought with Philip to the Athenians who fought at Marathon.

53. See Ellis 1976: 45, n. 4 and n. 6. On Argaeus, Beloch 1912–27: 3: 1: 255, n. 1 first suggested this identification. Heskel 1996: 40, n. 7 points to the comparative rarity of the name and that it was assigned to a mythical Argead ancestor (Paus. 2.28.3). As Heskel 1996: 40 observes, Argaeus must have been in exile for some period since all the ancient authors (Dem. 23.121; Diod 16.2.6, 3.3; Lib. 15.42, 20.23) say that it was Athenian intent to restore Argaeus, and Diodorus refers to the supporters of Argaeus who were turned over to Philip as exiles (16.3.6). Amyntas III had presumably exiled him, and one can only speculate (Heskel 1996: 41–43; Lane Fox 2011c: 337) about his whereabouts prior to the dispatch of the mission with Menias.

54. *Contra* Heskel 1996: 37–56, who claims that Argaeus "posed a serious threat to Philip's rule," citing Philip's concessions to the Athenians and subsequent policy, thus conflating the undeniable threat of Athenian power with that of their claimant. Had Argaeus been a significant threat, the citizens of Aegae would have rallied to him and Philip would have had a harder time defeating him.

55. Heskel 1996: 48 hypothesizes that Alorus, the home town of Ptolemy Alorites, must have opposed Philip and that, therefore, Argaeus stopped there to gather support. There is no evidence for either hypothesis. Ellis' suggestion (1976: 50), that Argaeus

hoped to appeal to the local elite in Aegae whose influence may have been limited by the move of the capital to Pella, is also speculative.

56. Heskel 1996: 49 assumes that he was killed in the battle. Heskel, inclined to inflate the importance of Argaeus, considers the defeat remarkable and that odds were in Argaeus' favor, whereas Griffith 1979: 212 more plausibly labeled it a "military picnic."

57. Diodorus' terminology (16.3.4) about these dealings of Philip with other kings has to do with gifts. Griffith 1979: 210–211 is doubtless right to think these activities of Philip combined wealth with diplomacy and, as Diodorus specifies, with promises. I am less sure than Griffith, however, about how much wealth Philip had at his command in the crisis and whether what wealth he had and offered was in cash. Some bribes, after all, involve the potential for future wealth.

58. See Ellis 1976: 52; Bosworth 2010: 91–102; *contra* Lane Fox 2011c: 341–342, who thinks Diodorus could be correct, though the circumstances at the beginning of Philip's reign doubtless speeded up and perhaps altered whatever had already begun. On the revolutionary nature of Philip's reforms, see Brice 2011 for discussion and references.

59. Errington 1990: 39–41.

60. Errington 1990: 39, believing Philip's mother to have been Lyncestian (see Chapter 2 for discussion of Eurydice's father's ethnicity), suggests that this lineage made it easier for Philip to incorporate the Upper Macedonian areas in his rule. Even if, as I have suggested, she was both Lyncestian and Illyrian, this would still be true.

61. Carney 2000a: 52–78.

62. Theopompus *FGrH* 115 F 29, preserved in Harpocration, contains a garbled reference, ultimately derived from a speech of Demosthenes, which may relate to Gygaea's son. The un-emended text translates, "they call Argaeus and Pausanias 'Archelaus.'" Hammond 1979: 175–176 suggests that the text should be emended and translated, "they call both Argaeus and Pausanias the son of Archelaus," whereas Heskel 1996: 39 suggests that the text meant to list the three claimants who attempted to overthrow Philip.

63. Ellis 1973: 353–354 suggests a date in the late 350s for Archelaus' attempt, an attempt he associates with outside support. Griffith 1979: 701 and Errington 1990: 39 assume that it happened at the beginning of Philip's reign. It seems odd, however, that Diodorus would mention the other claimants and fail to mention Philip's own half-brother. Goukowsky 1993: 54 suggested that the death of the first brother happened before the death of Perdiccas III, but after the death of Alexander II. There is no proof for this surmise, and it directly contradicts the only evidence there is, Justin's assertion (8.3.10) that Philip murdered him.

64. Howe 2018 suggests that for a long time they simply remained loyal; given the murderous nature of Argead dynastic politics, this seems unlikely.

65. Greenwalt 1988.

## Chapter 4

1. Herod. 5.18–21, 8.136; Thuc. 2.101.6; and Arist. *Pol.* 1311b refer to royal marriages; Pl. *Grg.* 471a–c; and Ael. *V. H.* 12.43 name Archelaus' mother, but they insist that she had servile status. Pl. *Grg.* 471a–c; and Ael. *V. H.* 12.43 name a wife of Archelaus (Cleopatra). Greenwalt 1988: 41 suggests that, assuming that Archelaus did marry his father's widow Cleopatra, the marriage may signify "that even as early as the fifth century the king's wife . . . had a demarcated public status of her own." Justin names as Amyntas III's other

wife, Gygaea (7.4.5), but we know of no action of hers. Justin also names (Eurynoe) the daughter of Amyntas III and Eurydice and tells us that she informed her father of the adulterous affair and murder plot of Eurydice and Ptolemy (Just. 7.4.7). Thus, apart from Eurydice herself, only her daughter takes any action and she appears only in Justin's account. See Greenwalt 1996 on the names of some royal women he describes as "proto-historical."

2. Molina Marín 2018: 21 rightly observes that adultery charges were easy to make and hard to refute, but then seems to take seriously the possibility (Molina Marín 2018: 83) that Ptolemy was the real father of all of Eurydice's boys. This seems implausible, particularly since there was another set of sons of Amyntas available.

3. Clement of Alexandria, *Protrepticus* 4.54, refers to a statue of Philip the Athenians dedicated at their shrine for bastards. See Ogden 1999: 34, n. 66.

4. Ogden 1999: 15 seems to find this the most convincing reason to doubt Justin's narrative.

5. As Mortensen 1992: 157 remarks, the scholiast's belief in the marriage may have led him to assume that Eurydice was involved in the murder. Mortensen less plausibly considers the possibility that he was trying to "reconcile the opposing traditions," though little reconciliation seems to happen.

6. Mortensen 1992: 159–160 concludes that this must mean that the author of the essay either did not know of charges that Eurydice had murdered some of her offspring or that he rejected them.

7. Mortensen 1992: 165–166, believing that the marriage happened but happened after the death of Alexander II, suggests that she married to protect her remaining sons, particularly Perdiccas, since he was in Macedonia whereas Philip was presumably safer in Thebes.

8. Greenwalt 2008: 93 thinks that Eurydice would not have worried about the continued safety of her remaining sons (particularly Perdiccas) from the violence of Ptolemy, but I see no reason for such confidence, even if one assumes he had murdered Alexander II for reasons of policy, not ambition.

9. McGinn 2008: 1–5 notes the common assumption in many cultures that widows are eager for both sex and wealth, and Walcott 1991 stresses worries present in many cultures about the sexuality of widows. McGinn 2008: 2 observes that widows were often understood as sources of tension because they were neither virgins nor wives and could function as "a lightning rod for the praise and blame of women."

10. Macurdy 1927: 212; 1932: 17–22, especially n. 22. The latter discussion more thoroughly rejected the testimony of Justin.

11. Ellis 1976: 43 simply mentions Iphicrates without any reference to Eurydice or any other Macedonian. Roisman 2010: 163 assumes that Ptolemy was involved in the appeal for aid to Iphicrates but does not mention Eurydice, thus reversing the ancient evidence.

12. Buckler 1980: 35–36; Borza 1992: 190–191 pictures Eurydice as returning to her ancestral roots and organizing the murders of her husband and sons so that her Illyrian-Lyncestian king would be empowered (however, in the addenda to the paperback edition [Borza 1992: 308], he seems to have changed his views because of Mortensen's arguments). This supposed policy makes no sense since no benefit would have come to Eurydice by its implementation. Errington 1990: 35–36 seems to doubt the story of the affair more than the story of Eurydice's murderous activities (though he does not wholeheartedly embrace the Justin narrative). Nonetheless he believes that Eurydice would have supported Ptolemy when he rebelled while Alexander II was in Thessaly. Why she

would have done this is unclear, given that Errington is not sure either that she had an affair with Ptolemy or that she tried to kill her sons.

13. Greenwalt 1988; Mortensen 1992.

14. For instance, Roisman 2010: 163 rejects the picture of Eurydice that Justin offers, but claims that "Scholars who portray her as exerting great influence over Macedonian politics rely on problematic evidence . . . ." He does not specify which scholars or why he considers inscriptional and literary evidence "problematic," but he certainly construes it quite narrowly. See Chapter 5 for further discussion.

15. See recent discussion and references in Müller 2016: 224–229.

16. Tod 1948: 2: 129, lines 6–7. See Hammond 1979: 178, 182.

17. See Mortensen 1992: 157, n. 2 for references to those who think that Diodorus, though he describes Ptolemy as a son of Amyntas and a brother of Alexander II and Perdiccas III, really meant son-in-law and brother-in-law. Hammond 1979: 182, n. 2, followed by Ogden 1999: 14–15, notes that the difference in Greek between "brother" and "brother-in-law" is much greater than in English and so confusion of the two is less likely to happen. Ogden therefore understands that Ptolemy is a son of Amyntas III and thus sees this as an additional amphimetric dispute. He suggests Syncellus, p. 500 Dindorf, may imply this.

18. *Contra* Anson 2009: 282–283, who doubts that he was the man who signed the treaty and that even if he was, doubts this meant he was an Argead. Anson does not discuss Pelopidas' treatment of Ptolemy and he also believes that Ptolemy married first Eurynoe and then Eurydice because he needed a link to the royal family, though we know members of the royal family sometimes intermarried.

19. Hammond 1979: 182–185, followed by Borza 1992: 190, suggests he was a son of Amyntas II, Errington 1990: 270–271, n. 2 rejects this notion, commenting that the name Amyntas is too common to deduce much. Ogden 1999: 15 also finds Hammond's suggestion unconvincing, as does Anson 2009: 282.

20. Anson 2009: 282 sees this as an indication that he was not an Argead.

21. Heckel 2006: 234–238, for instance, finds evidence for seven men named Ptolemy during the reign of Alexander the Great.

22. See Günther 1993: 315–316; Hunter: 1989: 43–47.

23. Le Bohec (-Bouhet) 2006: 193–196.

24. Hunter 1989: 39–42. Alexander's relationship with his mother, Olympias, is idealized; see Carney 2006: 49.

25. See Carney 2017. Some examples: Herod. 5.18–21, 8.126; Thuc. 2.101.6; Arist. *Pol.* 1311b; Diod. 16.91.4; Polyaen. 8.60; Arr. *FGrH* 156, F 9.22)

26. Alexander was going to force Cynnane, his half-sister, to marry again, but when the prospective groom died, he did not arrange another marriage and she supposedly did not want to remarry (Arr. 1.5.4-5; Polyaen. 8.60). Alexander's widowed full sister did not marry again during his lifetime; after his death she tried to arrange her own marriage to Leonnatus (Plut. *Eum.* 3.5) and Olympias tried to arrange her marriage to Perdiccas (Arr. *FGrH* 156, F 9.21).

27. Mortensen 1992: 157 thinks he reached this conclusion because he knew of the marriage and thought that therefore she must have been involved. My view would be that his belief in her involvement suggests that he accepted a tradition similar to that of Justin and that the scholiast's testimony should therefore be rejected. Dickey 2007: 53 has a high opinion of the scholiast; she thinks he was an ancient scholar, probably Didymus, and notes that the scholiast would have had access to material no longer available to us.

True enough, but the scholiast had a cultural context, doubtless including expectations about gender and behavior and older sources were not necessarily less biased.

28. Ogden 1999: 15, while not uncritical of the hostile tradition about Eurydice, pictures Eurydice siding with Ptolemy because she feared that he would win and hoped to save her own life, if at the expense of her three children; he draws a parallel to Arsinoë, accepting as historical the Phaedra plot about Arsinoë and Agathocles rejected by Lund 1994: 184–206; and Carney 1994: 123–131; 2000a: 173–178. It is unclear how this policy, if pursued, would have saved her.

29. Mortensen 1992: 165–166 not only is more certain than I that the marriage was historical but also sees it as more likely Eurydice's choice than I do. She reads it as primarily protective of her son Perdiccas, but also meant to maintain Eurydice's status as royal wife and to provide the potential for more royal children. She does not believe that the marriage was part of Pelopidas' second settlement of Macedonian affairs. She also pictures Eurydice as comparatively free even after the marriage to conduct herself independently.

30. Ogden 1999: 15. More recently (2011: 94, 102) he has termed it "step-mother marriage" though Eurydice was not likely the step-mother of Ptolemy.

31. Greenwalt 2008: 93, followed by Molina Marín 2018: 85, suggests that she married Ptolemy, after the murder of Alexander II, in order to protect her remaining sons, perhaps against other Argead claimants (he seems to assume that Pausanias had yet to appear), and because she was convinced that he did not intend harm to her other children. Even if Ptolemy had originally supported Alexander II and then abandoned him because of the Thessalian misadventure and/or his possible army reforms (so Greenwalt 2008: 93–96), it is not clear why Eurydice would have trusted him not to kill her other sons.

32. Müller 2016: 225–226, who points to her lack of real alternatives and rejects Fündling's (2014: 37) idea that she entrusted rule to him; there is no evidence that royal women had such power, though one can certainly imagine that she may have tried to influence the choice.

33. He already had one son and, for all we know, could have had more. Even if Eurydice were still fertile at the time of their marriage—she was probably toward the end of her child-bearing years—any baby born would have been far too young to function as any immediate concern in a succession battle. Molina Marín 2018: 85 worries that such a child would have been a threat to the succession of her existing sons, but, given the ages of her other sons, this would not seem to be a serious problem.

34. Lane Fox 2011b: 261 makes this plausible suggestion.

35. There are the usual speculations about his line of descent: he could have been a son or descendant of the king of the same name; some have even suggested that he was a son of Archelaus. See discussion and references in Müller 2016: 226, nn. 92–93.

36. Heskel 1997: 23–27 convincingly places Iphicrates' expedition soon after Alexander II's assassination, just prior to Pelopidas' second appearance in Macedonia. She dates the Iphicrates expedition between July and Autumn 368 and Pelopidas' return to November of 368.

37. Mortensen 1992: 157 points out that this means that Aeschines was himself not a witness to the encounter with Iphicrates; his speech, however, makes clear that there were a number of witnesses to the encounter, witnesses present when he spoke as part of the embassy.

38. As Carey 2000: 368 observes, Ptolemy had little choice in this switch, given the second incursion of Pelopidas.

39. Mortensen 1992: 158 and Ogden 1999: 15, though noting the problems with the ages of Philip and Perdiccas, consider Aeschines preferable to the version of Justin. Carey 2000: 103 thinks the business about Eurydice putting the brothers into Iphicrates' lap can't have been part of the original speech Aeschines delivered to Philip (and says it would have made the king smile if it happened), but I am not sure why it couldn't have been part of the original speech since it was flattering to his mother and sentimental about the family past.

40. The belief that Theopompus visited the court is based, primarily, on the letter of Speusippus. See discussion and references in Flower 1994: 18–21.

41. See *FGrH* 72 and Chapter 3 for a brief discussion of his fragment 4 about the *petzhetairoi*. Flower 1994: 21 suggests that he and Theopompus were both perhaps writing Greek histories and a *Philippika*.

42. As Howe 2018 does.

43. Macurdy 1932: 18–19 suggests that Justin took a simply "scandal-mongering" source and made the portrait of Eurydice even more negative because of his fascination with criminal royal women, willfully transferring Alexander II's murder from Ptolemy to Eurydice and inventing the murder of Perdiccas and adding other pathetic touches.

44. Yardley and Heckel 1997: 1 speak of him "omitting-or, at least, severely compressing—all that he did not find either intrinsically interesting or of use to the orator in search of historical examples." This generalization is helpful, but it does not pay attention to how often the focus is on women and their scandalous behavior.

45. Comploi 2002.

46. See discussion in Emberger 2008 and Frank 2018. Echoes of treatments of Roman imperial women and feelings about them seem to be present, and Frank argues particularly for memories of Cleopatra VII coloring Justin's account of Olympias.

47. See Carney 2006: 128–129 and 2013: 31–64, 137–138.

48. See Stern 2012 for a recent discussion and re-evaluation of Nepos' merits.

49. See discussion and references in Mortensen 1992: 161–163. This is not to imply that Theopompus was interested only in scandal (as Justin often does seem to be). Mortensen 1992: 162 suggests that he, like other Greek historians, might have given several different versions of events during this period, perhaps even favoring an alternate version.

50. Mortensen 1992: 161, citing Greenwalt 1988: 43 and 1989: 38 for context. Ogden 1999: 13–14.

51. Lane Fox 2011a: 210 and 2011b: 261, 268.

52. Knecht 1998: xii. Knecht 1998: 163–165 also notes that this image proved so compelling that it was perpetuated in treatments of other foreign queens of France.

53. Mortensen 1992: 157, though she seems to accept Eurynoe as historical, wonders why, if she were so murderous, Eurydice did not kill Eurynoe as well. As I've noted, Eurynoe may simply have died (Carney 2000a: 40) of natural causes and the role ultimately given Ptolemy as regent might suggest that he was Perdiccas III's uncle by marriage. Ogden 1999: 15 rightly points out that a marriage between Ptolemy and Eurynoe could have been "a conciliatory gesture," like the marriage of Archelaus' son Amyntas to a half-sister. Indeed, even if Ptolemy were simply an Argead, not a son of Amyntas, the marriage could still have been intended to tie another Argead strand back into the current main line.

54. Schaps 1977.

55. See discussion in Carney 2006: 50 and Mitchell 2007: 69–72. See also Jones 1999: 1–56 and Erskine 2002. Mosely 1973: 78 stresses the personal nature of the

diplomatic relations of kings. Sears 2013: 127 observes that diplomacy among Thracians and Macedonians often involved dynastic alliances sealed by marriage or adoption.

56. Jones 1999: 14 and Herman 1987: 29.

57. Blundell 1989: 31–42; Mitchell 1997: 1–26.

58. "Εὐρυδίκης δὲ τῆς μητρὸς αὐτῶν προδεδομένης ὑπὸ τῶν δοκούντων εἶναι² φίλων," Dilts 1997 prefers "δοκούντων αὐτῆς εἶναι" but some manuscripts read "αὐτοῖς" before "εἶναι." So, depending on the manuscript reading, they are either her *philoi* or their (i.e., her and her sons') *philoi*. Ogden 1999: 16, understanding the *philoi* as hers, thinks that this refers to Alexander II's murder, assuming that she had married Ptolemy and that the *philos* who betrayed her was Ptolemy, though surely it would, in that case, be his entire faction, not simply Ptolemy.

59. Mortensen 1992: 159 considers it "possible" that Alexander II's *philoi* were also those of Eurydice, but Aeschines' diction at 2.28 makes it clear that they were the same group, that they were, as Eurydice says, "ours."

60. Possibly for help with Thracian relations: see Ellis 1969: 7; Hammond 1979: 176; and Borza 1992: 183. Sears 2013: 126 suggests a date around 383, at the time Amyntas was restored to the throne.

61. Mortensen 1992: 158 points to the access this gave Eurydice.

62. Fündling 2014: 37 doubts that Alexander II's friends did summon Pelopidas, whereas Müller 2016: 228 thinks it possible that Philip, by then a hostage in Thebes, hoping to put pressure on Ptolemy, was behind the recourse to Pelopidas.

63. Macurdy 1927: 208; Hammond 1979: 184; Georgiados 1997: 197; and Roisman 2010: 163, who concludes that Ptolemy must have been involved because he benefited from Iphicrates' aid, but one may benefit from something without having done anything to acquire that benefit.

64. Müller 2016: 227 considers it possible that she took the initiative and wonders if she had funds to employ mercenaries in this action.

65. Borza 1992: 193 makes the point that if Ptolemy was the Ptolemy who had represented Amyntas in the treaty with Athens (see earlier discussion) when the Macedonians supported Athenian recovery of Amphipolis, Iphicrates, trying to do just that, might well help Ptolemy and Eurydice, reflecting on the earlier link and hoping to gain their support again. This is believable but rejects evidence we do have in favor of that we don't.

*Chapter 5*

1. Greenwalt 1988: 42.

2. Carney 2000a: 30.

3. Greenwalt 1988: 42 wonders if she paid for the Eucleia temple herself and concludes that she did.

4. See Kron 1996 on women, patronage, and their families, especially the point (Kron 1996:155) that in some cases males were obligated to fund the benefactions of the women of their family.

5. *SEG IX* 2. Rhodes and Osborne 2003: 486–493 date them to 330–326. See also Laronde 1987: 30–34. However, it has been argued that Olympias and Cleopatra appear this way in the inscription because they are functioning as heads of state. See references in Carney 2000a: 282, n. 6 and *SIG* I 252N 5–8, with n. 3. While I do not agree

with Palagia's (2010: 39) suggestion that Eurydice's failure to name her husband in her dedications automatically means that she was a widow, I do think she was a widow when the dedications were made.

6. The inscription is damaged and the date of Roxane's dedication is disputed. Roxane did not come to the Greek peninsula until well after Alexander's death in 323, but the dedication need not have been made by her in person. Themelis 2003 favors a date after Alexander's death, perhaps 319/18. Kosmetatou 2004 concludes it could be any time between 327 and 316. Mirón Pérez and Martinez López 2011: 45 date it to Roxane's widowhood and argue that it helped to legitimize her son and publicize her/his Hellenism. Müller 2012: 300 also favors a date after the death of Alexander. Harders 2014: 372, however, believes that the inscription dates to Alexander's reign because Roxane is termed γυνή (woman or wife) but apparent widows are sometimes referred to in the same way in Macedonian inscriptions (Le Bohec (-Bouhet) 2006: 194). I find the arguments for a post-Alexander date more convincing.

7. See Carney 1991: 157–172.

8. There are also a number of inscriptions that refer to a woman by her title and reference *both* her father and her husband. See Carney 2000a: 227.

9. Carney 2000a: 195–197.

10. Saatsoglou-Paliadeli 2000: 387–392. She suggests a date between 179/8 and the defeat of Perseus in 168. Since only a fragment of the inscription survives, it is possible that Perseus might have been referred to in a missing portion.

11. Tataki 1988: 207, 433. If, however, it dates to the third century or especially if dates to the second century, it is odd that the inscription does not refer to her as *basilissa*.

12. See Le Bohec (-Bouhet) 2006: 194–196 on the legal status of women in Macedonia, particularly in terms of property rights.

13. *Contra* Greenwalt 2008: 103, n. 49. Müller 2013 categorizes her use of the patronymic as symbolic capital.

14. *SIG* I 252N 5–8, with n. 3. She gave the sanctuary 190 *darics* to fund a dedication of a golden crown; quite possibly she paid for it from the plunder Alexander sent her after the siege of Gaza (Plut. *Alex.* 25.4). He also sent her plunder after Granicus (*FGrH* 151 F 1; Plut. *Alex.16.8*) and probably on other occasions.

15. *SEG IX* 2. See Carney 2006: 50–51 for a discussion of the possibility that they acted with and for Alexander.

16. Mortensen 1992: 159, n. 16.

17. The discovery of the Eurydice inscriptions at Vergina/Aegae has led to general agreement that the Eurydice referred to in this passage is the wife of Amyntas III: see Oikonomedes 1983; Robert and Robert 1984: 450–451; and Mortensen 1992: 159, n. 16.

18. Wilhelm 1949: 625–633, followed by Robert and Robert 1984: 450 and Le Bohec (Bouhet 2006: 191). Hammond 1994: 17, unaware of Wilhelm's emendation, considers it a dedication to the city's muses. Molina Marín 2018: 80, though aware of the emendation, seems to follow Hammond, though he says he accepts Wilhelm's emendation.

19. So Saatsoglou-Paliadeli 2000: 401–402, who understands it as a reference to Eurydice's residence in Aegae because she thinks that the noun *polietis* (citizen woman) is nominative in the text and thus appositive to Eurydice rather than dative, as Wilhelm emended it; Lane Fox 2011b: 268, though citing Mortensen and Wilhelm, agrees with Saatsoglou-Paliadeli.

20. Le Bohec (-Bouhet) 2006: 190–192 has an excellent discussion.

21. Oikonomedes 1983: 64 suggests that it was a statue of Eurydice herself, or one of Apollo, or perhaps a tablet with the Greek alphabet. Saatsoglou-Paliadeli 2000: 402

observes that, of the various options for terms that could refer to a statue, this text can't refer to either an ἄγαλμα (usually understood as a cult statue) or an εἰκών (usually understood as a portrait statue) for grammatical reasons, and that while ἀνδριάς (often assumed to apply only to statues of males) would fit the grammar (which requires a masculine pronoun), it would never apply to a female statue. Consequently, she concludes that it cannot have been a portrait statue (εἰκών) or a statue of Apollo (ἄγαλμα) and adds that a tablet with the alphabet would work with the grammar but has little archaeological support. She argues that *pothos* (a longing for something absent, in this case the longing for education) fits grammatically and mirrors the language of the dedication. See, however, Carney 2000a: 213 for occasions (e.g. Ath. 591b) where ἀνδριάς refers to a statue of a woman. Now, however, see Keesling 2017, who argues that ἀνδριάς was not used to refer to female images until after 200 BCE.

22. See discussion in Saatsoglou-Paliadeli 2000: 403, n. 113 who references a vase painting by the Meidias painter in which Pothos appears along with Mousaeus and the Muses.

23. Molina Marín 2018: 81 rightly notes the similarity but does not discuss the *topos* of *pothos* and scholarship about it. See discussion and references in Stewart 1993: 84–86. Stewart convincingly puts Alexander's *pothos,* as described in ancient authors, in a heroic context (Achillean and Heraclean), as a desire to surpass the deeds of others. Eurydice's inscription, if more discretely, implies a similar goal, as we shall see.

24. Mortensen 1992: 166 suggests Pella as a possibility as well. Saatsoglou-Paliadeli 2000: 402 argues that while there is no archaeological evidence for a sanctuary to the Muses at Aegae, as there is at Dion, there could have been one, particularly in the area around the mountains. See also Saatsoglou-Paliadeli 2011: 277, n. 40.

25. On the cult of the muses at Dion, see Pingiatoglou 2010. The location of the sanctuary has not yet been discovered, though sculpture and inscriptions relating to it have been found. She wonders if they were worshipped within the sanctuary of Zeus. See Murray 2005 for a discussion of the nature of the Muses.

26. Konishi 1993.

27. Saatsoglou-Paliadeli 2000: 401 says late 370s or early 360s.

28. Lane Fox 2011b: 263–264.

29. Carney 2000a: 28–29.

30. Greenwalt 1988: 41 deduces that she was probably the first Argead wife to be literate. Carney 2011: 197 understands the inscription/dedication as a way to publicize herself and her sons as well, in contrast to negative "publicity"; Molina Marín 2018: 80 sees it as a way to increase her prestige.

31. So Wilhelm 1949: 632. Le Bohec (-Bouhet) 2006: 191 thinks that the text means that her fellow female citizens have aided Eurydice in her education. She also notes that the term "citizen women" appears in a text from Dion—a list, possibly of members of a religious organization.

32. See Schmitt 1991; Savalli-Lestrade 2003: 70–71; Carney 2011: 197, n. 22.

33. Greenwalt 1988: 40–41.

34. Greenwalt 1988: 43; see also Molina Marín 2018: 79–81. However, Gygea may not have been Amyntas III's first wife or an Argead. See Chapter 2.

35. Drougou 2011: 189 speaks of the emphasis Philip put on the royal family, a practice continued by Hellenistic rulers, as were statues with heroic and/or divine characteristics.

36. Paus. 5.12.5; 6.20.9. See discussion and references in Carney 2013: 28–29.

37. See Saatsoglou-Paliadeli 1996 and recent overview in Kyriakou and Tourtas 2013: 299–301.

38. Kyriakou and Tourtas 2013: 300 point out that potsherds from the construction ditches of the Eucleia sanctuary confirm a date in the second half of the fourth century. A smaller temple, on a different axis, was added in the third century and there were some further alterations, including a new stoa, in the second century. There are also two peristyle structures, one (to the west of the first temple) from the fourth century. See Saatsoglou-Paliadeli 1996; Kyriakou and Tourtas 2015: 359; and Kyriakou 2014: 253.

39. Drougou 2011: 249–250 concludes that the connection between cult centers and structures related to the royal family can't have been accidental and thus that the combination served a political purpose.

40. On Philp's stagecraft, see references in Carney 2010a: 43–44.

41. Saatsoglou-Paliadeli 2000: 388–389; Drougou 2011: 249; Kyriakou 2014: 253 (who notes that the town planning here—theater, palace, and sanctuary in close relationship— is repeated in the placement of Hellenistic *basileia* (palaces)).

42. Drougou and Saatsoglou-Paliadeli 2000: 28–31; Drougou 2011: 249; Kyriakou and Tourtas 2013: 299–300; Kyriakou 2014: 252–258. Palagia 2016: 92–94 suggests that the young female head is also a representation of Eucleia, pointing out that in fifth-century Attic vase painting, Eucleia is represented as a young woman and concluding that there was not a single fixed version of Eucleia's iconography.

43. Saatsoglou-Paliadeli 1991: 12–16; Saatsoglou-Paliadeli 2000: 389–392 believed it to be a cult statue.

44. See Kyriakou and Tourtas 2013 and 2015 for overviews of the pits and a discussion of their significance and the time of each pit's creation. The 1990 pit (the one containing the body of the peplophorus statue and the controversial head we will discuss) seems to show special treatment of the female statue—difficult to move because of its size and weight—and vessels from the second century BCE through the early first century CE suggest ritualized behavior. Kyriakou and Tourtas 2015: 381 note that part of the sanctuary of Eucleia was reused in the first half of the second century, suggesting its continued significance in the period when the Macedonian kingdom was threatened by the Romans.

45. Excavations in 2008 and 2009 revealed two burial assemblies. See Saatsoglou-Paliadeli, Kyriakou, et al. 2008; Saatsoglou-Paliadeli, Papageorgiou, et al. 2008, Saatsoglou-Paliadeli, Kyriakou, et al. 2009 and Saatsoglou-Paliadeli, Papageorgiou, et al. 2009; Drougou 2011: 249, n. 24l; and Kyriakou 2014. In the first burial discovered, inside a large, lidded cylindrical bronze vessel was a gold pyxis (also lidded) containing a golden oak wreath, gold and purple fabric, and the remains of an adolescent male (14–18 years old). In 2009, another burial assemblage was found in the same ditch as the first, but this one contained two vessels, a silver funerary hydria and a silver Panathenaic vessel decorated with gold. The hydria held the cremated bones of an adult (of uncertain age and sex), covered in purple fabric, whereas the amphora held gold ornaments (some possibly part of a diadem), a gold olive wreath, and the remains of a very young child (3–7 years) of unknown sex. Saatsoglou-Paliadeli, Drougou, and Kyriakou all argue for the conclusion that these were burials of members of the royal family, probably including Heracles, Alexander the Great's son by Barsine (Kyriakou 2014 focuses on the similarities between the oak wreath in this burial and those of Tombs II and III from the Great Tumulus whereas Drougou stresses the importance of the vessel shapes). These assemblages do seem like condensed versions of the burials under the Great Tumulus at Vergina. The youth's bones are approximately correct for the age of Heracles. While there is some possibility that Heracles' mother, Barsine, accompanied him on his fatal trip to Macedonia (Just.15.2.3) and so one could surmise that the adult in the hydria was Barsine, the small child remains a puzzle.

46. See Saatsoglou-Paliadeli 2011: 277–278 for a recent description of this base.

47. Saatsoglou-Paliadeli 2000: 393, n. 43 concludes that it may have been part of an extensive reconstruction of the area in this period.

48. Saatsoglou-Paliadeli 2000: 393, n. 46 notes fragments of sculpture from the second half of the fourth century found in the sanctuary, possibly, she thought, remnants of whatever once stood on the base. The base sits on a low marble step (18 cm. high) and the base itself is 47 cm. high, 143 cm. long, and 97 cm. wide.

49. See Saatsoglou-Paliadeli 2000: 394, n. 4. It does also resemble a depiction on at least one funerary inscription (Saatsoglou-Paliadeli 2000: 393: n. 47). Saatsoglou-Paliadeli 2011: 278 simply refers to it as a "symbol of honor."

50. Andronikos 1984: 49–51. Oikonomedes 1983: 62 describes the inscription as being cut in "beautiful monumental letters of the early fourth century," but subsequent views have differed.

51. Saatsoglou-Paliadeli 2000: 394, nn. 49–50, commented at that time that dating them more firmly would depend on other finds from the sanctuary. In fact, as noted earlier, the sanctuary now appears to date to the second half of the fourth century.

52. Greenwalt 1988: 42 and Mortensen 1992: 164–165 discussed the date, but they did so before current views about the date of the palace and theater and the sanctuary were established.

53. Saatsoglou-Paliadeli 2000: 397.

54. Saatsoglou-Paliadeli 2011: 278.

55. Saatsoglou-Paliadeli 2011: 281.

56. Palagia 2016: 90–95.

57. Dr. Saatsoglou-Paliadeli will soon publish her findings on the statue body and head. Saatsoglou-Paliadeli 2011: 279–281 considers it the work of a major Athenian artist but is not yet sure if it is related to Eurydice's image in the Philippeum. She dates it early in the third quarter of the fourth century and believes that, if not an image of Eurydice, it must be that of another queen because she discerns a mature woman's features and so does not read the statue as a goddess or personification. We will discuss the head and face of the statue at greater length shortly. Paspalas 2011: 188 assumes that the other Eurydice statue base would also have supported a "Eucleia" statue. See also Drougou 2011: 188.

58. S. Dillon 2007: 65.

59. S. Dillon 2007: 66.

60. S. Dillon 2007: 76–80.

61. Connelly 2007: 85–87; S. Dillon 2007: 70.

62. Saatsoglou-Paliadeli 2011: 281. See Drougou and Saatsoglou-Paliadeli 2000: 30, Figure 25 for an image of the head and Kyriakou and Tourtas 2013: 312, Figure 19 for an image of the head and neck together. Schultz 2007: 230, nn. 65 and 66 and S. Dillon 2010: 78–79, not yet aware of Saatsoglou-Paliadeli's doubts about the fit of the statue and statue base, understood the statue as a portrait with features stressing age (lines from nose to lips). Schultz considers the statue face to be individualized and elderly, contrary to the usual representation of Eucleia, and also understands it as atticizing and heroizing, possibly a model for Eurydice's later image in the Philippeum.

63. Kyriakou and Tourtas 2015: 369 suggest that the change in the face might have originated in a portrait statue of Eurydice and that the final product found in this pit came from combining this statue with another.

64. See Palagia 2010: 39–40 and 2016.

65. It was found in the destruction layer of 1991 pit (the one with the snake sculpture), possibly confirming a connection to the cult the snake sculpture was related to (Kyriakou and Tourtas 2013: 313).

66. As Saatsoglou-Paliadeli 2000: 390 notes, the dedication is to a male, not a female deity.

67. On the cult generally, see Burkert 1985: 199–203; Lalonde 2006: 40–53; Dowden 2006: 65; and Ogden 2013: 272–283. Philip V made a dedication at Pella to Zeus Meilichius. See references in Saatsoglou-Paliadeli 2000: 391, n. 22.

68. Lalonde 2006: 55–56; Ogden 2013: 278, n. 33. M. Dillon 2002: 249 says that female interest in the cult derived from the god's role as provider of household needs.

69. Saatsoglou-Paliadeli 1991: 12–16; 2000: 289–292; Kyriakou and Tourtas 2015: 364.

70. Stafford 2008: 72–84 observes that in the fifth century, few personifications had sanctuaries of their own and that they often shared them with a major deity or had an altar within the other deity's temple or simply were epithets added to that of a major deity (e.g., Artemis Eucleia). This changed in the fourth century when personifications became increasingly popular.

71. Lalonde 2006: 61–62.

72. See the lengthy and speculative discussion in Sourvinou-Inwood 2003: 40–45.

73. See Smith 2011: 71 on the early military background of Eucleia, but she observes that, as time went on, Eucleia was less narrowly associated with military renown and more broadly understood. In fifth-century vase painting, however, Eucleia is sometimes associated with Aphrodite and has something of an erotic context, perhaps in terms of the need for maintaining good repute. See Borg 2005 and my further discussion. Given the stories that questioned Eurydice's good sexual repute (see Chapter 4), a dedication to this deity in the context of good sexual repute might be relevant.

74. Andronikos 1984: 51.

75. Borza 1992: 193.

76. Saatsoglou-Paliadeli 2000: 395, though conceding that it could have come during her marriage to Ptolemy and could involve Eucleia as protectress of marriage. This possibility seems less likely.

77. So Stafford 2008: 80, though she does observe that in late fifth-century vase paintings, Eucleia often appears with Eunomia, and by the fourth century and late Hellenistic period there is evidence for a shared cult (see Smith 2011: 74).

78. Borza 1992: 192–193, followed by Palagia 2016. Carney 2000a: 45 found this view appealing, but I am now more doubtful about this assumption of similarity.

79. Mortensen 1992: 167.

80. Saatsoglou-Paliadeli 1987: 740–742.

81. Lalonde 2006: 40–41 gives examples for Zeus Meilichius cults.

82. Palagia 2016 argues for a date in the troubled period after the death of Amyntas.

83. Lane Fox 2011b: 262 suggests putting it at the very beginning of Philip's reign, 360/59, during his early friendship with the Athenians. One doubts that any dedication in Philip's reign happened before the defeat of the Illyrians and, if the sanctuary is part of Philip's rebuilding of sections of Aegae, as I have argued, one would expect a somewhat later date.

84. See Carney 2015 (2007) and Chapter 6, as well as Carney 2006: 90–91; 2011: 197. Smith 2011: 71 remarks that Eucleia could give people a good reputation because of their ancestry, their marriage, or a victory of theirs. In a sense, all could have been at issue with Eurydice.

85. Borg 2005: 198, discussing Eucleia in terms of vase painting, comments that the goddess was both a demand for and a result of moderation in erotic passion, and so honored the good kind of married *eros*. Shapiro 1993: 77 and Smith 2011: 71–73 discuss vase painting showing Helen's bridal bath, apparently in reference to *eucleia* she is soon to lose.

86. Drougou 2011: 249. Stafford 2008: 81 notes that as personification cults grew more popular in the fourth century, a number had a political aspect.

87. Greenwalt 1988: 42 suggests the possibility of her funding the sanctuary, whereas Mortensen 1992: 167 raises the same possibility about the cult. Saatsoglou-Paliadeli 2000: 397 questions Mortensen's 1992: 167, n. 42 suggestion that Eurydice was the one to introduce the cult to Aegae and she particularly doubts that Mortensen's suggested connection to the Corinthian cult (via Eurydice's Bacchiad roots) is valid because, she argues, there is no evidence that Eucleia was worshipped as Artemis Eucleia in Corinth.

88. Kron 1996.

89. Greenwalt 1988: 42 makes this point.

90. See Carney 2006: 88–103, where Olympias' role in religious activity is discussed. A letter from Olympias to Alexander, referred to by Athenaeus (14.659f), had her offering to sell her son a slave familiar with Alexander's ancestral rites, both Dionysiac and Argead, and those that Olympias performed.

91. Kottaridi 2004. As with all the other the burials at Aegae, none of these burials are connected by inscriptions to named individuals, so judgments about whether they are royal are necessarily subjective. See a recent discussion and references in Saripanidi 2017: 81, 85, n. 84. Saripanidi doubts that the *phiali* (cups) in the burial demonstrate that the "Lady of Aegae" functioned as a priestess because of the wide presence during this period of such vessels in Macedonian burials, male and female, as well as those of children.

92. Saatsoglou-Paliadeli 2000: 397 deduces that Eurydice was a priestess of Eucleia and a permanent resident of Aegae and that she must have been buried there, at latest, in the third quarter of the fourth century.

93. Kron 1996: 140.

94. S. Dillon 2007: 65.

95. Kron 1996: 177, 181–182.

96. Saatsoglou-Paliadeli 2000: 400–401. The careful reburying of major sculpture and other items from the sanctuary after its destruction also confirms how important pious survivors considered its remains. See description and discussion in Kyriakou and Tourtas 2013 and 2015.

97. Mari 2011: 463, comments that the urban area around the Eucleia sanctuary was an "annex" of royal buildings and the royal power they conveyed; see also Drougou 2011: 244.

98. Saatsoglou-Paliadeli 2000: 397. She suggests that its existence "supports Eurydice's special relationship" with Aegae.

99. Saatsoglou-Paliadeli: 1993; 2000: 397–400.

100. Saatsoglou-Paliadeli 2000: 398.

101. Saatsoglou-Paliadeli 2000: 398. I have already discussed the two Daochus groups. Her belief that Eurydice's image stood at the far right in the group in the Philippeum has been reinforced by Schultz's reexamination of the remains of the Philippeum (Schultz 2007: 213–216).

102. Saatsoglou-Paliadeli 2011: 281.

103. Saatsoglou-Paliadeli 2000: 399; 2011: 279; it is not clear why she believes the one group precedes the other.

104. Schultz 2007: 216 considers the plinth cuttings of the existing statue (from the Eucleia sanctuary) and the Philippeum base similar in shape and size, but also notes (2007: 216, n. 66) some problems with believing them to be more or less simultaneous dedications.

105. On the unifying nature of semi-circular groups and particularly the Philippeum, see Carney 2015 (2007): 70 for references and, on the theatrical nature of such groups and particularly the Philippeum, see Schultz 2007: 211–213.

106. Petersen and Salzman-Mitchell 2012: 2–4, who put this association in the context of "public, if not politicized displays of motherhood," though they do not discuss Eurydice or royal Macedonian women.

### Chapter 6

1. Carney 2000a: 45 argued for 346, though I now believe 343 is a possibility. The text of the speech as we have it may also have been further revised before publication, not just in 343.

2. Andronikos 1987a: 84; Hammond 1991: 71; and Kottaridi 1999 accept the identification; Borza 1992: 308; Palagia 2002: 4; and Borza and Palagia 2008: 86 express doubts primarily because of their doubts about using the Panathenaic vase/s to date the entire tomb. Faklaris (forthcoming) discusses the tomb and its probable dating.

3. Andronikos 1994: 160 reports the finding of only one Panathenaic amphora, but subsequently fragments of three were recognized by Kottaridi during her study of the pyre (Kottaridi 2006: 157; Brecoulaki 2006a: 50, n. 1). See Kottaridi 2011b: 149, Fig. 168 for an image of these fragments.

4. For a relatively recent description of the tomb and its contents, see Kottaridi 2011c: 38–105. Dr. Kottaridi's publication of the tomb is forthcoming, so I am unable to include photographs from the tomb. The best currently available images of the exterior of the tomb, the back wall of the main chamber, the throne, and the painting on the back of throne appear in Kottaridi 2006: Plates 59–62.

5. Andronikos 1987b articulates this view at length. See Hatzopoulos 2008 for a history of the controversy and an argument in favor of the identification of Philip II as the primary occupant of Tomb II and for the development of the barrel vault in Greece before Alexander's invasion of the Persian Empire.

6. See Borza and Palagia 2008 for a history of the controversy and an argument in favor of the identification of Philip Arrhidaeus as the primary occupant of Tomb II and for the development of the barrel vault in Greece as consequence of Alexander's invasion.

7. The barrel vault is the only true constant in Macedonian tombs; while most have or had mounds above them, some may simply have been subterranean. Many have a trompe l'oeil palace or temple-like facade, but many do not. (Huguenot 2008: 42 notes that these facades hide the vault, but we don't know if this was done for aesthetic or cultural reasons.) They were usually made of isodomic porous blocks. Many had an antechamber and a main or burial chamber; see Huguenot 2008: 37–44 for general discussion of the type.

8. Palagia 2002: 4, discussing a possible later date for the tomb of Eurydice, notes that many tombs, in the twenty years of upset following Cassander's death, lack facades. Palagia 2014: 383 wonders if the owners made this choice hoping to avoid unwelcome attention during uncertain times.

9. Andronikos 1994: 147; Kottaridi 2006: 157.

10. For the Eurydice tomb, see Andronikos 1987a; 1988; 1994: 154–161; Rives-Gal 1996: 394–397; Kottaridi 2006; Brecoulaki 2006a: 49–76; Mangoldt 2012: 291–294; and Palagia 2017: 414–416.

11. Kottaridi 2011b: 142 identifies the occupant of the Rhomaios tomb as Thessalonice, the granddaughter of Eurydice. It has usually been assumed to be an early third century burial, but nothing specific ties it to Thessalonice.

12. See Kottaridi 2002: 78–79; 2006: 155–157; 2007: 38, n. 27; and 2011a for discussion and her deductions. None of her identifications are particularly implausible, but no specific evidence supports them. We shall discuss the general problem of determining which burials are royal shortly.

13. For the absence of a tumulus for the Rhomaios tomb see Andronikos 1984: 34–35, who does not find Rhomaios' explanation (washing away of fill by rain or destruction by plowing) plausible. On the lack of a mound for the Eurydice tomb, see Andronikos 1987c: 382, n. 54. See also Palagia 2014: 383.

14. Andronikos 1994: 155–156 wonders if the encasement of the vault was intended to recall a cist tomb or whether it indicated that the builders were not certain, without the unusual thickness, that the walls would withstand the thrust of the vault (he favors the latter view).

15. Andronikos 1994: 154 gives slightly different figures: 10.6–7 meters long and 7.5–7.95 meters wide. He notes that because of the activity of the ancient robbers, some of the plaster from the façade has fallen away and so a little of the vault is currently observable.

16. Miller 1993: 9 observes that the exterior entrance to Macedonian tombs was usually covered by large blocks that could be removed when re-entry was desired.

17. See Miller 1993: 44.

18. See Kottaridi 1999 and 2001 on these distinctive pyres. For this particular pyre, Kottaridi 1999: 632–634 mentions large iron nails, bronze cones and shields, bits of bronze *omphaloi* (central decorations, often on shields), as well as the knocker, and she provides a reconstruction of the door to the pyre (Kottaridi 1999: 641, Figs. 1–2). See Kottaridi 2011b: 148, Figure 167 for images of the many nails and fragments of door fixtures from the pyre.

19. Guimier-Sorbets and Morizot 2005: 141, n. 13. Huguenot 2008: 231–232 reports *skyphoi* (two-handled wine cups), *pinakes* (tablets), *lekanai* (wide, flattened, footed and lidded vases), *alabastra* (flasks for perfume or unguent), as well as the Panathenaic amphorae (vessels with narrow neck and two handles). See Kottaridi 1999: 633.

20. Kottaridi 1999: 633, n. 7; Huguenot 2003: 45 dislikes understanding the oil as functional for the burning of the pyre.

21. Guimier-Sorbets and Morizot 2005: 139–140.

22. Kottaridi 2006: 158. See Huguenot 2008: 231, n. 1799 for references to cist Tomb I at Derveni that had a pyre with a simple, podium-like architecture; it was not an enclosed structure. See also Themelis and Touratsoglou 1997: 151–155, Figures 44–45.

23. Guimier-Sorbets 2005: 137–138, 145.

24. Guimier-Sorbets 2005: 139; Guimier-Sorbets 2006: 122. Huguenot 2008: 232–233 doubts that the Macedonian dead were the literally or formally heroized, but thinks things like depictions of banquets, an image showing the dead being offered a crown,

and an image of a *naiskos*, are all signs of privilege. She argues that in the Hellenistic period, the title of "hero" was given for political and social merits, especially military, but suggests that though no proof exists of hero cults in Macedonia, the development of a military class able to have these ostentatious tombs probably favored heroization and maybe pioneered it. She thinks that tombs guaranteed memory rather than heroization in a specific way.

25. Brecoulaki 2006a: 50.

26. Andronikos 1994: 156. Palagia 2017: 415 warns that we must await further study of skeletal remains to determine if the skeletons were purposefully interred or were tomb robbers. The position of the bodies noted by Andronikos, if correct, particularly that of the one found face down, implies that these were not purposeful burials, thus making the tomb robber suggestion fairly plausible.

27. Andronikos 1994: 156.

28. Andronikos 1994: 156 believed that no funerary offerings had been deposited in the antechamber, and it is possible that the metal fragment found there came from a burial in the main chamber and was dropped in the antechamber by departing robbers.

29. Lane Fox 2011d: 8 comments that even if the piece of iron found is from a helmet—and this he says is not certain—it was found on top of ceramic roof tiles from the late Hellenistic period and so concludes it belonged to a later intruder, not an original occupant.

30. Palagia 2010: 38, n. 23 and 2017: 426, n. 43.

31. Kottaridi 2006: 158–159 suggests that the whiteness of the walls and blue of the ceiling may allude to the land of the dead. See, later in this chapter, possible connections between the typical vaulted ceiling of Macedonian tombs and Orphic belief.

32. See Kottaridi 2006: Plate 59, 2. Brecoulaki 2014 stresses the connection between bright color and expense and concludes that the use of such color in Macedonian court material culture was an indication of the *truphe* (wealth or luxury), past and future, of the occupant of the tomb.

33. Andronikos 1994: 156.

34. Kottaridi 2006: 157.

35. Kottaridi 2006: 159–161 notes the similarities in detail to the decorations found on *klinai* and observes that the throne's Paros marble resembled the color of ivory.

36. See Kottaridi 2006: Plate 61, 5.

37. See Kottaridi 2006: 163–164 and 2007: 41–43 for analysis of the painting. It featured an unprecedented and to some degree unrealistic composition (the pairs of galloping horses pull in two different directions), but one that enables the viewer to look directly at the gods. Kottaridi also points out that the colors of the Persephone/Hades painting are more muted and subtle than the decorative use of color on the walls and on the rest of the throne. See further Paspalas 2011: 193, especially n. 72, on the unconventional nature of the composition and theme and the suggestion that it relates to beliefs of the Macedonian elite about the afterlife.

38. Kottaridi 2006: 165–166, who connects the burial to Orphic beliefs, and more speculatively pictures "the queen" supervising the construction of her tomb, thus integrating her religious beliefs into the structure and outfitting of the tomb. (Huguenot 2008: 48 concludes that Macedonian tombs were probably ordered and begun considerably before the death of the occupant because of the demands of designing and constructing them, a practice that would fit Kottaridi's vision.) Kottaridi 2007: 43 considers Eurydice a priestess. There is no evidence that Eurydice was a priestess, though she could have been one (see Chapter 5). Kottaridi also suggests that the mature version of Persephone

depicted on the throne reflected Eurydice's age, whereas the Persephone of Tomb I depicted Persephone as young woman and perhaps reflected the age of the woman buried there.

39. Brecoulaki 2006a: 59, 66, also relates the light effects and gilding to aspects of divinity in Greek tradition.

40. Brecoulaki 2006a: 53.

41. Andronikos 1994: 160. Guimier-Sorbets and Morizot 2005: 145 note that tomb decorations often indicate that baldaquins were associated with the prosthesis *kline* or with the cremation urn, as was apparently the case in this tomb. Guimier-Sorbets and Morizot 2006: 126 suggest that the Eurydice tomb's thick walls allowed for a structure to hold the fabric of the baldaquin in the vault, though this supposition might be at odds with Kottaridi's idea already discussed of the blue false ceiling.

42. Kottaridi 2006: 158.

43. Rose 2001 refers to seven or more, while Palagia 2002 mentions six statuettes.

44. Andronikos 1987a: 84.

45. Guimier-Sorbets and Morizot 2006: 126–127 suggest practical considerations: a wooden *kline* would not support cremation vessels in any lasting way, whereas a stone throne could and might have seemed more prestigious.

46. Andronikos 1994: 150 seems to agree.

47. Huguenot 2003: 49–50 argues against the banqueting notion, pointing out, among other things, that there are certainly *klinai* in female burials (e.g., the woman in the antechamber of Tomb II at Vergina). Moreover, women may have reclined in some circumstances.

48. Huguenot 2008: 49.

49. Borza 1992: 308 first articulated doubts about using the Panathenaic fragments to date the construction of the tomb (seeing them as possible heirlooms). He limited their significance to the establishment of a terminus post quem. He also wondered whether she lived until 344/3; I have already discussed the likely date of her death. Huguenot 2003: 37 and 2006a: 49 points to the use of Panathenaic vases as objects of commerce (see Neils 1992: 48–50; Tiverios 2000 and 2007 on these vases and on the market for these vases) and as heirlooms and so doubts that they can be used to date the construction of the tomb or to determine gender.

50. See Kyriakou 2014: 257–258. Drougou 2011: 249, n. 24.

51. See my discussion earlier in this chapter.

52. I originally doubted that the occupant was a woman (Carney 2000a: 243) because of the absence of specific evidence, but the discovery of jewelry fragments, as I have noted, surely demonstrates that a woman was buried there, though she may possibly have been accompanied by a male.

53. Palagia 2017: 416 concludes that there is not yet enough proof that a woman was the only occupant of the tomb: she mentions that the helmet, the *kline* and the Panathenaic amphorae could mean that there was a male burial in the tomb as well (though the burial discovered in the Eucleia ditch with the remains of a young child in a metal "Panathenaic" amphora seems to confute this point).

54. See a recent discussion of this problem in Palagia 2017: 411–417. She finds compelling indications of royalty in the iconography of the lion hunt on the façade of Tomb II and to some degree in the building of the Great Tumulus over Tombs I, II, and III, but considers the funerary goods of Tombs II and III comparable to elite burials at Derveni. See further discussion and references in Carney 2015 (2001).

55. See Themelis and Touratsoglou 1997.

56. Carney 2015 (2001).

57. See Connelly 2007: 44–45 for a discussion of elite women as priests. It is likely that royal women performed ritual functions, probably in connection with a royal cult, but that does not necessitate that they were priests (Carney 2000a: 24–44, 2006: 95).

58. See discussion and references in Huguenot 2003. At Vergina there are three stone thrones (in the Eurydice, Rhomaios, and Bella Tumulus II tombs), though the Bella Tumulus throne has no stone back, only a painted one. See also Andrianou 2009: 12–29. Andrianou 2009: 129 suggests that thrones may relate to Orphic symbolism, particularly to the role of Dionysus in aiding the dead to reach the afterlife. Huguenot 2008: 115–119 argues that an understanding of thrones as seats of royal power entered Macedonian culture post-Alexander, through Achaemneid influence. Palagia 2018, suggested that Alexander adopted the throne as a royal symbol, that after his death it stood for his presence, and that the presence of the throne in subsequent periods in Macedonia indicates a royal burial.

59. Huguenot 2003: 37 points out that the Eleusis painter was active in both the second and third quarters of the fourth century and so, as with the Panathenaic vases, she doubts that the *lekythoi* can be used to date construction of the tomb. Kottaridi 2006: 157 states that the painter "reached his acme a little before midcentury," but concedes that only the amphorae are precisely dated.

60. Huguenot 2003: 37 considers this body of pottery more important, though she notes that it has not yet been published.

61. Huguenot 2008: 46–47 cautions against depending on either pottery or coins for dating a tomb.

62. Andronikos 1987a: 84; followed by Brecoulaki 2006a: 49–50.

63. On the location of Olympias' burial place, see Carney 2006: 104–105.

64. Philip's remaining wives were Audata (Carney 2000a: 57–58), Phila (Carney 2000a: 59–60), Nicesipolis (Carney 2000a: 60–61), Philinna (Carney 2000a: 61–62), Meda (Carney 2000a: 68), and Cleopatra (Carney 2000a: 72–75). Amyntas, the son of Philip's brother Perdiccas, was probably born in the mid to late 360s (Heckel 2006: 23).

65. Huguenot 2008: 45 considers the arguments for the Eurydice identification "not incontestable but plausible," but she does not first analyze other possible candidates in the course of her discussion.

66. Huguenot 2008: 45 concludes that they do not seem to, at least on the basis of current evidence.

67. Andronikos 1994: 147; Guimier-Sorbets and Morizot 2006: 127.

68. Huguenot 2008: 42, n. 62 notes that while the living can't generally see the tomb façade—concluding that that façade must be for dead—some facades seem meant to be seen by the living, at least for a time, giving as an example the great tomb at Lefkadia, which shows weather damage and repairs. Palagia 2011: 479 and 2014: 383 asserts that the tomb facades remained visible for generations.

69. Huguenot 2008: 44.

70. Miller 1993: 9–14 discusses the possible prototypes and emphasizes the illusionary nature of the facades and of Macedonian architecture generally. See also Guimier-Sorbets and Morizot 2006: 124. Palagia 2011: 479 favors an interpretation of them as imitations of palace propylaea.

71. Andronikos 1987b: *passim*; 1994: 147–149. Andronikos interprets two large cist tombs (at Katerini and Palatitsia) as midway points of this evolution. The Katerini tomb had no vault or entry door, but two rooms and a door connecting the rooms. (Paspalas 2011: 192, n. 65 doubts that this tomb dates as early as Andronikos once believed it did.)

The tomb at Palatitsia was divided into two parts by square pillars. Both tombs were covered by shorter slabs, apparently in the vain hope of making the roof stronger. However, Andronikos also connects the Macedonian tomb form to beliefs about the afterlife, whereas Haddad 2015 seems narrowly focused on engineering as a motivator.

72. See Themelis and Touratsoglou 1997: 28–39 and Fig. 6 (a diagram of the objects in situ in the tomb).

73. Andronikos 1994: 153–154, who suggests a connection between the more archaic society of Macedonia and this practice and wonders if the practice also related to a greater desire to please the dead and a stronger belief in life after death.

74. Huguenot 2008: 1: 234–236.

75. Miller 1993: 17–19 warns about overconfidence in asserting any particular understanding of the nature of beliefs and thus the function of the tombs and in assuming these beliefs did not change over time.

76. Palagia 2014: 383 is convincing here.

77. Huguenot 2008: 233–234 suggests this, associating it with Orphic belief, noting the appearance in many tombs (not in Eurydice's tomb but in, for instance, Tomb II's antechamber) of golden stars, apparently once decorating fabric attached to the ceiling. Huguenot connects the symbolism of the stars to transition from the chthonian world to the heavenly.

78. Hatzopoulos 2006: especially 133–138. He also focuses (2006: 134) on the cults of Demeter and Persephone, citing Andronikos' discussion of the popularity of the cult of Hades in Macedonia and noting that Persephone can intercede with judges in the underworld. S. G. Cole 2003: 194–197 discusses the frightening goddess/queen of the underworld, Persephone.

79. Guimier-Sorbets 2002: 162–163 suggests that this scene implies a connection to heroization of the dead as well as to the possibility that the occupant was an initiate and that this, in turn, was a kind of female heroization. See my earlier discussion for doubts about literal heroization in the context of these tombs.

80. Miller 1993: 18 notes that it, unlike other tombs, does not suggest a "contained environment" but rather invites the viewer into the afterlife, which is behind, somehow, the final wall.

81. See Palagia 2016: 79–87 for a discussion of the dominance of Persephone, queen of the underworld, in Macedonian funerary art. She includes the tomb of Persephone at Vergina (Tomb I), the Eurydice tomb, and the Tomb of the Palmettes at Lefkadia. Franks 2012: 77–97 discusses various readings of the landscape of the frieze of Tomb II; she finds evidence that it can be understood as sacred but does not suggest that it relates to the afterlife.

82. See my lengthier discussion in Carney 2015 (2007). See also Lapatin 2001: 117, n. 198 and Schultz 2007.

83. See Schultz 2007.

84. Schultz 2007.

85. Schultz 2007: 213–219.

86. See Palagia 2010: 35–36 for references to the various attempts to correct the lacuna in the text, though not necessarily for her conclusions.

87. *Contra* Lane Fox 1974: 504 and Palagia 2010 who argue, on different grounds, that the statue did "depict" Philip's last wife. Lane Fox, while recognizing that the image could represent Philip's mother, suggests that Philip might, instead, have included his last wife because he was so enthusiastic about her. Palagia sees the inclusion of both

Olympias and Cleopatra/Eurydice as a "gesture of reconciliation" directed at Olympias and Alexander (Palagia 2010: 37).

88. Heckel 1981b: 54.

89. Schultz 2007: 208–209.

90. Schultz 2007: 209–210 makes a convincing case that the Philippeum could have been completed by summer 336 and that Philip would have wanted to complete it in time for the Olympic games of that year, thus highlighting his presentation for an international audience.

91. See discussion and references in Carney 2015 (2007): 66.

92. Schultz 2007: 230, n. 63 notes that the oath the members of the Corinthian League had to swear not to overthrow Philip's kingdom or that of his descendants. As he observes, the Philippeum witnesses this oath, in effect, of obedience to a dynasty.

93. See Carney 2015 (2007): 67–70.

94. On the long and complicated career of Olympias, see Carney 2006, especially 19–41.

95. See Carney 2000b: 24, n. 17; 2015 (2007): 83, n. 26; and Mirón Pérez 1998: 223. Mirón Pérez considers the possibility that the move was intended as an honor meant to associate the two images not only with Hera but also with images of other gods and heroes placed in the same structure, though she also reflects on the possibility that it could have been a move of a negative sort meant to destroy the dynastic image the Philippeum had created and intended to disassociate the women from power. Whereas I once preferred a late fourth-century date (which did not really explain the removal of Eurydice), I now think the removal happened closer to Pausanias' own day.

96. The wife of Nestor and daughter of Clymenus (*Od.* 3.451–452); the wife of Creon in Sophocles' *Antigone* (1183–1243); the mother of Laomedon and daughter of a king (Apollodorus 3.12.3); the daughter of Lacedaemon, wife of Acrisius the king of Argos and mother of Danaë; one of the daughters of king Amphiarus of Argos (Paus. 5.17.7–8).

97. Bremmer 1991: 16. Tataki 198: 354, though the name does not appear in Beroea until the second century, describes it as "widely diffused in Macedonia." She includes it in the category of "names local to Macedonia." See Tataki 1988: 354, n. 181 for citations from various parts of Macedonia.

98. Plato (*Symp.* 179 d–e) tells the story of Orpheus' visit to the underworld in a failed attempt to save his unnamed wife, as does Euripides' *Alcestis* 356–360. Pseudo-Moschus (a second-century-BCE poet) 3.115–125 is the earliest version that names Orpheus' wife "Eurydice." Ovid (*Metamorphoses* 10.1–85) names her Eurydice, as do Virgil (*Georgics* 4.453–527) and Pausanias (9.30.6). See the discussion of the evolution of the Orpheus myth in Bowra 1952; Lee 1965; Sansone 1985: 254; and Bremmer 1991. Lee 1965: 406, n. 15 points out that the name is also associated with the queen of Hades.

99. Bremmer 1991: 16–17; Molina Marín 2018: 88.

100. On significant names and name-changing for royal women, see Greenwalt 1999a and Carney 2000a: 32–34, 58, 62–63, 74. Simply because Olympias, according to Plutarch, was known by four names, we cannot assume that marriage was the reason for all or perhaps any of her name changes, or that she herself had nothing to do with the changes.

101. See Greenwalt 1999a.

102. Justin (9.7.13) mentions only one other name, whereas Plutarch knows of three others (Plut. *Mor.* 401a–b). See also Heckel 1981.

103. Badian 1982a: 100 suggests that, though his birth name had been held by earlier Argeads, the change was made because none of those so named had been king and because he needed to stress his connection to his father. Greenwalt 1999a: 454–458 deduces

from Curtius' account that the name change happened not at some ceremony associated with his accession, but a little before that occasion, as part of the partisan effort that brought him to the throne, and so Greenwalt interprets it as an attempt to recast him as a more public figure. Greenwalt rightly observes that while this is the only known male example of a name change, name choice had long had political significance for royal males, particularly in the absence (until nearly the end of the Argead era) of the use of a royal title.

104. Badian 1982a: 101–103, though the best Persian evidence for name changes is for men, not women.

105. So Badian 1982a: 104–105 *contra* Berve 1926b: 229 and Heckel 1983: 41. Badian points out that we have only Photius' summary of this passage, not Arrian himself, that Arrian himself made mistakes about names, and that Photius certainly does.

106. Ellis 1976: 47–48 seems to assume that Philip would only have changed his wife's name to that of his mother under compulsion, perhaps because Ellis accepted the "bad Eurydice" story (see Chapter 4).

107. *Contra* Badian 1982a: 105–106. See Chapter 3.

108. Berve 1926b: 213; Heckel 1978: 155–156, who attributes the information to Ptolemy, and believes that Arrian never made a mistake in citing information from Ptolemy. He concludes (followed by Prestianni-Giallombardo 1981) that both names were hers, but believes that her first name was Cleopatra and that it was changed to Eurydice, whereas Berve (and others; see Heckel 1978: 156, n. 6 for references) thought the reverse was true.

109. Tarn 1948: 2: 262, n. 1 and Badian 1982a.

110. Heckel 1983–1984: 196 suggests this possibility.

111. Badian 1982a: 103 rightly points out that the idea that she could have changed it is merely speculation.

112. Macurdy 1932: 25 concludes that the name "had a tendency to become dynastic," on the basis of this slender evidence. Her suggestion is particularly unconvincing because she assumes that there was only one "queen" at a time in the Macedonian court.

113. Badian 1982a: 106–107, *contra* Heckel 1978.

114. Heckel 1978: 157 tries to solve this problem by arguing that "Eurydice" was "only gradually developing into a dynastic name" and practice was not yet standard.

115. So Bosworth 1980: 282.

116. *Contra* Heckel 1983: 41.

117. See Carney 1987b; 2000a: 132–137.

118. Badian 1982a: 101 is probably correct about this.

119. Badian 1982a: 101 oddly refers to Philip's mother Eurydice as "the most recent non-controversial Macedonian queen no longer alive." Eurydice was (see Chapters 3 and 4) very controversial indeed. Moreover, he considers any possible connection between name choice and Adea Eurydice's political role extremely speculative, despite that fact that she virtually immediately began to act in an aggressive way.

120. Greenwalt 1999a: 459–460 rejects the idea that either Perdiccas or the army chose her name. I agree but not because I doubt, as he does, that the army knew much about Philip's mother and her role (the remains at Vergina might suggest the opposite—see Chapter 5) but because it is difficult to imagine an assortment of soldiers collectively coming up with the idea.

121. Badian 1982a: 101, n. 9 considers her birth name somehow undignified and unroyal, as well as likely Illyrian, like that of her mother. Heckel 1983: 40–41 argues convincingly that the name is not Illyrian and not inappropriate, translating it as meaning

not "Sweetie," as Badian did, but "fearless," an appropriate choice, as Heckel notes, for Cynnane to have made for her daughter.

122. Heckel 1983: 41, *contra* Badian 1982a: 101, 106, asserts that it was. Her unusual actions and military image do not suggest any desire to reject her partially Illyrian origins.

123. *Contra* Greenwalt 1999: 460–462. Olympias was, at the time, back in Molossia, her homeland, and Alexander IV, her grandson, was a newborn or possibly not yet born. Doubtless Adea Eurydice planned from the start, as her mother probably had, to oppose the other side of the royal family, but her first problems were with the generals she had to deal with in person, not with the distant Olympias.

124. Greenwalt 1999a: 457 speaks of royal names as "political symbols" and 1999a: 462 admires her use of the past to master the present.

125. See Marquardt 1985.

126. Carney 1993b: 315–316.

# Bibliography

Akamatis, I. M. 2011. "Pella." In Lane Fox 2011e, 393–408.

Anatonaccio, C. 2003. "Hybridity and the Cultures within Greek Culture." In C. Dougherty and L. Kurke (eds.), *The Cultures within Ancient Greek Culture: Contact, Conflict, Collaboration*, 57–74. Cambridge.

Andrianou, D. 2009. *The Furniture and Furnishings of Ancient Greek Houses and Tombs.* Cambridge.

Andronik(c)os, M. 1984. *Vergina: The Royal Tombs and the Ancient City.* Athens.

Andronikos, M. 1987a. "Βεργίνα Ανασκαφή 1987." *AEMTH* 1: 81–88.

Andronikos, M. 1987b. "Some Reflections on the Macedonian Tombs." *BSA* 82: 1–16.

Andronikos, M. 1987c. "Η ζωγραφική στην αρχαία Μακεδονία." *AE* 126: 363–382.

Andronikos, M. 1988. "Βεργίνα Ανασκαφή 1988 στο νεκροταφείο." *AEMTH* 2: 1–4.

Andronikos, M. 1994. "The 'Macedonian' Tombs." In R. Ginouvès (ed.), *Macedonia from Philip II to the Roman Conquest*, 145–190. Princeton, NJ.

Anson, E. M. 1997. "Ethnicity and the Greek Language." *Glotta* 85: 5–30.

Anson, E. M. 2009. "Philip II, Amyntas Perdicca, and Macedonian Royal Succession." *Historia* 58: 276–286.

Archibald, Z. H. 2010. "Macedonia and Thrace." In Roisman and Worthington 2010, 326–341.

Archibald, Z. H. 2013. *Ancient Economies of the Northern Aegean, Fifth to First Centuries BC.* Oxford: Oxford University Press.

Badian E. 1982a. "Eurydice." In W. L. Adams and E. N. Borza (eds.), *Philip II, Alexander the Great Philip II, Alexander the Great, and the Macedonian Heritage*, 99–110. Washington, DC.

Badian, E. 1982b. "Greeks and Macedonians." *Studies in the History of Art* 10: 33–51.

Baughn, E. P. 2013. *Couched in Death: Klinai and Identity in Anatolia and Beyond.* Madison.

Beloch, J. 1912–27. *Griechische Geschichte.*, 2nd edn, 4 vols., 8 parts. Strasburg, Leipzig, and Berlin.

Berve, H. 1926a. *Das Alexanderreich auf prosopographischer Grundlage*, Vol. 1. Munich

Berve, H. 1926b. *Das Alexanderreich auf prosopographischer Grundlage*, Vol. 2, Munich.

Billows, R. A. 1990. *Antigonos the One-Eyed and the Creation of the Hellenistic State*. Berkeley.

Bissa, E. M. A. 2009. *Governmental Intervention in Foreign Trade in Archaic and Classical Greece*. Leiden: Brill.

Blundell, M. W. 1989. *Helping Friends and Harming Enemies: A Study in Sophocles and Ethics*. Cambridge.

Boatwright, M. T. 1991. "Plancia Magna of Perge: Women's Roles and Status in Roman Asia Minor." In S. B. Pomeroy (ed.), *Women's History and Ancient History*, 249–272. Chapel Hill.

Borg, B. E. 2005. "Eunomia or 'Make Love Not War'? Meidian Personfications Reconsidered." In E. Stafford and J. Herrin (eds.), *Personification in the Greek World: From Antiquity to Byzantium*, 193–210. Aldershot.

Borza, E. N. 1992 (paperback ed.). *In the Shadow of Olympus: The Emergence of Macedon*. Princeton.

Borza, E. N. 1995a. "The Natural Resources of Early Macedonia." In C. G. Thomas (ed.), *Makedonika*, 37–56. Claremont, CA.

Borza, E. N. 1995b. "Timber and Politics in the Ancient World: Macedon and the Greeks." In C. G. Thomas (ed.), *Makedonika*, 85–112. Claremont, CA.

Borza, E. N., and O. Palagia. 2008. "The Chronology of the Macedonian Royal Tombs at Vergina." *Jahrbuch des Deutschen Archäologischen Instituts* 122: 81–125.

Bosworth, A. B. 1971. "Philip II and Upper Macedonia." *CQ* 21, 1: 93–105.

Bosworth, A. B. 1980. *A Historical Commentary on Arrian's History of Alexander*. Oxford.

Bosworth, A. B. 2010. "The Argeads and the Phalanx." In E. D. Carney and D. Ogden (eds.), *Philip II and Alexander the Great: Father and Son, Lives and Afterlives*, 91–102.

Bowra, C. M. 1952. "Orpheus and Eurydice." *CQ* 46: 113–126.

Brecoulaki, H. 2006a. *La Peinture Funéraire De Macédoine, Emplois et Fonctions de la Couleur IVe—Iie s. av. J.-C.*, Vols. 1 and 2. Meletemata 48. Athens.

Brecoulaki, H. 2006b. "La peinture funéraire en Macédoine." In A.-M. Guimier-Sorbets, M. B. Hatzopoulos, and Y. Morizot (eds.), *Rois, Cités, Nécropoles: Institutions, Rites Et Monuments en Macédoine*. Meletemata 45, 47–61. Athens.

Brecoulaki, H. 2014. "'Precious Colours' in Ancient Greek Polychromy and Painting: Material Aspects and Symbolic Values." *Revue Archéologique* 57: 3–35.

Bremmer, J. 1991. "Orpheus from Guru to Gay." In P. Borgeaud (ed.), *Orphisme et Orphée, en l'honneur de Jean Rudhardt*, 13–30. Geneva.

Brice, L. J. 2011. "Philip II, Alexander the Great, and the Question of the Macedonian Revolution in Military Affairs.'" *AncW* 42, 2: 137–147.

Buckler, J. 1980. *The Theban Hegemony*. Harvard Historical Studies 98. Cambridge, MA.

Burkert, W. 1985. *Greek Religion*. Oxford.

Carey, C. (trans.) 2000. *Aeschines*. Austin.

Carney, E. D. 1987a. "Olympias." *AncSoc* 18: 35–62.

Carney, E. D. 1987b. "The Career of Adea Eurydice." *Historia* 36: 496–505.

Carney, E. D. 1991. "'What's in a Name?': The Emergence of a Title for Royal Women in the Hellenistic Period." In S. B. Pomeroy (ed.), *Women's History and Ancient History*, 157–172. Chapel Hill.

Carney, E. D. 1993a. "Olympias and the Image of the Virago." *Phoenix* 47: 29–55.

Carney, E. D. 1993b. "Foreign Influence and the Changing Role of Royal Macedonian Women." *AM* 5, 1: 313–323.

Carney, E. D. 1994. "Arsinoë before she was Philadelphus." *AHB* 8, 4: 123–131.

Carney, E. D. 1995. "Women and *Basileia*: Legitimacy and Female Political Action in Macedonia." *CJ* 90, 4: 367–391.

Carney, E. D. 2000a. *Women and Monarchy in Macedonia*. Norman.

Carney, E. D. 2000b. "The Initiation of Cult for Royal Macedonian Women." *CP* 95: 21–43.

Carney, E. D. 2004. "Women and Military Leadership in Macedonia." *AncW* 35: 184–195.

Carney, E. D. 2006. *Olympias, Mother of Alexander the Great*. New York.

Carney, E. D. 2010a. "Putting Women in Their Place: Women in Public under Philip II and Alexander III and the Last Argeads." In E. D. Carney and D. Ogden (eds.), *Philip II, Alexander III: Father and Son, Lives and Afterlives*, 43–54. New York.

Carney, E. D. 2010b. "Women in Macedonia." In Roisman and Worthington 2010, 409–427.

Carney, E. D. 2011. "Being Royal and Female in the Early Hellenistic Period." In A. Erskine and L. Llewellyn-Jones (eds.), *Creating the Hellenistic World*, 195–220. Swansea.

Carney, E. D. 2013. *Arsinoë of Egypt and Macedon: A Royal Life*. Oxford and New York.

Carney, E. D. 2015 (1980) "Alexander the Lyncestian: The Disloyal Opposition" and "Afterword." In E. D. Carney, *King and Court in Ancient Macedonia: Rivalry, Treason and Conspiracy*, 127–140. Swansea, UK.*

Carney, E. D. 2015 (2007). "The Philippeum, Women, and the Formation of Dynastic Image." and "Afterword." In E. D. Carney, *King and Court in Ancient Macedonia: Rivalry, Treason and Conspiracy*, 61–90. Swansea, UK.*

Carney, E. D. 2015 (1992). "The Politics of Polygamy: Olympias, Alexander and the Murder of Philip" and "Afterword." In E. D. Carney, *King and Court in Ancient Macedonia: Rivalry, Treason and Conspiracy*, 167–190. Swansea, UK.*

Carney, E. D. 2015 (2001). "Were the Tombs under the Great Tumulus at Vergina Royal?" and "Afterword." In E. D. Carney, *King and Court in Ancient Macedonia: Rivalry, Treason and Conspiracy*, 109–126. Swansea, UK.*

Carney, E. D. 2015 (1983). "Regicide in Macedonia" and "Afterword." In E. D. Carney, *King and Court in Ancient Macedonia: Rivalry, Treason and Conspiracy*, 155–165. Swansea, UK.*

Carney, E. D. 2017. "Argead Marriage Alliances." In S. Müller, T. Howe, and R. Rollinger (eds.), *The History of the Argeads, New Perspectives*, 139–150. Wiesbaden.

Carney, E. D. 2018. "Royal Women as Succession Advocates." In T. Howe, and F. Pownall (eds.), *Greek and Roman Sources: From History to Historiography*. Swansea, UK.

Cawkwell, G. L. 1978. *Philip of Macedon*. London.

Chilidis, K. 2008. "New Knowledge Versus Consensus—A Critical Note on the Their Relationship Based on the Debate Concerning the Use of Barrel Vault in Macedonian Tombs." *European Journal of Archaeology* 11: 75–103.

Christesen, P., and S. C. Murray. 2010. "Macedonian Religion." In Roisman and Worthington 2010, 428–445.

Cole, J. W. 1974. "Perdiccas and Athens." *Phoenix* 28: 55–72.

Cole, S. G. 2003. "Landscapes of Dionysos and Elysian Fields." In M. B. Cosmopoulos (ed.), *Greek Mysteries: The Archaeology and Ritual of Ancient Greek Secret Cults*, 193–217. London.

Comploi, S. 2002. "Frauendarstellungen bei Fremdvölkern in den 'Historiae Philippicae' des Pompeius Trogus/Justin." In C. Ulf and R. Rollinger (eds.), *Geschlechter, Frauen, Fremde Ethnien in Antiker Ethnographie, Theorie und Realität*, 331–359. Innsbruck.

Connelly, J. B. 2007. *Portrait of a Priestess: Women and Ritual in Ancient Greece*. Princeton.

Corvisier, J.-N. 2002. *Philippe II de Macédoine*. Paris.

De Shong Meador, B. 2001. *Inanna, Lady of Largest Heart: Poems of the Sumerian High Priestess*. Austin.

De Shong Meador, B. 2010. *Princess, Priestess, Poet: The Sumerian Temple Hymns of Enheduanna*. Austin.

Dell, H. J. 1980. "Philip and Macedonia's Northern Neighbors." In M. B. Hatzopoulos and L. D. Loukopoulos (eds.), *Philip of Macedon*, 90–99. Athens.

Dickey, E. 2007. *Ancient Greek Scholarship: A Guide to Finding, Reading, and Understanding Scholia, Commentaries, Lexica, and Grammatical Treatises*. Oxford.

Dillon, M. 2002. *Girls and Women in Greek Religion*. New York and London.

Dillon, S. 2007. "Portraits of Women in the Early Hellenistic Period." In P. Schultz and R. von den Hoff (eds.), *Early Hellenistic Portraiture: Image, Style, Context*, 63–83. Cambridge.

Dillon, S. 2010. *The Female Portrait Statue in the Greek World*. Cambridge.

Dilts, M. R. 1992. *Scholia in Aeschinem*. Stuttgart and Leipzig.

Dilts, M. R. 1997. *Aeschinis Orationes*. Stuttgart and Leipzig.

Dowden, Ken. 2006. *Zeus*. London.

Drougou, S. 2011. "Vergina—The Ancient City of Aegae." In Lane Fox 2011e, 243–256.

Drougou, S., and C. Saatsoglou-Paliadeli. 2000. *Vergina: Wandering through the Archaeological Site*. Athens.

Dušanić, S. 1980. "Plato's Academy and Timotheus' Policy, 365–354 B.C." *Chiron* 10: 111–144.

Dušanić, S. 1980–1981. "Athens, Crete and the Aegean after 366/5 B.C." *Talanta* 12–13: 7–29.

Dzino, D. 2008. "'The People Who Are Illyrians and Celts': Strabo and the Identities of the 'Barbarians' from Illyricum." *Arheološki vestnik* 59: 371–380.

Dzino, D. 2012. "Contesting Identities of Pre-Roman Illyricum." *Ancient West & East* 11: 69–95.

Engels, J. 2010. "Macedonians and Greeks." In Roisman and Worthington 2010, 81–98.

Ellis, J. R. 1969. "Amyntas II, Illyria and Olynthos 393/2–380/79." *Makedonika* 9: 1–8.

Ellis, J. R. 1973. "The Step-Brothers of Philip II." *Historia* 22: 350–354.

Ellis, J. R. 1976. *Philip II and Macedonian Imperialism*. London.

Emberger, Peter. 2008. "Schwache Männer—starke Frauen? Große Frauengestalten des Altertums im Geschichtswerk des Pompeius Trogus / Iustinus" *Grazer Beiträge* 26: 31–49.

Errington, R. M. 1990. *A History of Macedonia*. Berkeley.

Erskine, A. 2002. "O Brother, Where Art Thou? Tales of Kinship and Diplomacy." In D. Ogden (ed.), *The Hellenistic World: New Perspectives*, 97–116. London.

Faklaris, P. B. Forthcoming. "Προβλήματα του λεγομένου 'τάφου της Ευρυδίκης' στη Βεργίνα." *Archaiologikon Deltion*.

Fernández Nieto, F. J. 2006. "La designción del successor en el antiguo reino de Macedonia." In V. Alonso Troncoso (ed.), *ΔΙΑΔΟΧΟΣ ΤΝΣ ΒΑΣΙΛΕΙΑΣ: La figura del successor en la realeza helenística*, 29–44. Madrid.

Flower, M. A. 1994. *Theopompus of Chios: History and Rhetoric in the Fourth Century BC*. Oxford.

Frank, R. 2018. "A Roman Olympias: Powerful Women in the *Historiae Philippicae* of Pompeius Trogus." In T. Howe and F. Pownall (eds.), *From History to Historiography: Ancient Macedonians in the Greek and Roman Sources*. Swansea, UK.

Franks, H. M. 2012. *Hunters, Heroes, Kings: The Frieze of Tomb II at Vergina*. Princeton, NJ.

Fündling, J. 2014. *Philipp II. Von Makedonien*. Darmstadt.

Georgiados, A. 1997. *Plutarch's Pelopidas: A Historical and Philological Commentary*. Stuttgart and Leipzig.

Geyer, F. 1930. *Makedonien bis zur Thronbesteigung Philipps II*. Historische Zeitschrift Beiheft 19. Munich.

Goukowsky, P. 1993. "Les maisons princières de Macédoine de Perdiccas II à Philippe II." In P. Goukowsky and C. Brixhe (eds.), *Hellenica Symmkia: Histoire, Archéologie, Epigraphie*. Etudes de Archéologie Classique 3, 43–66, Nancy:.

Graninger, D. 2010. "Macedonia and Thessaly." In Roisman and Worthington 2010, 306–325.

Greaney, G. L. 2005. *De Falsa Legatione/On the False Embassy. Aeschines. A Translation with Rhetorical Notes*. Lewiston, NY.

Greenwalt, W. S. 1984. "The Search for Arrhidaeus." *AncW* 10: 69–77.

Greenwalt, W. S. 1988 "Amyntas III and the Political Stability of Argead Macedonia." *AncW* 18: 35–44.

Greenwalt, W. S. 1989 "Polygamy and Succession in Argead Macedonia." *Arethusa* 22: 19–45.

Greenwalt, W. S. 1996. "Proto-Historical Argead Women: Lan (ice?), Cleonice, Cleopatra, Prothoe, Niconoe." *AHB* 10: 47–50.

Greenwalt, W. S. 1999a. "Argead Name Changes." *AM* 6, 1: 453–462.

Greenwalt, W. S. 1999b. "Why Pella?" *Historia* 48: 158–183.

Greenwalt, W. S. 2007. "The Development of a Middle Class in Macedonia." *AM* 7: 87–96.

Greenwalt, W. S. 2008 "Philip and Olympias on Samothrace." In T. Howe and J. Reames (eds.), *Macedonian Legacies: Studies in Ancient Macedonian History and Culture in Honor of Eugene N. Borza*, 79–106. Claremont, CA.

Greenwalt, W. S. 2010. "Macedonia, Illyria and Epirus" In Roisman and Worthington 2010, 279–305.

Griffith, G. T. 1979. "Part Two." In N. G. L. Hammond and G. T. Griffith, *A History of Macedonia*. Vol. 2. Oxford.

Grzybek, E. 1986. "Zu Philipp II und Alexander dem Grossen." *AM* 4: 223–229.

Guimier-Sorbets, A.-M. 2001. "Mobilier et décor des tombes macédoniennes." In R Frei-Stolba and K. Gex (eds.), *Recherches récentes sur le monde hellénistique. Actes du Colloque en l'honneur de Pierre Ducrey, Lausanne 20–21 novembre 1998*, 217–229. Bern.

Guimier-Sorbets, A.-M. 2002. "Architecture et décor funéraires, de la Grèce à l'Egypte: L'expression du statut héroïque du défunt." In C. Muller and F. Prost (eds.), *Identités et cultures dans le monde méditerranéen antique, Mélanges F. Croissant*, 159–180. Paris.

Guimier-Sorbets, A-M., and Y. Morizot. 2005. "Des bûchers de Vergina aux hydries de Hadra, découvertes récentes sur la crémation en Macédoine et à Alexandrie." *Ktema* 30: 137–152.

Guimier-Sorbets, A-M., and Y. Morizot, Y. 2006. "Construire l'identité du mort: L'architecture funéraire en Macédoine." In A.-M. Guimier-Sorbets, M. B. Hatzopoulos, and Y. Morizot (eds.), *Rois, Cités, Nécropoles: Institutions, Rites Et Monuments en Macédoine*. Meletemata 45, 117–130. Athens.

Günther, L.-M. 1993. "Witwen in der griechishen Antike—Zwischen *oikos* und *polis*." *Historia* 42: 308–325.

Haddad, N. A. 2015. "Critical Assessment of the Barrel Vault Geometry and Structure of the Oldest Macedonian Tomb of Eurydice in Vergina." *Mediterranean Archaeology and Archaeometry* 15, 2: 143–162.

Hall, Jonathan M. 1997. *Ethnic Identity in Greek Antiquity*. Cambridge.

Hall, Johnathan. 2001. "Contested Ethnicities: Perceptions of Macedonia within Evolving Definitions of Greek Identity." In I. Malkin (ed.), *Ancient Perceptions of Greek Ethnicity*, 159–186. Washington, DC.

Hall, Johnathan. 2002. *Hellenicity: Between Ethnicity and Culture*. Chicago.

Hammond, N. G. L. 1979. "Part One." In N. G. L. Hammond and G. T. Griffith, *A History of Macedonia*. Vol. 2, 3–200. Oxford.

Hammond, N. G. L. 1991. "The Royal Tombs at Vergina: Evolution and Identities." *BSA* 86: 69–82.

Hammond, N. G. L. 1994. *Philip of Macedon*. Baltimore.

Harders, A.-C. 2014. "Königinnen ohne König. Zur Rolle und Bedeutung der Witwen Alexanders im Zeitalter der Diadochen." In H. Hauben and A. Meeus (eds.), *The Age of the Successors and the Creation of the Hellenistic Kingdoms (323–276 B.C.)*, 345–378. Leuven.

Harris, E. M. 1989. "Iphicrates at the Court of Cotys." *AJP* 110, 2: 264–271.

Harris, E. M. 1995. *Aeschines and Athenian Politics*. Oxford.

Hatzopoulos, M. B. 1982. "The Oleveni Inscription and the Dates of Philip II's Reign." In W. L. Adams and E. N. Borza (eds.), *Philip II, Alexander the Great and the Macedonian Heritage*, 21–42. Lanham, MD:.

Hatzopoulos, M. B. 1985. "La Béotie et la Macédoine à l'époque de l'hégémonie thébaine: Le point de vue macédonien." In P. Roesch and G. Argoud (eds.), *La Béotie antique*, 247–257. Paris.

Hatzopoulos, M. B. 1986. "Succession and Regency in Classical Macedonia." *AM* 4: 279–292.

Hatzopoulos, M. B. 1987. "Strepsa: A Reconsideration." In M. B. Hatzopoulos and L. D. Loukopoulou, *Two Studies in Ancient Macedonian Topography*, Meletemata 3, 40–44. Athens.

Hatzopoulos, M. B. 1989(1985–86). "Ἡ ὁμηρεία τοῦ Φιλίππου τοῦ ʿΑμύντα στις Θήβες." *Archaiognosia* 4: 37–57.

Hatzopoulos, M. B. 1996. *Macedonian Institutions Under the Kings. Vol. 1 and 2.* Meletemata 22. Athens.

Hatzopoulos, M. B. 2006. "De vie à trépas: Rites de passage, lamelles dionysiaques et tombes macédoniennes." In A.-M. Guimier-Sorbets, M. B. Hatzopoulos, and Y. Morizot (eds.), *Rois, Cités, Nécropoles: Institutions, Rites Et Monuments en Macédoine*. Meletemata 45, 131–141. Athens.

Hatzopoulos, M. B. 2007. "Perception of the Self and the Other: The Case of Macedonia." *AM* 7: 51–66.

Hatzopoulos, M. 2008. "The Burial of the Dead (at Vergina), or The Unending Controversy on the Identity of the Occupants of Tomb II." *Tekmeria* 9: 91–118.

Hatzopoulos, M. B. 2011a. "Macedonia and Macedonians." In Lane Fox 2011e, 43–50.

Hatzopoulos, M. B. 2011b. "Macedonians and Other Greeks." In Lane Fox 2011e, 51–78.

Heckel, W. 1978. "Cleopatra or Eurydice?" *Phoenix* 32: 155–158.

Heckel, W. 1980. "Marsyas of Pella, Historian of Macedon." *Hermes* 108: 444–462.

Heckel, W. 1981a. "Polyxena, the Mother of Alexander the Great." *Chiron* 11: 79–96.

Heckel, W. 1981b. "Philip and Olympias (337/6 B.C.)." In G. S. Shrimpton and D. J. McCargar (eds.), *Classical Contributions: Studies in Honour of M. F. McGregor*, 51–57. Locust Valley, NY.

Heckel, W. 1983. "Adea-Eurydike." *Glotta* 61 (1–2): 40–42.

Heckel W. 1983–84. "Kynnane the Illyrian." *RSA* 13–14: 193–200.

Heckel, W. 2002. "The Politics of Distrust: Alexander and His Successors." In D. Ogden (ed.), *The Hellenistic World: New Perspectives*, 81–96. London.

Heckel, W. 2006. *Who's Who in the Age of Alexander the Great*. Malden, MA.

Heinrichs, J. 2012. "Münzen als Krisensymptome? Zur makedonischen Silverprägung unter Amyntas III und Perdikkas III (ca. 393–359)." *ZPE* 181: 117–139.

Herman, G. 1987. *Ritualised Friendship and the Greek City*. Cambridge.

Heskel, Julia. 1996. "Philip II and Argaios. A Pretender's Story." In R. W. Wallace and E. M. Harris (eds.), *Transitions to Empire: Essays in Greco-Roman History, 360–146 B.C. in Honor of E. Badian*, 37–56. Norman.

Heskel, Julia. 1997. *The North Aegean Wars, 371–360 BC*. Historia Einzelschriften 102. Stuttgart.

Hoffmann, O. 1906. *Die Makedonen*. Göttingen.

Hornblower, S. 1991. *The Greek World 479–323 BC*. London and New York.

Howe, Timothy. 2018. "A Founding Mother? Eurydike I, Philip II and Macedonian Royal Mythology." In T. Howe and F. Pownall (eds.), *Ancient Macedonians in the Greek and Roman Sources: From History to Historiography*. Swansea, UK.

Huguenot, C. 2003. "Les trônes dans les tombes macédoniennes: Réflexions sur les coutumes funéraires de l'élite macédonienne" In B. Boissavit-Camus, F. Chausson, and H. Inglebert (eds.), *La mort du souverain entre Antiquité et haut Moyen Age*, 29–51. Paris.

Huguenot, C. 2008. *La Tombe aux Érotes et la Tombe d'Amarynthos, Architecture funéraire et presence macédonienne en Gréce centrale*. Eretria 19, Vols. 1 and 2. Lausanne.

Hunter, V. 1989. "Women's Authority in Classical Athens: The Example of Kleobule and Her Son (Dem. 27–29)." *Echos du Monde Classique/Classical Views* 33: 39–48.

Jacoby, F. 1962. *Die Fragmente der griechischen Historiker*, Vol. 2B, 1 and 2. Leiden.

Jones, C. P. 1999. *Kinship Diplomacy in the Ancient World*. Cambridge, MA.

Kallet, L. 1983. "Iphicrates, Timotheos and Athens, 371–360 B.C." *GRBS* 24, 3: 239–252.

Kapetanopoulos, E. 1994. "Sirras." *AncW* 25, 1: 15–26.

Keesling, C. M. 2017. "Greek Statue Terms Revisited: What Does ἀνδριάς Mean?" *GRBS* 57: 837–861.

King, C. 2010. "Macedonian Kingship and Other Political Institutions." In Roisman and Worthington 2010, 373–391.

King, C. 2018. *Ancient Macedonia*. New York.

Knecht, R. J. 1998. *Catherine De'Medici*. New York.

Konishi, Haruo. 1993. "Muse Goddess of Literacy." *LCM* 18: 116–121.

Kosmetatou, E. 2004. "Rhoxane's Dedications to Athena Polias." *ZPE* 146: 75–80.

Kottaridi, A. 1999 "Βασιλικές πυρές στη νεκρόπολη των Αιγών." *AM* 6: 631–642.

Kottaridi, A. 2001. "Το έθιμο της καύσης και οι Μακεδόνες. Σκέψεις με αφορμή τα ευρήματα της νεκρόπολης των Αιγών." In N. C. Stampolides (ed.), *Καύσεις στην εποχή του Χαλκού και την πρώιμη του Σιδήρου*, 359–371. Athens.

Kottaridi, A. 2002. "Discovering Aegae, the Old Macedonian Capital." In M. Stamatopolou and M. Yeroulanou (eds.), *Excavating Classical Culture: Recent Archaeological Discoveries in Greece*, 75–81. Oxford.

Kottaridi, A. 2004. "The Lady of Aigai." In D. Pandermalis (ed.), *Alexander the Great: Treasures from an Epic Era of Hellenism*, 139–148. New York.

Kottaridi, A. 2006. "Couleur et signification: L'usage de la couleur dans la tombe de la reine Eurydice." In A.-M. Guimier-Sorbets, M. B. Hatzopoulos, and Y. Morizot (eds.), *Rois, Cités, Nécropoles: Institutions, Rites Et Monuments en Macédoine*.

Meletemata 45, 155–168, pl. 59–62. Athens. N.B. The first version of the title of this article appears in the table of contents, whereas the title on the first page of the article is "Couleur et sens: l'emploi de la couleur dans la tombe de la reine Eurydice."

Kottaridi, A. 2007. "L'épiphanie des dieux des Enfer dans la nécropole royale d'Aigai." In S. Descamps-Leguime (ed.), *Peinture et Couleur Dans Le Monde Grec Antique*, 26–45. Paris.

Kottaridi, A. 2011a. "Queens and Princesses and High Priestesses: The Role of Women at the Macedonian Court." In A. Kottaridi (ed.), *Heracles to Alexander the Great: Treasures from the Royal Capital of Macedon, a Hellenic Kingdom in the Age of Democracy*, 93–126. Oxford.

Kottaridi, A. 2011b. "Burial Customs and Beliefs in the Royal Necropolis of Aegae." In A. Kottaridi (ed.), *Heracles to Alexander the Great: Treasures from the Royal Capital of Macedon, a Hellenic Kingdom in the Age of Democracy*, 131–152. Oxford.

Kottaridi, A. 2011c. *Macedonian Treasures: A Tour through the Museum of the Royal Tombs of Aigai* (trans.) A. Doumas. Athens.

Köves-Zulauf, Thomas. 2007. "Orpheus und Eurydike." *ACD* 43: 5–28.

Kron, U. 1996. "Priesthoods, Dedications and Euergetism. What Part Did Religion Play in the Political and Social Status of Women?" In P. Hellström and B. Alroth (eds.), *Religion and Power in the Ancient Greek World*, 139–182. Uppsala.

Kyriakou, A. 2014. "Exceptional Burials at the Sanctuary of Eukleia at Aegae (Vergina): The Gold Oak Wreath." *BSA* 109: 251–285.

Kyriakou, A., and A. Tourtas. 2013. "After Destruction: Taking Care of Remains at the Sanctuary of Eukleia at Vergina." In J. Driessen (ed.), *Destruction, Archaeological Philological and Historical Perspectives*, 299–318. Leuven.

Kyriakou, A., and A. Tourtas. 2015. "Detecting Patterns through Context Analysis: A Case Study of Deposits from the Sanctuary of Eukleia at Aegae (Vergina)." In D. C. Haggis and C. M. Antonaccio (eds.), *Classical Archaeology in Context: Theory and Practice in Excavation in the Greek World*, 357–384. Berlin.

Lalonde, G. V. 2006. *Horos Dios: An Athenian Shrine and Cult of Zeus*. Monumenta Graeca et Romana, Vol. 11. Leiden.

Lane Fox, R. 1974. *Alexander the Great*. New York.

Lane Fox, R. 2011a. "399–369." In Lane Fox 2011e, 209–234.

Lane Fox, R. 2011b. "The 360's." In Lane Fox 2011e, 257–270.

Lane Fox, R. 2011c. "Philip of Macedon, Accession, Ambition and Self-Presentation." In Lane Fox 2011e, 335–366.

Lane Fox, R. 2011d. "Introduction: Dating the Royal Tombs at Vergina." In Lane Fox 2011e, 1–34.

Lane Fox, R. (ed.). 2011e. *Brill's Companion to Ancient Macedon: Studies in the Archaeology and History of Macedon, 650 BC–300 AD*. Leiden.

Lapatin, K. 2001. *Chryselephantine Statuary in the Ancient Mediterranean World*. Oxford.

Laronde, A. 1987. *Cyrène et la Libye hellénistique*. Paris.

Le Bohec (-Bouhet), S. 2006. "Réflexions sur la place de la femme dans la Macédoine antique." In A. M. Guimier-Sorbets, M. B. Hatzopoulos, and Y. Morizot (eds.), *Rois, cités, nécropoles: Institutions, rites et monuments en Macédoine*, 187–198. Athens.

Le Bohec (-Bouhet), S. 2007. "Philippe II et les Dieux." *AM* 7: 333–344.

Lee, M. O. 1965. "Orpheus and Eurydice. Myth, Legend, Folklore." *C&M* 26: 402–412.

Louko(u)poulou, L. D. 2011. "Macedonia in Thrace." In Lane Fox 2011e, 367–376.

Lund, H. 1994. *Lysimachus, A Study in Early Hellenistic Kingship*. London.

Macurdy G. H. 1927. "Queen Eurydice and the Evidence for Woman-Power in Early Macedonia." *AJP* 48: 201–214.

Macurdy, G. H. 1932. *Hellenistic Queens*. Baltimore.

Mangoldt, H. von. 2012. *Makedonische Grabarchitektur: Die Makedonischen Kammergräber und ihre Vorläufer*. Vols. 1 and 2. Berlin.

March, D. A. 1995. "The Kings of Makedon: 399–369 B.C." *Historia* 44: 257–282.

Mari, M. 2011. "Traditional Cults and Beliefs." In Lane Fox 2011e, 453–465.

Marquardt, P. 1985. "Penelope '*Polutropos*.'" *AJP* 106, 1: 32–48.

Mattingly, H. B. 1968. "Athenian Finance in the Peloponnesian War." *BCH* 92: 450–485.

McGinn, T. A. J. 2008. *Widows and the Patriarchy: Ancient and Modern*. London.

Meeus, A. 2009. "Some Institutional Problems Concerning the Succession to Alexander the Great: *Prostasia* and Chiliarchy." *Historia* 58: 287–310.

Metzler, D. 1980. "Eunomia und Aphrodite. Zur Ikonologie einer attischen Vassengruppe." *Hephaistos* 2: 73–88.

Miller, M. 1986. "The Macedonian Pretender Pausanias and His Coinage." *AncW* 13: 23–27.

Miller, S. G. 1993. *The Tomb of Lyson and Kallikles: A Painted Macedonian Tomb*. Mainz.

Millett, P. 2010. "The Political Economy of Macedonia." In Roisman and Worthington 2010, 472–504.

Mirón Pérez, M. D. 1998. "Olimpia, Eurydice y el origen del culto dinastico en la Grecia helenistica." *FlorIlib* 9: 215–235.

Mirón Pérez, M. D. 2000. "Transmitters and Representatives of Power: Royal Women in Ancient Macedonia." *AncSoc* 30: 35–52.

Mirón Pérez, M. D., and Martinez López, C. 2011. "Benefactoras y filánthropas en las sociedades antiquas." *Arenal, Revista de historia de las mujeres* 18, 2: 243–275.

Mitchell, L. G. 1997. *Greeks Bearing Gifts: The Public Use of Private Relationships in the Greek World*. Cambridge.

Mitchell, L. G. 2007. "'Born to Rule?' Succession in the Argead Royal House." In W. Heckel, L. Tritle, and P. Wheatley (eds.), *Alexander's Empire: Formulation to Decay*, 61–74. Claremont, CA.

Molina Marín A. I. 2018. "Reina y madre. Eurídice I y la concepción clánica del poder en Macedonia." In B. Antela Bernárdez, C. Zaragozà Serrano, and A. Guimerà Martínez (eds.), *Dolor y Placer: las mujeres en la Antigüedad*, 75–90. Alcalá de Henares, Madrid.

Moore, K. R. 2016. "Of Philosophers and Kings: Concerning Philip II of Macedon's Alleged 'Debt' to Plato." *Anabasis: Studia Classica et Orientalia* 7: 1–22.

Morgan, J. 2008. "Women, Religion, and the Home." In D. Ogden (ed.), *A Companion to Greek Religion*, 297–310. Malden, MA.

Mortensen, C. 1991. "The Career of Bardylis." *AncW* 22, 1: 49–59.

Mortensen, C. 1992. "Eurydice: Demonic or Devoted Mother?" *AHB* 6: 156–171.

Mosley, D. J. 1973. *Envoys and Diplomacy in Ancient Greece*. Wiesbaden.

Müller, S. 2011. "Oikos, Prestige und wirtschaftliche Handlungsräume von Argeadinnen und hellenistischen Königinnen." In J. E. Fries and U. Rambuschek (eds.), *Von wirtschaftlicher Macht unter militärischer Stärk: Beiträge zur archäologischen Geschlechter*. Frauen, Forschung-Archäologie 9, 96–114. Münster.

Müller, S. 2012. "Stories of the Persian Bride: Alexander and Roxane." In R. Stoneman, K. Erickson, and I. Netton (eds.), *The Alexander Romance in Persia and the East*, 295–310. Groningen.

Müller, S. 2013. "Das symbolische Kapital von Argeadinnen und Frauen der Diadochen." In C. Kunst (ed.), *Matronagr. Soziale Netzwerke von Herrscherfrauen im Altertum in diachoner Perspektive*, 31–42. Osnabrück.

Müller, S. 2014. *Alexander, Makedonien und Persien*, Frankfurter Kulturwissenschaftliche Beiträge Band 18, Frankfurt.

Müller, S. 2016. *Die Argeaden: Geschichte Makedoniens bis zum Zeitalter Alexander des Grossen*. Paderborn.

Murray, P. 2005. "The Muses: Creativity personified?" In E. Stafford and J. Herrin (eds.), *Personification in the Greek World: From Antiquity to Byzantium*, 147–160. Aldershot.

Natoli, A. F. 2004. *The Letter of Speusippus to Philip II. Introduction, Text, Translation and Commentary*. Historia Einzelschrift 176. Stuttgart.

Neils, Jennifer. 1992. "Panathenaic Amphoras: Their Meaning, Makers, and Markets." In J. Neils (ed.), *Goddess and Polis: The Panathenaic Festival in Ancient Athens*, 29–52. Princeton.

Ogden, D. 1999. *Polygamy, Prostitutes and Death: The Hellenistic Dynasties*. London.

Ogden, D. 2011. "The Royal Families of Argead Macedon and the Hellenistic World." In B. Rawson (ed.), *A Companion to Families in the Greek and Roman World*, 92–107. Malden, MA.

Ogden, D. 2013. *Drakōn: Dragon Myth and Serpent Cult in the Greek and Roman Words*. Oxford.

Oikonomides A. N. 1983. "A New Inscription from Vergina and Eurydice the Mother of Philip II." *AncW* 7: 62–64.

Oikonomides, A. N. 1988. "Rebellions and Usurpers in the Ten Years after the Death of Amyntas III of Macedon (370–360 BC.)." *CB* 64: 41–44.

Otto, T. 2009. "Rethinking Tradition: Invention, Cultural Continuity and Agency." In J. Wassmann and K. Stockhaus (eds.), *Experiencing New Worlds*, 36–57. London.

Palagia, O. 2002. "'The Tomb of Eurydice,' Plundered." *Minerva* 13, 1: 4.

Palagia, Olga. 2010. "Philip's Eurydice in the Philippeum at Olympia." In E. D. Carney and D. Ogden (eds.), *Philip II and Alexander the Great*, 33–41. New York.

Palagia, O. 2011. "Hellenistic Art." In Lane Fox 2011e, 477–494.

Palagia, O. 2014. "Commemorating the Dead: Grave Markers, Tombs, and Tomb Paintings, 400–430 BCE." In M. M. Miles (ed.), *A Companion to Greek Architecture*, 374–389. Chichester.

Palagia, O. 2016. "Visualising the Gods in Macedonia from Philip II to Perseus." *Pharos* 22: 73–98.

Palagia, O. 2017. "The Royal Court in Ancient Macedonia: The Evidence for Royal Tombs." In A. Erskine, L. Llewellyn-Jones, and S. Wallace, S. (eds.), *The Hellenistic Court: Monarchic Power and Elite Society from Alexander to Cleopatra*, 409–431. Swansea.

Palagia, O. 2018. "Alexander the Great, the royal throne and the funerary thrones of Macedonia." *Karanos* 1: 23–34.

Papazoglou, F. 1965. "Les Origines et la Destinée de L'État Illyrien: Illyrii Proprie Dicti." *Historia* 14: 143–179.

Parker, V. 2003. "Sparta, Amyntas, and the Olynthians in 383 B.C.: A Comparison of Xenophon and Diodorus." *RhM* 146: 113–137.

Paspalas, S. A. 2011. "Classical Art." In Lane Fox 2011e, 179–207.

Petersen, L. H., and P. Salzman-Mitchell. 2012. "Introduction: The Public and Private Faces of Mothering and Motherhood in Classical Antiquity." In L. H. Petersen and P. Salzman-Mitchell (eds.), *Mothering and Motherhood in ancient Greece and Rome*, 1–22. Austin.

Pingiatoglou, S. 2010. "Cults of Female Deities at Dion." *Kernos* 23: 179–192.

Pownall, F. A. 2004. *Lessons from the Past: The Moral Use of History in Fourth-Century Prose*. Ann Arbor.

Prandi, L. 1998. "A Few Remarks on the Amyntas 'Conspiracy'." In W. Will (ed.), *Alexander der Grosse. Eine Welteroberung und ihr Hintergrund*, 91–101. Bonn.

Prestianni-Giallombardo, A.-M. 1973–1974. "Aspetti Giuridici e Problemi Cronologici della Reggenza di Filippo II di Macedonia." *Helikon* 13–14: 191–204.

Prestianni-Giallombardo, A.-M. 1976–77. "'Diritto' matrimoniale, ereditario e dinastico nella Macedonia di Filippo II." *RSA* 6–7: 81–118.

Prestianni-Giallombardo, A.-M. 1981. "Eurydike-Kleopatra. Nota Ad Arr., *Anab.*, 3,6,5." *AnnPisa* 3: 295–306.

Price, Simon. 2012. "Memory and Ancient Greece." In B. Smith and R. R. R. Smith (eds.), *Historical and Religious Memory in the Ancient World*, 15–36. Oxford.

Psoma, S. 2012. "Innovation or Tradition? Succession to the Kingship in Temenid Macedonia." *Tekmeria* 11: 73–87.

Rhodes, P. J., and R. Osborne. 2003. *Greek Historical Inscriptions, 404–323 B.C.* Oxford.

Rives-Gal, G. 1996 (2002). *Funérailles, politique et idéologie monarchique dans le royaume de Macédoine de Philippe II à Démétrios Poliorcète (336–83 av. J.-C)*. Toulouse.

Robert, J., and Robert, L. 1984. "Vergina-Aigai." *REG* 97: 450–451.

Roisman, J. 2010. "Classical Macedonia to Perdiccas III." In Roisman and Worthington 2010, 145–165.

Roisman, J., and I. Worthington (eds.). 2010. *A Companion to Ancient Macedonia.* Malden, MA:.

Rose, M. 2001. "Royal Tomb Robbery." *Archaeology* 54, 6: 16.

Saatsoglou-Paliadeli, C. 1987. "Εὐρυδίκα Σίρρα Εὐκλεία." In *ΑΜΗΤΟΣ: Τιμητικος τόμος για τον καθηγητή Μανόλη Ανδρόνικο.* Vol. 2, 733–744. Thessaloniki.

Saatsoglou-Paliadeli, C. 1990. "Βεργίνα 1990. Ανασκαφή στο Ιερό της Εύκλειας." *AEMTH* 4: 21–34.

Saatsoglou-Paliadeli, C. 1991. "ΒΕΡΓΙΝΑ 1991. Ανασκαφή Το Ιερό της Εύκλειας στη Βεργίνα." *AEMTH* 5: 9–21.

Saatsoglou-Paliadeli, C. 1993a. "Σκέψεις με αφορμή ένα εύρημα από τα Παλατίτσια." *AM* 5, 3: 1339–1371.

Saatsoglou-Paliadeli, C. 1993b. "Βεργίνα Ανασκαφή στο ιερό της Εύκλειας." *AEMTH* 7: 51–59.

Saatsoglou-Paliadeli, C. 1996. "Το Ιερό της Εύκλειας στη Βεργίνα." *AEMTH* 10A: 55–67.

Saatsoglou-Paliadeli, C. 2000a. "Queenly Appearances at Vergina-Aegae: Old and New Epigraphic and Literary Evidence." *AA* 3: 387–403.

Saatsoglou-Paliadeli, C. 2011. "The Arts at Vergina-Aegae, the Cradle of the Macedonian Kingdom." In Lane Fox 2011e, 271–296.

Saatsoglou-Paliadeli, C. Kyriakou, E. Mitsopoulou, and A. Tourtas, 2008. "Παλαιές υπο χρεώσεις και νέα ευρήματα στις Αιγές." *AEMTH* 22: 177–182.

Saatsoglou-Paliadeli, C., A. Kyriakou, E. Mitsopoulou, and A. Tourtas. 2009. "Πολύτιμα ταφικά σύνολα από την αγορά των Αιγών I. Η αρχαιολογική εικόνα και η ιστορική ερμηνεία της." *AEMTH* 23: 117–122.

Saatsoglou-Paliadeli, C., P. Papageorgiou, G. Maniates, S. Triantaphullou, M. Babelides, A. Kyriakou, and A. Tourtas, A. 2008. "Μικροανασκαφή σ' ένα αναπάντεχο εύρημα από την αγορά των Αιγών η διεπιστημονική προσέγγιση." *AEMTH* 22: 183–190.

Saatsoglou-Paliadeli, C., P. Papageorgiou, G. Maniates, S. Triantaphullou, M. Babelides, A. Kyriakou, and A. Tourtas. 2009. "Πολύτιμα ταφικά σύνολα από την αγορά των Αιγών II: η διερεύνηση στο εργαστήριο. " *AEMTH* 23: 123–130.

Sansone D. 1985. "Orpheus and Eurydice in the Fifth Century." *C&M* 36: 53–64.

Saripanidi, V. 2017. "Constructing Continuities with a 'Heroic' Past: Death, Feasting and Political Ideology in the Archaic Macedonian Kingdom." In A. Tsingarida and E. S. Lemos (eds.), *Constructing Social Identities in Early Iron Age and Archaic Greece,* Études D'Archéologie 12, 73–170. Brussels.

Savalli-Lestrade, I. 2003. "La place des reines à la cour et dans le royaume à l'époque hellénistique." In R. Frei-Stolba, A. Bielman, and O. Blanchi (eds.), *Les femmes antiques entre sphère privée et sphère publique: Actes du diplôme d'études avancées, Universités de Lausanne et Neuchâtel,* 59–76. Bern.

Sawada, N. 2010. "Social Customs and Institutions: Aspects." In Roisman and Worthington 2010, 392–408.

Schaps, D. 1977. "The Women Least Mentioned: Etiquette and Women's Names." *CQ* 27: 323–330.

Schmitt, H. H. 1991. "Zur Inszenierung des Privatslebens des Hellenistischen Herrschers." In J. Seibert (ed.), *Hellenistische Studien. Gedenkschrift für H. Bengston*, Münchener Arbeiten zur Alten Geschichte 5, 77–86, Munich.

Schultz, P. 2007. "Leochares' Argead Portraits in the Philippeion." In P. Schultz and R. von den Hoff (eds.), *Early Hellenistic Portraiture: Image, Style, Context*, 205–233. Cambridge.

Scullion, S. 1994. "Olympian and Chthonian." *CA* 13: 75–119.

Sears, M. A. 2013. *Athens, Thrace, and the Shaping of Athenian Leadership*. Cambridge.

Shapiro, H. A. 1993. *Personifications in Greek Art: The Representation of Abstract Concepts 600–400 B.C.* Bern.

Smith, Amy C. 2011. *Polis and Personification in Classical Athenian Art*. Leiden.

Sourvinou-Inwood, C. 1996. *"Reading" Greek Death: To the End of the Classical Period*. Oxford.

Sourvinou-Inwood, C. 2003. *Tragedy and Athenian Religion*. Lanham, MD:.

Sprawski, S. 2010. "The Early Temenid Kings to Alexander I." In Roisman and Worthington 2010, 127–144.

Stafford, E. 2000. *Worshipping Virtues: Personification and the Divine in Ancient Greece*. Swansea.

Stafford, E. 2008. "Personification in Greek Religious Thought and Practice." In D. Ogden (ed.), *A Companion to Greek Religion*, 71–85. Malden, MA.

Stern, S. R. 2012. *The Political Biographies of Cornelius Nepos*. Ann Arbor.

Stewart, A. 1993. *Faces of Power: Alexander's Image and Hellenistic Politics*. Berkeley.

Stipčević A. 1963. *The Art of the Illyrians,* (trans.) L. White. Milan.

Stylianou, P. J. 1998. *A Historical Commentary on Diodorus Siculus, Book 15*. Oxford.

Tarn, W. W. 1948. *Alexander the Great*. Vols. 1 and 2. Cambridge.

Tataki, A. B. 1988. *Ancient Beroea: Prosopography and Society*. Meletemata 8. Athens.

Themelis, P. 2003. "Macedonian Dedications on the Akropolis." In O. Palagia and S. V. Tracy (eds.), *The Macedonian in Athens 322–229 B.C*, 162–172. Oxford.

Themelis, P., and J. Touratsoglou. 1997. ΟιΤάφοι του Δερβενίου. Athens.

Thomas, C. 2010. "The Physical Kingdom." In Roisman and Worthington 2010, 65–80.

Tiverios, M. 2000. Μακεδόνες καί Παναθήναια: Παναθήναϊκοί αμφορείς απο το βορειοελληνικό χώρο. Athens.

Tiverios, M. 2007. "Panathenaic Amphoras." In O. Palagia and A. Choremi-Spetsieri (eds.), *The Panathenaic Games*, 1–20. Oxford.

Tod, M. N. 1948. *Greek Historical Inscriptions*. Vols. 1 and 2. Oxford.

Tronson, A. 1984. "Satyrus the Peripatetic and the Marriages of Philip II." *JHS* 104: 116–156.

Unger, G. F. 1882. "III Miszellen." *Philologus* 41: 159–161.

Walcott, P. 1991. "On Widows and Their Reputation in Antiquity." *Symbolae Osloenses* 66: 5–26.

West, W. C. 1977 "Hellenic Homonoia and the New Decree from Platea." *GRBS* 18: 307–319.

Wilhelm, A. 1949. "Ein Weihgedict der Grossmutter Alexanders des Grossen." Παγκάρπ πεια. *Mélanges Henri Grégoire*. Vol. 2, 625–633. Brussels.

Woodhull, M. L. 2012. "Imperial Mothers and Monuments in Rome." In Petersen and Salzman Mitchell 2012, 225–251.

Worthington, I. 2008. *Philip II of Macedonia*. New Haven.

Yardley, J. C., and W. Heckel. 1997. *Justin: Epitome of the Philippic History of Pompeius Trogus: Vol. 1, Books 11–12: Alexander the Great*. Oxford.

Zahrnt, M. 2006. "Amyntas III: Fall und Aufstieg eines Makedonenkönigs." *Hermes* 134: 127–141.

Zahrnt, M. 2007. "Amyntas III und die Griechischen Mächte." *AM* 7: 239–251.

Zahrnt, M. 2009. "The Macedonian Background." In W. Heckel and L. A. Tritle (eds.), *Alexander the Great: A New History*, 7–25. Hoboken, NJ.

*E. D. Carney, 2015. *King and Court in Ancient Macedonia: Rivalry, Treason and Conspiracy*. Swansea, UK, is a collection of some of my old articles, each with an "Afterword." In this bibliography, items in this collection are cited by the date of publication of the collection, but with the original date of publication in parentheses.

# Index

Figures are indicated by an italic *f* following the page number.

in Palatitsia, 92–95, 93*f*
by Roxane, 139n6
defeats, in formation of national identity, 47
deities, 88–90, 91, 102–3
Demosthenes, 35, 36, 56, 125n49
denigration of mothers of potential
 successors, 11–12
Derdas, 20–21, 122n15
Derveni tombs, 104–5
Dickey, E., 135–36n27
Diodorus Siculus, 15, 17–18, 19
 assassination of Alexander II, 35, 59
 assassination of Ptolemy, 41–42
 claimants to throne during Philip II's
  reign, 47–48
 death of Perdiccas III, 55–56
 doublets in, 20, 123–24n30
 Pausanias, 38–39
 reign of Alexander II, 33, 34–35
 reign of Amyntas III, 19–20, 21
 reign of Ptolemy, 38
Dion, cult of muses at, 140n24, 140n25
diplomacy, 71–73
double game, 5–6
doublets in Diodorus, 20, 123–24n30
Drougou, S., 141n39, 141n42, 141n45
dynastic crisis, 1
dynastic monuments, 108–11

education of children by Eurydice, 79–80
education of Eurydice, 79–82,
 140n30, 140n31
Eleusis painter, 149n59
Elimeia, 20–21
elite class, 8, 72–73
Ellis, J. R., 133n63
Enheduanna, 1–2
*epitropos*, 120n24, 129n19
 Ptolemy as, 38, 39–41, 66
Errington, R. M., 134–35n12
ethnicity of Eurydice, 23–27, 125n49, 125n50
Eucleia, 143n73, 143n77
 priestess of, 86–87, 91, 144n91, 144n92
 in vase paintings, 144n85
Eucleia sanctuary, 82–92, 83*f*, 138n3
 artifacts from, 141n42, 141n44, 142n48,
  142n57, 142n62, 142n63
 burial assemblies, 141n45
 dates of, 141n38

Laodice's dedication at, 78
reburying of sculptures from,
 96–97, 144n96
Euripides, 88–89
Eurydice
 adultery of, 54–55
 ancestry of, 23–24
 assassination of Alexander II, 35, 36
 assistance of Iphicrates, 64–67
 daughter of, 133–34n1
 death of, 75, 92, 97–98
 description of, 74–75
 ethnicity of, 125n49, 125n50
 evidence related to life and actions
  of, 2–5
 in extant sources, 71–75
 identity of, 23–27
 legitimacy of sons, 11–12
 marriage to Amyntas III, 22–23, 27–29
 marriage to Ptolemy, 4, 37, 56, 60–64,
  134n7, 136n28, 136n29, 136n30,
  136n31, 136n32
 murder of sons, 55–58, 134n5, 134n6
 narrative sources, 2–5
 negative view of, 137n43
 opposition to Pausanias, 38–40
 *philia* networks, 71–72, 73–74
 during Philip II's reign, 51–52
 promotion of status of, 126–27n72
 propaganda and extant sources on, 67–71
 role in Athenian intervention after assassination of Alexander II, 38
 sons of, 6, 18, 28–30 (*see also sons
  by name*)
 statue in Philippeum, 108–9, 110–11
 support for Ptolemy, 134–35n12, 136n28
Eurydice, use of name by others, 111–15,
 152n114
Eurynoe, 54, 133–34n1, 135n18, 137n53
extant sources, 67–75

facades
 in Tomb of Eurydice, 101–2
 in tombs, 106–7, 108, 145n7,
  146n8, 149n68
factions in Macedonian court, 3, 72–73
foreign support for kings, 9–10, 48–49
fourth-century propaganda, 67–71
Fox, L., 69–70, 124n37, 147n29, 150–51n87

Schultz, P., 151n90, 151n92
sexual infidelity. *See* adultery
sexuality of widows, 57–58, 134n9
Sirras, 24, 77, 78–79, 125n48, 125n52
snake sculpture, 84–85, 88
sources
    for life of Eurydice, 2–5, 67–75
    for reign of Amyntas III, 15–17
Spartans, 20–21
Speusippus, 130n36
Stafford, E., 143n70, 143n77
stars, in tombs, 150n77
statue grouping at Palatitsia, 92–95
statue podia
    in Eucleia sanctuary, 85–86
    in Palatitsia, 92–95, 93f
step-mother marriage, 136n30
Strabo, 23–24
Stratonice, 78
succession
    advocates, 10–12, 29–30
    of Alexander II, 28–30
    of Eurydice's sons over Gygaea's, 29–31
    king's preference in, 120n28, 126n71
    pattern of, 9–10
    of Perdiccas III, 38
    of Philip II, 44–46
*Suda*, 38–40, 66, 69
symbolic capital, 30

Teleutias, 20–21
Thebes, 33, 34–35, 38, 40–41
    cult to Artemis Eucleia, 89–90
    Perdiccas III's alliance with, 42
Theopompus, 3, 67, 69, 133n62,
        137n40, 137n49
Thessaly, 7, 21–22, 33–34, 40–41, 51, 128n7,
        128n8, 128n9
Thrace, 7, 51
thrones, in tombs, 102–5, 149n58
Timotheus, 42
Tomb of Eurydice, 2, 96–97, 98
    blue ceiling in, 101–2, 147n31, 147n32
    chronology of Macedonian
        tombs, 106–8
    description of, 99–103, 146n14, 146n15
    facade in, 108
    gender of person in, 103–5
    identifying as belonging to
        Eurydice, 105–6

jewelry in, 102–3, 104, 148n52
Persephone/Hades painting, 102–3,
        104–5, 107–8, 147n37, 147–48n38
    as shared tomb, 104–5, 148n52, 148n53
    skeletal remains found in, 101, 147n26
tombs. *See also* Tomb of Eurydice
    barrel vault, 98–99, 106, 145n7
    chamber, 107
    cist, 106–7, 149–50n71
    Derveni, 104–5
    facades in, 101–2, 106–7, 108, 145n7,
        146n8, 149n68
    Katerini, 149–50n71
    Macedonian development of, 106–8
    Rhomaios, 100, 103–4, 146n11
    Tomb Alpha at Derveni, 107
    Tomb II at Vergina, 98–99, 103–4
Tourtas, A., 141n38, 142n63
treachery, 4

Upper Macedonia, 6–7, 18–19, 23–24, 49

vase painting, 144n85
Vergina, Greece
    Eucleia sanctuary, 82–92
    Great Tumulus at, 98–99, 104–5
    thrones in tombs in, 149n58
    Tomb II at, 98–99, 103–4
widows
    remarriages of, 60–61, 62–63
    view of, 57–58, 134n9

women
    dedication of Eurydice associated
        with, 79–81
    gender stereotyping, 4, 68–69
    inscriptions from, 77–78
    name changes of, 111–15, 151n100
    polygamy within Macedonian
        monarchy, 10–12
    role in Macedonian monarchy, 10–13
    role in religion, 91, 149n57
Worthington, I., 130n34

Xenophon, 20–21, 22

Yardley, J. C., 137n44

Zahrnt, M., 21
Zeus Meilichius, 88

Printed in the USA
CPSIA information can be obtained
at www.ICGtesting.com
CBHW080847090224
4154CB00020B/127